LLOYD GEORGE

FAMILY LETTERS 1885–1936

Lloyd George, Mrs. Lloyd George, Mair, and Megan, *c.* 1904

LLOYD GEORGE
FAMILY LETTERS
1885–1936

Edited by
KENNETH O. MORGAN

Published jointly by
UNIVERSITY OF WALES PRESS, CARDIFF
and
OXFORD UNIVERSITY PRESS, LONDON
1973

University of Wales Press,
Merthyr House, James Street, Cardiff

Oxford University Press, Ely House, London W. 1

GLASGOW NEW YORK TORONTO MELBOURNE WELLINGTON
CAPE TOWN IBADAN NAIROBI DAR ES SALAAM LUSAKA ADDIS ABABA
DELHI BOMBAY CALCUTTA MADRAS KARACHI LAHORE DACCA
KUALA LUMPUR SINGAPORE HONG KONG TOKYO

ISBN 0 19 211717 3

© *1972 The National Library of Wales and the*
First Beaverbrook Foundation
Editing © *1973 Kenneth O. Morgan*

Printed in Great Britain by
The Camelot Press Ltd, London and Southampton

TO
GLANMOR WILLIAMS

CONTENTS

ILLUSTRATIONS

* Copyright Radio Times Hulton Picture Library

INTRODUCTION

'Who shall paint the chameleon, who can tether a broomstick?' asked J. M. Keynes in a despairing attempt to explain, or explain away, David Lloyd George.[1] The Welshman's uniquely elusive personality has continued to defy historians ever since. During his early career, Lloyd George was less a subject for biography than for hagiography. Writers, usually Welshmen like J. Hugh Edwards or Beriah Gwynfe Evans, wrote sentimental accounts of the 'cottage-bred boy' on his progress 'from village green to Downing Street'. But since the controversial events which brought Lloyd George to the premiership on 6–7 December 1916, there has been a complete transformation. Writers of most political persuasions have been consistently hostile, viewing Lloyd George, on the model of Baldwin's famous speech at the Carlton Club in October 1922, as a 'dynamic force' with the elemental power to deprave or destroy British institutions. In this, if in little else, Baldwin's judgement has survived his own lifetime. A bitter vignette which has had especial influence was Keynes's 'essay in biography' which finally appeared in 1933 and which depicted Lloyd George as an a-moral 'goat-footed bard' 'rooted in nothing', 'a vampire and a medium in one'. Lloyd George's private life has received even more hostile attention, particularly since his eldest son's revelatory version of his father's life of amorous adventure appeared in 1960.[2] Until the mid-1960s, therefore, Lloyd George as man and statesman was at a low ebb.

In some measure, this was because his case tended to go by default. Much of the primary evidence for the major crises of his career comes from opponents, often from Asquithians more bitter towards Lloyd George than was Asquith himself. The Coalition Liberals and other possible supporters were too often silent. Beaverbrook's verdict, that Lloyd George above all demanded sole possession of 'the driver's seat' was ambivalent.

---

[1] J. M. Keynes, 'Lloyd George', *Essays in Biography* (Hart-Davis, 1951 edn., pp. 32–3).

[2] Richard Lloyd George (2nd Earl), *Lloyd George* (Muller, 1960).

Lloyd George himself was a notoriously bad correspondent: letters from him are hard to unearth. Even so, since 1967 when the Lloyd George Papers in the Beaverbrook Library were opened, there has been a steady revision of the judgement of historians on Lloyd George's career and reputation. Works of major scholarship—especially those by younger historians remote from the old conflicts over the Maurice debate or the 'coupon election', take a more detached and often more sympathetic view of his outlook and character. The emergence of new materials such as the Lloyd George Papers is, of course, central to this change. Another immensely valuable source now available is the recently-published diary of Frances Stevenson, Lloyd George's private secretary, mistress, and ultimately second wife, which spans his career from September 1914 onwards.[1] Until recently, however, no sources were at hand which covered his career as a whole. In particular, his formative years as a politician and a Cabinet minister between 1886 and 1914 receive only scant coverage in the Lloyd George Papers (a reflection of his chaotic methods of work until Frances Stevenson began her secretarial duties). This gap is reflected in the fifty-odd biographies of him, all of which, with the exception of Watkin Davies's valuable and much-neglected study,[2] are notably weak on this earlier period. But two unique collections of manuscript material have now been uncovered. One, the papers of his brother, William George, remains in private hands. The other, perhaps the richest hoard of all, comprises the papers of Mrs. Lloyd George at Bryn Awelon, Criccieth, of which Lady Megan Lloyd George was the trustee. The copyright of these papers is owned jointly by the First Beaverbrook Foundation and by the National Library of Wales: they were purchased by the National Library in 1969. They include over 2,000 letters or fragments from Lloyd George to his first wife, together with collections relating to their children, Olwen, Gwilym, and Megan, a diary for 1887, and many notebooks and other items. It is this unique mass of family correspondence, including in all over 2,300 letters in Lloyd George's own hand (the only major collection of his personal correspondence now available) which forms the substance of this book, and its chief justification.

[1] A. J. P. Taylor (ed.), *Lloyd George: a Diary by Frances Stevenson* (Hutchinson, 1971). See also Frances Lloyd George, *The Years that are Past* (Hutchinson, 1967).
[2] W. Watkin Davies, *Lloyd George, 1863–1914* (Constable, 1939).

The core of this volume consists of the letters to Mrs. Lloyd George from 1885 onwards. I have drawn freely on these and have tried to include every item that seems to me to be of historical interest. I have managed to date some from internal evidence; in most of the rest, the dating is clear enough. In addition, I have included a few other sources that bear on this family correspondence—some revealing diary entries for the year 1887 (when the flow of letters temporarily dried up); two letters (for 1895 and 1899) from William George to his brother; some of Lloyd George's letters to his youngest daughter and political heir, Megan, between 1912 and 1936; and a few letters from Mrs Lloyd George and from Lady Megan which help to illuminate the final phase after 1922. But, unless otherwise indicated, all the other material in this volume is drawn from the letters from Lloyd George to his first wife.

David Lloyd George's early life is familiar enough and there is no need to review it in detail here. He was born in Manchester in January 1863, the second child and elder son of William George, formerly the master of Hope Street Unitarian school, Liverpool. But he was taken, after the death of his father, to the tiny village of Llanystumdwy in southern Caernarvonshire, when only eighteen months old. Here he was brought up by his formidable uncle, the shoemaker-preacher Richard Lloyd, and educated, much to his own disgust, in the local Anglican elementary school. In 1877 he was articled to Messrs. Breese, Jones, and Casson, solicitors, in Portmadoc; he set up practice on his own in Criccieth in 1884. It was at about this time that he first met Margaret Owen of Mynydd Ednyfed farm, Criccieth.

Born in November 1866, Margaret was his junior by almost four years. She is obviously a much more obscure figure, although many aspects of her personality and views can be gleaned from the correspondence.[1] In a humble way she was herself something of a political animal. Within her own circumscribed world at Criccieth, she was a shrewd judge of political personalities: indeed, it was on people rather than on issues that she preferred to pass judgement. She seldom offered advice on the key decisions of her husband's career. A devout Calvinist Methodist, she was an instinctive Liberal who backed her

[1] There is an affectionate portrait by her son (Richard), Viscount Gwynedd (2nd Earl Lloyd-George), *Dame Margaret* (Allen & Unwin, 1947). It rather exaggerates her lack of interest in politics.

husband up staunchly during such crises as the Cymru Fydd affair in 1896 and his opposition to the Boer War in 1899–1902. Later on, she became increasingly absorbed with management of the home and with bringing up their five children, born to them between 1889 and 1902.[1] However, as late as February 1921, she could throw herself into a most bitter by-election in Cardiganshire and make over sixty speeches on behalf of Ernest Evans, the Lloyd George Liberal (who won the seat). In 1928 she took some part in securing the Liberal nomination in Anglesey for her younger daughter, Megan (who was later elected and sat for that constituency from 1929 to 1951). But the letters suggest that Mrs. Lloyd George, the wife of a supremely political man, immersed in public events and personal manœuvre to the exclusion of almost all else, became more withdrawn from her husband's career after 1902, more anxious to retreat into the warm reassuring circle of her Criccieth home, and the local activities of the chapel, the Women's Institute, and the Ladies' Lifeboat Guild. Only in connection with some limited aspects of Welsh local politics did she continue to share her husband's interests for the remainder of her married life: for example, she was elected chairman of the Criccieth Urban District Council after the first world war. Apart from this, she would probably have been happier had he given up politics altogether, and settled down as a country attorney.

The letters in this volume throw light on Lloyd George's personality and viewpoint in many ways. They are especially full for the years 1890–1902; thereafter the correspondence becomes more episodic. In this respect, the letters offer a fascinating contrast with the Frances Stevenson diary. That begins in September 1914, at the start of a new phase in Lloyd George's career inaugurated by total war. It chronicles a man at the top, operating at the very hub of political power. But these letters to Mrs. Lloyd George trace, in the main, the progress of a man on his way to the top, one who viewed the

---

[1] The five Lloyd George children were:
1. Richard (who succeeded his father as 2nd Earl), born 15 February 1889, died 1 May 1968 leaving a son and a daughter.
2. Mair Eluned, born 2 August 1890, died 30 November 1907.
3. Olwen (now Lady Carey-Evans), born 3 April 1892: two sons and two daughters.
4. Gwilym (created Viscount Tenby 1957), born 4 December 1894, died 14 February 1967, leaving two sons.
5. Megan, born 22 April 1902, died 14 May 1966, unmarried.

power structure very much as a Welsh Baptist outsider thrusting his way through an alien, Anglo-Saxon world. In the Frances Stevenson diary again, Lloyd George's political philosophy is somewhat taken for granted, the legacy of his earlier years of struggle and conflict. These letters to his first wife, however, reveal some of the components of that philosophy: they depict what made him a radical and a democrat, and the crucial part that rural Wales played in that process in his stormy journey to the summit. The picture that emerges here of the younger Lloyd George is not, perhaps, an altogether attractive one. His ambition and vanity, his ruthless energy and belligerence, all carefully fanned by the uncompromising Uncle Lloyd, are there from the start; it is notable how frequently the verb 'to smash' appears in Lloyd George's letters, long before it was appropriated by student demonstrators. Yet the picture is not simply one of a soulless automaton. The energy and the belligerence were always at the service of higher political objectives as well as of self-promotion: they always had a purpose to serve. These letters also reveal an affectionate husband, a devoted parent, and an engaging (if often very demanding) friend. Despite the frequent tiffs with his wife—usually the result of her reluctance to join him in London and look after him there—Lloyd George had a deep and abiding concern for his family in Criccieth, for his endlessly loyal brother William, and especially for his devoted Uncle Lloyd, always encouraging and driving him on. His concern for his home in Wales was rooted not only in personal affection, but in the social and spiritual values that it represented. Frances Stevenson sensed this on 3 December 1914 when she wrote of 'the passionate attachment which he feels for Wales and which lies at the bottom of all his work'.[1] It was an attachment which she could sense but could not adequately explain, since Wales was, inevitably, for her a closed and basically hostile world. Lloyd George's continuing involvement with social and political issues in Wales can therefore be traced throughout this book. The reader should bear in mind, of course, that this aspect is probably somewhat exaggerated in these letters as Lloyd George was likely to emphasize topics that would be of especial interest to his wife back in Criccieth.

Since Lloyd George's private life has been the subject of so

[1] *Lloyd George: a Diary by Frances Stevenson*, p. 15.

much ill-informed and ill-natured speculation, I have tried to document both the happier and unhappier phases of his relations with his first wife as fairly as I can, the flashes of irritation and bad temper, with the long periods of warm affection. In a sense, more could have been said of the happier phases as I have omitted much domestic detail from the earlier letters which is of very slight historical interest. I hope what I have included shows that, in spite of all crises (and they were usually not very different from those which punctuate the course of most marriages), Lloyd George remained very close to his wife and her world at least down to his becoming Chancellor in 1908 (shortly after the death of their beloved eldest daughter, Mair Eluned). The letters to Mrs. Lloyd George become more patchy thereafter. This is in large measure, of course, a result of the fact that they were living together at 11 Downing Street and had no need to write, partly a result of the toll taken of a minister's private correspondence by government business. Only with the permanent entry of Frances Stevenson into Lloyd George's life at the end of 1912 did a definite rift begin to develop between him and his wife. A gulf had arisen originally not because of his affairs with other women (usually wildly exaggerated by later writers and often a theme for teasing humour in these letters) but rather because of his wife's very human and very Welsh aversion to London, and to her husband's London-based world of political manœuvre—a world that Uncle Lloyd, by contrast, understood and even admired. For years, Lloyd George had known long periods of feeling alone and neglected, breakfast-less in a cold house in London.[1] Frances Stevenson could provide the instant affection, constant reassurance, and intuitive political sympathy that he needed to survive. Even so, relations with Mrs. Lloyd George were a good deal more cordial than Miss Stevenson's, inevitably, quite different account as recorded in her diary suggests. (Incidentally, there is no direct reference to Miss Stevenson in the letters to Mrs. Lloyd George.) There was never a formal separation, still less a divorce, while a personal bond like Megan's search for a safe seat in 1928 could renew the ties between husband and wife. They celebrated their golden wedding together on a family holiday on the French riviera in January 1938, despite some years of partial estrangement.

[1] See for instance, Lloyd George to Mrs. Lloyd George, 21 August 1897 (p. 112).

These letters, however, will be of most value to the historian not for their domestic detail but rather for their evidence of Lloyd George's political outlook and methods. They illuminate many aspects of his earlier ventures in politics between 1885 and 1902. His contempt for class and privilege comes out very plainly—whether it be the absurd pretensions of 'royal flunkeys' or the arrogance and conceit of a London Welsh *nouveau riche* draper's wife. As late as September 1911 Lloyd George was totally unimpressed by the pomp and circumstance of Balmoral: he remained his own man. The unrepentant architect of the alleged 'honours scandal' of 1922 is already foreshadowed. Lloyd George's complex attitude towards Welsh institutions is also revealed: even in Wales itself he was something of an outsider. An instance of this is his massive contempt for the puritanism of the chapels and the petty snobberies of the nonconformist deacons in the *sêt fawr* (deacons' seat). At the same time, they represented, he felt, almost in spite of themselves the upsurge of the Welsh democracy and the nonconformist *pays réel* first liberated at the 'great election' of 1868: a measure like the disestablishment of the English church in Wales was thus a vital objective. Again, while not a religious man at all in the conventional sense—he veered between a deistic worship of nature and a stern rationalism worthy of his Unitarian father—he could respond to the messianic appeal of the 1904 religious revival. Perhaps this was because it originated with the chapel laity rather than with the priestly caste: as he once told a Welsh friend, 'I hate a priest, Daniel, whenever I find him.'[1] Other facets of the real Lloyd George that emerge are his constant involvement with the local and national newspaper press, and his unique sophistication in handling them; his self-assured treatment of, and early ascendancy over, older parliamentary colleagues; his powerful and carefully nurtured gifts of oratory; his sense of how and when to veer between party loyalism and instant revolt; his skill in mounting popular campaigns—and, perhaps as in the Cymru Fydd crisis of 1895–6 or in the 'fusion' moves of 1920, a tendency to exaggerate the lasting impact of paper organizations or of the short-term euphoria at public

---

[1] Memoir by D. R. Daniel, 'D. Lloyd George: Canghellaur y Trysorlys' (covering the period from 1908), (Nat. Lib. Wales, Daniel Papers, 2912, p. 52). In pp. 4–25 of this document there is a searching discussion of Lloyd George's religious outlook.

meetings. The slow crystallization of political commitment through official party channels was a world for which he never had much sympathy nor, perhaps, understanding. He chose to commune with the masses rather than haggle with agents: Nuremberg rather than Nevin was the model. These letters show also a Lloyd George whose concern for social questions, particularly those relating to industrial communities, evolved only very slowly. After the immense class cleavage revealed in the Penrhyn quarry dispute between 1896 and 1903, he remained largely caught up in the old, immemorial conflicts of church and chapel, tenant farmer and Tory landlord. Even after his conversion to social reform during his visit to Germany in the summer of 1908, he remained an Old Liberal in Wales although a New Liberal in England, a sectarian in the one and a social reformer in the other. In all these crucial matters, his letters to his wife afford important clues.

But, like every other historical source, they have their limitations. They are patchier after 1906 although clusters of letters survive to provide important first-hand evidence on such matters as Britain's entry into war in August 1914, the formation of the first wartime coalition in May 1915, and the downfall of the Lloyd George peacetime administration in 1921–2. These letters shed light on some of Lloyd George's political priorities, but very far from all of them. His dawning vision of a higher political synthesis to transcend petty partisanship—the commitment to a dream of coalition in 1910 and again in 1920 somewhat on the lines of Theodore Roosevelt's 'New Nationalism'—is not illustrated at all. Neither are his increased involvement with foreign affairs after the Agadir crisis in 1911, his direction of military and naval strategy during the first world war, nor his attempt to remodel the structure of international relations between 1918 and 1922, apart from a few stray references. For these and other matters, the student must turn to Frances Stevenson's revealing diary. On the other hand, these letters do show aspects of his career on which that fascinating document is largely silent—or even positively misleading (as in its exaggeration of the isolation of late nineteenth-century rural Wales, or the poverty of Lloyd George's own childhood). In this historical sense, as well as in the delicate and often painful personal tensions that they record, the Frances Stevenson diary and the Lloyd George family correspondence complement each other as sources for the life of a great statesman.

In editing these letters, I have largely retained the abbreviations and other idiosyncrasies of the originals, and have revised punctuation and spelling only when the sense absolutely demands it. The passages in Welsh—often highly revealing—I have translated freely—perhaps too freely for Celtic scholars— in the footnotes or, in the case of shorter passages, in the text. All the letters originate from London unless otherwise indicated. The letters or parts of letters I have omitted have been rejected not because they are scandalous but because they are banal. Many of them deal with matters of trivial domestic detail that shed no light at all on Lloyd George or anyone else. I have also omitted most of the letters that relate to Lloyd George's various travels abroad, except when they turn to public issues. Most of the details in them merely provide a flood of conventional tourist information that is not worth publishing—presumably a dutiful attempt to supply his wife with what Lloyd George imagined that she would like to know. It is when he turns to politics that these letters become vivid and absorbing, and it is on this that I have largely concentrated. This family correspondence is essentially political rather than personal.

Finally I must thank the First Beaverbrook Foundation and the National Library of Wales for their joint invitation to me to edit these letters, and Mr. A. J. P. Taylor and Mr. David Jenkins, the respective librarians for those two institutions, for their constant help and encouragement throughout. I am also much indebted to Mr. Taylor for reading through my manuscript and making some valuable comments. I am very grateful to Lady Olwen Carey-Evans for important information on the Lloyd George family, and I have also benefited from conversations with Lady Valerie Daniel and the third Earl Lloyd-George of Dwyfor. The staff of the manuscript and all other departments of the National Library of Wales have been, as always, a model of helpfulness, patience and courtesy, while the admirable schedule of the Lloyd George Papers prepared by Mr. Daniel Huws greatly assisted me in my research throughout. Publication was greatly aided by the advice of Mr. John Bell of Oxford University Press, and of Dr. Brinley Jones of the University of Wales Press: it is especially gratifying for me to have this book published jointly by the presses of the two universities in which I have spent my entire academic career.

My manuscript benefited from the patient scrutiny of Miss Audrey Bayley of Oxford University Press. Mr. Bryn Parry of the Caernarvon Record Office gave valuable guidance on the illustrations. My greatest debt is to my father for assistance with the index and other technical matters, and to both my parents for their constant help towards and interest in my work.

As a result of my work on these letters, Lloyd George's career became alive for me in a totally new way. Although I have been exploring it as a professional historian for the past fifteen years, these letters offered me a vast range of new insights into a creative, restless and strangely contemporary statesman. I can only hope that the reader will find them equally rewarding, and that the apparatus I have provided will be of some help to his study of them. Lloyd George remains an enigma, with a political style unique in recent history. An ultimate understanding of him will probably always baffle the historian. But after the publication of these letters he is, I hope, a little less enigmatic than before.

The Queen's College, Oxford　　　　　　　KENNETH O. MORGAN
August 1972

CHAPTER 1

Courtship, Marriage, and into Parliament

(1885–90)

David Lloyd George of Llanystumdwy first met Margaret Owen of Criccieth in the spring of 1884, he and his family having taken up residence in Morvin House, Criccieth. His diary first refers to her in June of that year, and a prolonged and complicated courtship then began. Margaret's parents were far from encouraging and placed innumerable obstacles in the way of her seeing David. For many months they forbade him to come to Mynydd Ednyfed farm during the daytime. The Owens were prominent Methodists and viewed with disfavour a youthful adherent of the Campbellite Baptists. In addition, Richard Owen, Margaret's father, a respectable and wealthy farmer, saw himself as a pillar of local society, and read with alarm of the young Lloyd George's flamboyant speeches with their sarcastic attacks on the gentry, the Church, and established institutions in general. Until the late summer of 1887, therefore, the courtship dragged on inconclusively, with young David having to use a sympathetic farm servant to smuggle in his letters and to arrange nocturnal appointments with Margaret. Another problem was that his uncle and guardian, the shoemaker Richard Lloyd, was himself unenthusiastic about Margaret Owen as a suitable wife for his favourite nephew. Just as the Owens had tried to involve Margaret with local Methodist farmers, so 'Uncle Lloyd' attempted to divert David's roving and discriminating gaze towards eligible Baptist girls in the neighbourhood. An additional source of tension was that David himself, as the earlier letters below indicate, made it very plain from an early stage that his courtship must be a controlled operation, one that would not frustrate the young solicitor's wider ambitions 'to get on' in the law and in politics.

Despite all these problems, however, affection between David and Margaret steadily deepened. At first his letters had addressed her as 'Dear Miss Owen': this is the style of his first letter to her to survive, written from the Drury Lane Theatre on 20 May 1885. By February 1887, this formal mode of address had at last changed to 'Dearest Maggie': his own letters he signed henceforth as 'Dei'. After delicate negotiations with Margaret's parents, who continually urged delay, David obtained their permission to marry their daughter: this was on 2 November 1887. After some debate as to whether the wedding should take place in Criccieth or in Llanystumdwy, they were married at the Pencaenewydd Methodist chapel just outside Criccieth, the service being conducted jointly by the minister of Margaret's Methodist chapel and by Uncle Lloyd. Even at this early stage, David

Lloyd George had a flair for the creative compromise. After a ten-day honeymoon in London, which included visits to such attractions as the Globe Theatre and to Spurgeon's Tabernacle, they settled down in a farmhouse let by Margaret's parents in Criccieth. When David became an M.P. he set up a solicitor's business in the City of London, and they took a series of flats there, the first being in Essex Court in the Temple. Their first child, a son named Richard after Uncle Lloyd, was born on 15 February 1889; their second child, a daughter, Mair Eluned, on 2 August 1890. The first was to be christened in a Baptist chapel, the second in a Methodist chapel, another compromise. By then, though, David Lloyd George had been elected to parliament.

Almost from the outset of their lengthy courtship, David had made it very clear to Margaret that his energies and ambitions were being directed towards a career in politics. This was the end which his hard work in the solicitor's office was designed to serve. He had first been directly involved in politics in the 1880 general election, on behalf of the Liberal candidate for Caernarvonshire. From 1881 he began to acquire valuable experience in public speaking before the Portmadoc Debating Society: his first effort there to be reported in the press appeared in the *North Wales Express* on 3 February 1882. He also began to find outlets in the local Welsh-language press as a pugnacious commentator on current political issues. In 1885 he became caught up in Liberal politics in neighbouring Merioneth when he backed Morgan Lloyd (shortly to turn Liberal Unionist) in a contest for the Liberal nomination. He reinforced his standing in Merioneth politics in a striking speech at a meeting at Ffestiniog, a quarrying town, in support of the Irish Nationalist, Michael Davitt, on 12 February 1886. The Liberal schism over Irish home rule troubled Lloyd George as it did so many others in Wales. He thought of attending the inaugural meeting of Joseph Chamberlain's Radical Union at Birmingham that May, but a fortunate accident caused him to miss his train. By the time of the general election of July 1886 he was firmly back in the Gladstonian fold, and there he stayed.

The Caernarvon Boroughs, the constituency which included Criccieth, with Bangor, Conway, Caernarvon, Pwllheli, and Nevin as its other components, was won by the Conservatives in the 1886 election. An increasingly numerous body of Liberals, particularly in the southern part of the county, now suggested that the fiery young Criccieth solicitor might serve as a suitable candidate next time. He took an active part in the anti-tithe campaign in southern Caernarvonshire in 1886–7, and made a range of belligerent speeches on Church disestablishment, land reform, temperance, and other bitterly controversial questions. His fame now spread far beyond his own Caernarvonshire: in 1888, in a celebrated court case, he defended some nonconformists from Llanfrothen who had ventured to bury their own dead in the parish churchyard, in defiance of the rector. In the High Court, Lord Chief Justice Coleridge gave judgement for the defendants. In the first county council elections in January 1889, in which the Liberals swept Caernarvonshire and most other Welsh counties, Lloyd George was elected an alderman at the age of 25. A few weeks earlier, he had been adopted as Liberal candidate for the Caernarvon Boroughs. Then in March 1890 the sitting Conservative member, Edmund Swetenham, died, and a bitter contest ensued. Caernarvon Boroughs was anything but a secure Liberal seat. Bangor had a powerful Anglican interest associated with the cathedral, while Conway was uncertain in its allegiance. Lloyd George depended heavily on his power base in the three small southern boroughs of Pwllheli, Nevin, and his own Criccieth. In addition he was under attack from his own supporters. The Rev. Evan Jones, minister of Moriah chapel, Caernarvon, and a powerful Methodist patriarch, insisted that Lloyd George declare in advance of the poll that he would refuse the Liberal whip unless the next Liberal government were to pass Welsh disestablishment concurrently with, or immediately after, Irish home rule. After a desperately close contest, and after two somewhat dubious recounts, on 11 April 1890 David Lloyd George was declared member for Caernarvon Boroughs by a majority of eighteen votes.

Already he was a highly controversial figure. He was hard-hitting and uncompromising, frequently the target of severe criticism in the Welsh press. Still, a series of eloquent triumphs on the platform, notably a temperance address at the Free Trade Hall in Manchester on 4 June, steadily built up his reputation. He made his maiden speech in the Commons a few days later, on 14 June, a colourful attack on the government's proposals to compensate holders of liquor licences. It made an immediate impact on Welsh opinion—after all, the Brewer ranked with the Bishop and the Squire in the 'Unholy Trinity' of Liberal demonology. His second speech in the House was an onslaught on the money provided under the supplementary estimates for lesser members of the royal family: it aroused a private protest from the Queen herself, but cheered the radicals and the Irish. When parliament went into summer recess later in August, Lloyd George's standing as an articulate backbencher was becoming assured.

(undated—probably 1885) (from Criccieth)

Without any preamble or beating about the bush, let's straight to the topic. Here I am under the very disagreeable necessity—through no fault of my own you must admit—of addressing you for the hundredth time during a not very protracted courtship in a remonstrative spirit. Appealing to the love I have for you or that you have professed for me seems to be but vanity itself in your sight. I am now going to appeal to your sense of fairness & commiseration. I have repeatedly told you how I am steeped to the lips in an accumulation of work— that I am quite entangled & confounded by my office arrears— that I have to work late every evening & then get up early the following morning to effect some measure of disentanglement. You know how very important it is for a young fellow starting in business that he should do his work not only efficiently but promptly. Another thing you have been told is that clients from Criccieth & the surrounding districts can only see me in the evenings & that they generally ask me to make appointments with them beforehand. And yet notwithstanding that you have been fully & emphatically acquainted with all these considerations the only assistance you give me is this—that in the course of a *week's* time you have disappointed in *three* appointments made by you, that at the last moment, when my business arrangements had been made to suit those appointments, that moreover you kept me on Friday evening to loiter about for about 30 minutes before you even took the trouble to acquaint me with your intention to make a fool of me at your mother's nod. Now letting love stand aside for the nonce—even a general sense of philanthropy might dictate to you that such conduct is scarcely kind on your part. I am sure you will recognise that it is not in keeping with your usual kindliness of spirit. I must really ask you for a little sympathy in my struggles to get on.

Another thing—you well know how you lecture me about my lack of self respect. Well how is it you conduce to this quality to me? By showing me the utmost disrespect. You stick me for half an hour in a conspicuous spot to wait for you & having made an exhibition to all passers by, you coolly send word that it is your mother's pleasure I should go home to avoid another disappointment. Now once for ever let us have an end of this long standing wrangle. It comes to this. My supreme idea is to get on. To this idea I shall sacrifice everything—except I trust honesty. I am prepared to thrust even love itself under the wheels of my Juggernaut, if it obstructs the way, that is if love is so much trumpery child's play as your mother deems courtship to be. I have told you over and over that I consider you to be my good angel—my guiding star. Do you not really desire my success? If you do, will you suggest some course least objectionable to you out of our difficulty? I am prepared to do anything reasonable & fair you may require of me. I can not—earnestly—carry on as present. Believe me— & may Heaven attest the truth of my statement—my love for you is sincere & strong. In this I never waver. But I must not forget that I have a purpose in life. And however painful the sacrifice I may have to make to attain this ambition I must not flinch—otherwise success will be remote indeed. . . .

8 March 1886 (probably from Criccieth)

I send you enclosed ticket in order to demonstrate to you

that I can keep my promises better than a young lady of my acquaintance can.

Will you come out of your drawing class at 7 tomorrow evening? I shall be there at that hour to meet you.

Kindly recollect that the directions I gave you on a previous occasion as to escort from the concert fully apply. Mr. Hopkinson has especially desired me to see that all young ladies are provided with due escort home after the performance is over! I can assure you that you may implicitly trust to my providence in this respect. . . .

1 May 1886 (from Blaenau Ffestiniog)

Enclosed I send you ticket for the Debating Society. Please recollect that the Society displays its usual consideration for young ladies in providing for them suitable escort after the meeting. So there is no necessity for making any arrangements for ambuscades of servants to waylay you on the way home.

29 July 1886 (from Criccieth)

[He apologizes for failing to keep an appointment with her: he was unavoidably detained by a heated argument in a case at Caernarvon County Court.]

Will you come up to the top of the Foel by 7.15 p.m. *this* evening. I have heaps of interesting things to impart you. Nothing unpleasant though. You will come up won't you? I know you can manufacture excuses by the score—& difficulties by the myriad—ond peidiwch codi bwganod am un tro.[1] Believe me the best plan is—first of all to decide upon doing a thing—secondly to discover the best method of doing it. . . .

(undated—probably 1886) (from Criccieth)

[He would like to meet her at the Foel the following day.]

You will please remember that rain will not deter me in the least from coming up at the appointed hour. A shower of rain is of course a very serious matter for very delicate people—that is why they have so mortal a dread of it undoubtedly—but I do not class myself amongst valetudinarians. I had a splendid bouquet of asters for you tonight. Now they will wither in resentment.

---

[1] But don't raise bogeys for once.

28 August 1886 (from Criccieth)

I trust that you received due amusement & entertainment in the preaching meetings—instruction or edification you would scarcely dare to hope for in the Association games. Who won the buckle? Who raved most deliriously about the agonies of the wicked's doom & about the bliss of every true Calvinist's predestination? I hope you have sunk no deeper in the mire of the Cyffes Ffydd[1] & other prim orthodoxies—Believe me.

I have done pretty well at Portmadoc & am consequently inclined to take a rather hopeful view of the ways of Providence just now. That is why I have for the present set aside the true orthodox gloom.

Write me your answer to the question I gave you on Wednesday evening (or Thursday morning—I am not sure which it was!). Do, that's a good girl. I want to get *your own* decision up on the matter. The reason I have already given you. I wish the choice you make—whatever it be—to be really yours & not anyone else's. . . .

P.S. I have a series of adventures to detail to you—*on sight*. I have also relegated all sentiment for a tete-a-tete. It disfigures a letter.

25 September 1886 (from Blaenau Ffestiniog)

[He invites her to hear a lecture by Mr. Williams.]

The proceedings will—or ought to be anyhow—opened with a stroll. What say you to the road between Wernddu & "Cebol's"[2] palatial portals about 6.30?

You will notice that I have marked on the ticket that the lecture commences at 7. As a matter of arrangement it will not open until 8. So that there is ample time given for a *rehearsal* a la Dinas. . . .

You can square your mother by reminding her that Mr. Williams is one of the etholedigion [elect] & that Gruffydd ap Cynan[3] was an eminent Methodist divine who flourished before Christ & in fact initiated him into the true principles of Calvinism. That ought to propitiate her.

---

[1] The 'Confession of Faith', the doctrinal declaration drawn up by the combined Association of the Calvinist Methodists at Aberystwyth in 1823.

[2] Apparently J. T. Jones, Criccieth

[3] An eleventh-century prince of Gwynedd.

(undated—apparently October 1886) (from Criccieth)

I am pleased also to perceive that you intend enjoying yourself in London in the only truly sensible style—by going to the theatres in the evening. But I fear that you are going beyond the threshold of the Cyffes Ffydd etc.

If you wish good thorough dramatic enjoyment go to the Lyceum to see Faust. You must book a seat one or two days before hand to get a comfortable seat there. It is so popular. . . . Another excellent performance is that of Sophia at the "Vaudeville". But take care that you don't fall in love with the young fellow in black—Tom Jones' cousin & arch-type who teaches & professes to follow the dictates of "moral philosophy". He is so good—& a member withal, I believe, of the "Hen Gorph" & as canting a hypocrite as ever adorned a "set fawr".[1] Another excellent drama you will get at the Adelphi, "The Harbour Lights". . . . I went to the Gaiety also to see Dorothy—that is tolerably good. But if you want an exquisitely funny comedy go to the Savoy to see "The Mikado". To perfectly enjoy this you must, however, get a book of words. The music is entrancing. . . .

I now leave off to go to Chapel. I may write more upon my return—of my spiritual experiences &c. under the Weinidogaeth [ministry]. I wish to goodness I were there with you. . . .

8 December 1886 (from Criccieth)

I trust you will have something to report to me tomorrow of the result of an interview with your mother. As I have already intimated to you it is but of trivial consequence to me what your mother's views of me may be—so long of course as they do not affect yours. All I wish for is a clear understanding so that we may afterwards see for ourselves how we stand.

You will appreciate my anxiety to bring the matter to an issue with your mother. I somehow feel deeply that it is unmanly to take by stealth & fraud what I am honestly entitled to. It has a tinge of the ridiculous in it, moreover.

This being done, you will not be troubled with any more lectures & I am confident I shall be thereby encouraged to act in such a way as will ensure your requited Confidence.

---

[1] 'Hen Gorff' (literally 'old body') is the familiar name for the Calvinistic Methodists. 'Set fawr' is the deacons' seat in a chapel.

25 February 1887 (from the Savoy theatre, London)

After a severe & exciting day's work I have now gone to seek recreation & repose to one of those glorious institutions "where the weary cease from troubling & the wicked are at rest" (Job III 20). We had a very stiff day's work today. Our opponents had retained an eminent Queen's Counsel to oppose us. He subjected old Richard Thomas to a cross-examination of about 3 hours duration & I fear succeeded in considerably damaging the old man. The poor old chap is getting old & fuddled. To make matters worse my London agent who has attended to this matter had to leave the Court before the case was half over & I had without of course ever having had any experience in these courts to conduct our case myself. You may imagine that I felt rather anxious being pitted all alone against a Q.C. of high standing—without either experience or preparation as I had left the whole thing to my agent. However I did my best & got up after the Q.C. to re-examine R. T. and try & put together into some sort of coherency the thing of shreds of patches into which the smart Q.C. had torn our story. I am not sanguine of success—but the sheriff's agent who was present admitted that I had done exceedingly well & that I had succeeded in completing [completely?] disposing of one at least very important point laboured by my opponent. That is his opinion & he further remarked that *if* the old man had not made a mess of it on some very important points we might succeed. I did not swear [at?] the old man though he thoroughly deserved it, did he not? However I recollect that if I swore I would break a solemn promise I had made to a little girl I am extremely fond of.

(undated—probably 1887) (from Criccieth)

[He clears himself of any charge of impropriety arising from his visiting a girl, the daughter of a fishmonger, who was implicated in a breach of promise case.]

One of the few religious dogmas of our creed I believe in is —fraternity with which you may couple equality. My God never decreed that farmers & their race should be esteemed beyond the progeny of a fishmonger & strange to say Christ— the founder of our creed—selected the missionaries of his noble teaching from amongst fishmongers. Do you really think that the Christ who honoured & made friendship with Zebedee the fishmonger's son would disdain the acquaintance of a poor toiling fishmonger's daughter. And who are lawyers & farmers daughters that they should presume to despise that class from amongst which the prince of eternity selected his friends. If proof was required of the utter hollowness of what is known as respectable Christianity let him but study the silly scorn of classes for their supposed inferiors. The barbarous castes of the Heathen Hindoo are but a faint imitation. . . . You seem to think that the supreme function of a wife is to *amuse* her husband —to be to him a kind of twin or plaything to enable him to while away with enjoyment his leisure hours. Frankly, that is simply prostituting marriage. My ideas are very different—if not superior—to yours. I am of opinion that woman's function is to soothe & sympathize & not to amuse. Men's lives are a perpetual conflict. The life I have mapped out will be so especially —as lawyer & politician. Woman's function is to pour oil on the wounds—to heal the bruises of spirit received in past conflicts & to stimulate to renewed exertion. Am I not right? If I am then you are pre-eminently the girl for me. I have a thorough belief in your kindliness & affection.

As to setting you free, that is a matter for your choice & not mine. I have many times impressed upon you that the only bond by which I have any desire to hold you is that of love. If that be lost then I would snap any other bond with my own hand. Hitherto my feelings are those of unflinching love for you & that feeling is a growing one.

You ask me to choose—I have made my choice deliberately & solemnly. I must now ask to make your choice. I know my slanderers—those whom you allow to poison your mind against me. Choose between them & me—there can be no other alternative.

May I see you at 7 tomorrow? . . .

David Lloyd George's Diary, 30 August 1887

By the bye I am in a very queer state of mind upon this question [his marriage]. My urge is strong for a marriage straight away—say in [an] hour. On the other hand I am anxious that it should not come off until the spring at the earliest. Maggie I believe to be in a very similar state of mind but on the whole I think she wd. prefer the earlier date.

However my present view is that prudence dictates spring as the date & I rather imagine that the event will be postponed to that season. I shd. however like to be in a position to ask the old folks consent *now*. One very good reason for postponement is that there is no available house for one's residence—except Cefniwrch wh[ich] neither of us cares for. The only thing to be said for it is this, that if it is to be let furnished for a short period we might have another house by the end of that period. It is when I am with Maggie that I find myself most anxious for marriage. Her society has a wonderful charm for me & I believe she now much prefers me to her parents. She will tell me so occasionally. . . .

It is evident that I have a higher opinion of Maggie's qualifications than her mother has. I think she is worthy of something better than a farmer. A farmer's wife is only a portion of his stock.

Diary, 3 September 1887

Long talk [with Margaret Owen] as to my night visits. Told her that I was not enamoured of them especially as my uncle seemed to be feel them so sorely—but they were our only resource since her mother was not civilized enough to permit my visiting her during decent hours. I suggested that she shd. tell her mother that I intended to come up at 8 every evening & she said that she had been thinking of the same thing, that she was thoroughly tired of our midnight meetings as they involved a sense of transgressing respectable rules. She finally promised to tell her mother on Monday without fail. She *may* do so.

Diary, 4 September 1887

Got an invitation this morning. I mean to cultivate [Caernarvon] Boroughs as, if the Unionist Govt. holds together another 3 yrs., I may stand a good chance to be nominated as Liberal candidate. There are two or three impressions I must be careful to make in the meantime. 1st & foremost that I am a good speaker. 2ndly that I am a sound & thorough politician. 3rdly that I can afford to attend to parliamentary duties. To succeed in the first I must avail myself of every opportunity to speak in public so as to perfect myself & attain some reputation as a speaker. To succeed in the 2nd point I must put into those speeches good sound matter well arranged so as to catch the year [*sic*] of the intelligent who always lead & gain the name of sound as well as fluent speaker. I must also write political articles on Welsh politics so as to show my mastery of them. To attain the 3rd reputation I must (1) attend to my business well so as to build up a good practice (2) practise economy so as to accumulate some measure of wealth (3) get all my cases well advertised (4) subscribe judiciously.

Diary, 1 November 1887

I then had a talk with Mr. & Mrs. Owen—they pleaded for delay—that they had made up their minds not to stay at Mynydd Ednyfed . . . but that they could not get anything like a good price for the stock these bad times especially this time of the year & that they cd. not get a tenant worth anything to buy their assets at such short notice—that if they sold their things under value it would be *our* loss in the end—they wished us to wait for a yr. or so —that we were quite young &c. The old man also said 'Fedra i roi dim arian i chi rwan dim ond hynny sydd gyda hi ei hunan'.[1] I suppose he meant that he had no cash until he sold the stock. I was not prepared for this sort of talk. I thought the old man very cunningly tried to persuade me to delay by showing me it was in my own interest. In the course of conversation Mrs. Owen said something about building a house. I then told her we had made up our minds to live at Port[mado]c as we could get no house at Criccieth. She replied that she did not like us to go to Portmadoc to live. I told them when R. O. [Mr. Richard Owen] said something about money that I wanted no money as I had of course before coming to that point seen that I wd. have sufficient myself without any extraneous aid (I am not sure whether it would have been better to plead poverty—but I wanted to show them that I took no commercial views of my engagement). The interview ended by their asking me to reconsider the matter & see them again about it. They then went to bed & left me with Maggie who was in the kitchen during the interview. . . .

Diary, 8 November 1887

I told my mother [about his marriage] before I started— the poor old woman cried and said she felt my leaving very much. She then gave me some very good advice about being

[1] I can't give you any money now apart from what she's got herself.

kind to Maggie, never saying anything nasty to her when I lost my temper, to be attentive to her if & when she was ill, that sort of thing. She praised M. very much from what she had heard from M. E. G. [Mary Ellen George].

26 November 1887

'Your mother has not said anything to the contrary.' No, perhaps not, but we must not marry on the strength of inferences. We ought to know *definitely* whether they object & also where they propose we should go in the interval between our marriage & their leaving Mynydd Ednyfed. Unless they tell us to stay with them we must lose no time in looking out for a house & furniture. . . .

They were married on 24 January 1888.[1] *David Lloyd George's ambitions now turned increasingly towards a political career. In July he was proposed as prospective Liberal candidate for the Caernarvon Boroughs by the Liberal associations of Pwllheli, Criccieth, and Nevin. With the aid of friends such as D. R. Daniel, he built up support in Bangor, Caernarvon, and Conway also, and easily captured the nomination of the Caernarvon Boroughs Liberal Association. He described himself now as 'a Welsh Nationalist of the Ellis type' although some local Liberals feared him as a crypto-socialist.*[2]

'*Monday*' (some time in the spring or summer of 1889)

Find to my unmitigated disgust that I can't get off. It is all due to that fellow Ellis Griffith.[3] Been hunting him up all this afternoon—been to his chambers, where he ought to have been, found he was not there, the clerk could give me no information as to his whereabouts. I then hied to his private lodgings with a similar result. At last I got hold of Ellis (M.P.)[4] who told me Griffith had gone off for the day to see some boating match or other & that I had no chance whatever of

[1] Lloyd George wrote a brisk business-like letter to his friend D. R. Daniel, on his wedding day (N.L.W., Daniel Papers, 2747). He dealt only cursorily with his wedding: 'yr ydwyf am gychwyn i wlad bell—*gwell* hefyd disgwyliaf' (I'm setting off for a far-off land—a *better* one, too, I hope). A letter written to Daniel a few days later during his honeymoon was solely concerned with a newspaper, *Udgorn Rhyddid*, with which they were both connected.

[2] Lloyd George to D. R. Daniel, 5 July 1888 (Daniel Papers, 2751). One Liberal at Pwllheli had said that Lloyd George was 'too extreme, addicted to socialistic ideas'. In fact, Daniel himself was a sympathizer with socialism.

[3] Ellis Jones Griffith (1860–1926): Liberal member for Anglesey, 1895–1918, and for Carmarthen, 1923–4; under-secretary at the Home Office, 1912–15; a barrister, he was transmuted into Sir Ellis Jones Ellis-Griffith in 1918.

[4] Thomas Edward Ellis (1859–99): Liberal member for Merioneth, 1886–99; a junior whip, 1892–4, and Liberal chief whip, 1894–9; a Welsh patriot, mourned after his premature death as 'Wales' lost leader'.

seeing him today. As it is extremely important I should see him in London I *must* stay over tomorrow. This is a nuisance, a confounded nuisance. You have not the slightest idea what a wretched place this London is when you have no company. I heartily wish I were down with you & little Dick. . . .

3 September 1889 (from Llandrindod Wells)

The meeting is just over & I have been penned up in a foul room from 9 up till now with an interval of ¾ of an hour for dinner. It was a very lively meeting & resolutions were passed which will severely shock our mild Welsh M.P.'s & all the meek & mild Liberals of the Principality in general. [1]

In March 1890 the Conservative member for Caernarvon Boroughs, Edmund Sweten-ham, died. Lloyd George was the Liberal candidate in the by-election that followed. His opponent was a popular local squire, H. J. Ellis Nanney. Caernarvon Boroughs was a highly marginal seat and Lloyd George, with internecine divisions among his own supporters, particularly the Methodists of Caernarvon, faced a very stern contest.

21 March 1890 (from Bangor)

Home tomorrow I hope by 11 train. They are all ready & eager for the fight.

7 April 1890 (from Caernarvon)

I shall be there [Bangor] canvassing all day tomorrow. On Wednesday I shall be at Pwllheli & Nevin. On Thursday I intend taking a run through all the Boroughs. On Friday—it is then I shall be in real want of your kind affectionate face—I shall be at Carnarvon. I am half inclined to go fishing in the Seiont whilst the count is on.

I really can't tell you how we are getting on. I am awfully afraid that the Bangor people are not working systematically as they ought to.

I attended the Baptist chapel on Sunday evening. One 'blaenor' [deacon] made a regular electioneering speech in the 'Seiat' [fellowship meeting]. I also spoke but not upon politics. They were highly delighted that I went there, poor people, &

[1] There is a lengthy account of this meeting of the Executive Committee of the Welsh National Council in the minute-book of the North Wales Liberal Federation (in the editor's possession). Among other things, resolutions were passed attacking the collection of tithe, condemning those Welsh Liberal M.P.s who absented themselves from the tithe debates, and warning Gladstone that failure to push on with Welsh disestablishment might call into question the loyalty of Wales to the Liberal Party.

made much of me. I was much touched by their kindly enthusiasm. One important blaenor is a Tory but it was he who immediately I entered the chapel whilst the congregation was at it singing left the 'set fawr' [deacons' seat] & brought me a hymn book.

Perhaps you will see the 'hen langc'[1] & tell him from me that he must be calm on Friday & not take it very much to his heart if we lose on Friday. Personally I am quite resigned to a defeat for I am convinced that a few so-called moderates deliberately intend betraying us. I have received private & confidential information on this point. Never mind. Woe unto them. Dr. John Thomas[2] & Dr. Herber [Evans][3] have already suspected it & so have the "Hwntws".[4] It is a general rumour throughout South Wales that a few of the Hen Gorph are going to turn tail. There is an article upon it in the South Wales Daily News. The result will be an outcry which may do good. Never mind. I am in good spirits.

On polling day, 11 April 1890, after two recounts, Lloyd George emerged as the victor, capturing the seat by a majority of eighteen votes. He was introduced to the House on Budget Day, 17 April.

(undated—apparently 17 April 1890)

This is the first letter which I write as an introduced member of the House of Commons & I dedicate it to my little darling. I snatch a few minutes during the delivery of Goschen's budget to write her. I was introduced amid very enthusiastic cheers on the Liberal side, by Mr. Acland[5] and Stuart Rendel.[6]

[1] Old boy: i.e. 'Uncle Lloyd', Lloyd George's shoemaker uncle, Richard Lloyd (1834–1917). There is a biography of him in Welsh, William George, *Richard Lloyd* (Cardiff, 1934). Lloyd George severely criticized this book, saying that his brother had 'used Uncle Lloyd as a vehicle for expressing his own narrow views on religion' (*Lloyd George: a Diary by Frances Stevenson*, p. 288). Lloyd George always considered his uncle to be a model of tolerance and open-mindedness.

[2] Dr. John Thomas (1821–92): eminent Independent minister and political activist; minister of Tabernacle chapel, Liverpool since 1854.

[3] Rev. E. Herber Evans (1836–96): eminent Independent minister; at this time, minister of Salem chapel, Caernarvon.

[4] South Walians.

[5] Arthur Herbert Dyke Acland (1847–1926): Liberal member for Rotherham, 1885–99; vice-president of Committee of Council on Education, 1892–5; active in the Welsh education movement and a very close friend of Tom Ellis.

[6] Stuart Rendel (1834–1913): Liberal member for Montgomeryshire, 1880–94; an English Anglican, he became first chairman of the Welsh Parliamentary Party in 1888; created Baron Rendel, 1894; friend of Gladstone and backer of Lloyd George.

J. T. Roberts,[1] who came up with us for the express purpose of seeing this ceremony, was overjoyed at the reception. He seemed to feel that he came in somehow for a portion of the cheer.

Cymru Fydd came to the station to meet us. Mr. Alfred Davies,[2] a member of the London County Council, had his carriage to drive us to the House. A very swell 'landau'.

Sir John Puleston[3] came up to me & very kindly invited me to dine with him at 7.30. I told him I couldn't come without Roberts, he then extended his invitation to Roberts.

It will interest you to know that Goschen has *taken off* 2d. in the lb. [*sic*] duty on tea. I am glad now we didn't buy that chest—it will be cheaper now by a few shillings at least.

7 May 1890

I got on beyond my highest expectations at Finsbury tonight. I started very nervous & not intending to hold out more than 10 or 15 minutes but I must have spoken for about $\frac{3}{4}$ of an hour. I roused the audience to such a pitch of enthusiasm that they would hardly allow me to proceed & when I left they rose to their feet & flourished their hats. In proposing me a vote of thanks the most profuse compliments were lavished upon my "eloquence, wit" &c. One speaker, a member of the London County Council & a great swell, said he was perfectly fascinated.

14 May 1890

Send me the "Faner"[4] will you? Vincent Evans[5] I am told has been criticising me in his "superior" fashion. I told him last night to his face he assiduously cracked up Tom Ellis & Ellis Griffith & ran down everyone else in their way.

16 May 1890

[Ellis Griffith had been compelled to say something about

---

[1] Lloyd George's election agent in 1890.

[2] Alfred Davies (1848–1907): a wealthy London Welshman; later Liberal member for Carmarthen District, 1900–6.

[3] Sir John Henry Puleston (1829–1908): Conservative member for Devonport, 1874–92; a Welshman, he was shortly to be nominated to fight Lloyd George in Caernarvon Boroughs in the 1892 general election.

[4] i.e. *Baner ac Amserau Cymru*, the leading Welsh-language weekly newspaper, founded in 1859 and edited and owned by the veteran, Thomas Gee of Denbigh.

[5] E. Vincent Evans (1851–1934): a prominent Welsh journalist who contributed a column to the *Faner* at this period; later on, he became very friendly with Lloyd George and, as a result, became a Companion of Honour in 1922.

Lloyd George's West Norwood speech in his 'Welsh Notes' in the *Faner*.]

But although he was present & knew in his heart of hearts that it was a success from an oratorical point of view he hasn't the grace to say so. . . . Your Dafydd *will* get on despite them. I have just met Ellis. Poor fellow he is far from well. Good sort Ellis. 'Tis a pity these fellows make a tool of him.

(undated—May 1890)

Cofia ysgrifenu ata i yfory.[1] I feel *very* VERY lonely. Never thought I should feel it so keenly. I went straight from Euston to my agents & after my business there went to my rooms. So very keenly did I feel the absence of my genial Maggie's welcoming face that I could not help bursting into tears.

I am awfully digalon [dejected]. Write me a long letter old darling. Kiss little Dick for me. . . .

Stuart Rendel came up to me just as I was finishing this letter & congratulated me on my Tabernacle speech. He said he had been told by a very good judge who was present & who didn't know me a bit that it was admirable & that I had created a very good impression. Tell Uncle will you? The Western Mail publishes my speech verbatim & has a long article upon it.

27 May 1890

I am rather afraid the Government will not adjourn until Friday. Our own men obstruct business so grossly that the Govt. threaten to keep us together over Friday & recall us to our duties the following Thursday. This is simply atrocious but it is our side's fault entirely. Healy[2] & Harcourt[3] seem to have entered into a conspiracy of obstruction. The Irish members spoke last night for 3 hours on a silly question of granting an additional pension to some girls who happened to be the daughters of a fellow who had invented an improved gun. I voted with the govt. against it. I fancy all they wanted was to prevent the Gov[t]. getting into the proper business of the House that night. They wasted the whole of yesterday afternoon in the same fashion.

[1] Remember to write to me tomorrow.

[2] Tim Healy (1855–1931): Irish Nationalist member, 1880–1918; first Govenor-General of the Irish Free State, 1922–8.

[3] Sir William Harcourt (1827–1904): Liberal member, 1868–1904; Home Secretary, 1880–5, Chancellor of the Exchequer, 1886 and 1892–5; Liberal leader, 1896–8.

Thank you for the Faner extracts. Vincent [Evans] displays his spleen liberally. He can't help cracking me up but he does it very faintly. . . .

5 June 1890

Your old Dei scored the greatest success of his life at the Free Trade Hall last night. The Hall was packed with an audience numbering several thousands. Caine[1] spoke first, Canon Hicks[2] came next then—nervous & fearful as to results—Dick's Tada was called. Immediately I got up the audience cheered again & again. In fact they gave me what the "Manchester Guardian" calls an ovation on rising. This set me up. When I said I was a native of Manchester they renewed the cheers. It would be a long story to take you through all my speech. I spoke for half an hour amid continued & long continued cheers. There was not a bit they failed to take up. I hardly uttered two consecutive sentences but that they cheered. . . . During my closing sentences a hush fell over the whole place. I spoke fiercely—feeling myself mind you intensely every word I uttered & charging my sentences with all the intensity of my heart—both in voice & action & when I sat down there came a sight which I shall never forget—the whole dense & immense audience seemed for a moment stunned but recovering they sprang up as one man & flung hats, handkerchiefs, sticks, hands—anything they could get hold of. For several minutes there was nothing but din & confusion, the Chairman in vain appealing for order. I trembled like a leaf with passion for a long while. I was overwhelmed with congratulation. Caine said "You have made your reputation in England with that speech". Mrs. Caine said the speech inspired her for her work in London. The poor Welshmen of Manchester—many of whom had gone there to listen to me, postponing their chapel meeting for the purpose I was told—were beyond themselves with joy & crowded to the platform to shake hands with me & to say they were "proud of their countryman". One Englishman said "God

[1] William S. Caine (1842–1903): president of the British Temperance League and vice-president of the United Kingdom Alliance; Liberal, then Liberal Unionist member between 1880 and 1903; the father-in-law of two Welsh Liberals, Herbert Lewis and Herbert Roberts (*q.v.*, pp. 62, n. 2, 73, n. 1).

[2] Rev. E. L. Hicks (1843–1919): canon of Manchester Cathedral; bishop of Lincoln from 1910; a Liberal churchman, partly of Welsh descent.

bless you". I saw Mrs. Gee's daughter on the platform. She was delighted.[1]

10 June 1890

On Saturday evening I dined at Stuart Rendel's. All the Welsh M.P.'s had been invited to meet the G.O.M. [Gladstone] I had a long talk with the old gentleman, mostly about compensation. . . . After chapel I went to Mr. D. H. Evans'. Evans is a young Welshman who keeps a drapery establishment in Oxford St. Although he is only 33 yrs. of age & started with £500 now he has already amassed a large fortune. He lives in a small house in Regents Park, keeps a liveried valet or butler to serve. He showed me one of his pictures, a Landseer picture of a dog which cost him *£800*!! He had also a Turner which must have cost him some hundreds. He had numerous R.A.'s & in fact I should fancy his picture gallery alone must have aggregated £10,000 in value.

But what about him. Well he is a light-headed featherbrained fellow with some good nature & much practical shrewdness. Concerning her, she is clever but purse proud & consequently contemptible. Of course she was alright with [Alfred] Thomas[2] & I—we are M.P.'s & therefore fit company for a beatified draper's wife, but I hated and despised her from the moment she talked about the Welsh society in London being 'led by drapers' assistants'. I asked fiercely—"Why not drapers' assistants? Every great movement has been initiated by men of that class". Unless she improves on acquaintance I shan't go there often altho' she be a Baptist. . . .

After two months in the House, Lloyd George made his maiden speech on 14 June 1890, on the Local Taxation Bill. It was a sparkling attack on the compensation due to holders of liquor licences.

12 June 1890

When am I to get little Dick's photo? I want it so badly. I

---

[1] i.e. the daughter of Thomas Gee (1815–98), see p. 25, n. 4 above. The extraordinary effect of Lloyd George's speech at this temperance meeting is confirmed in 'Welsh Note from Manchester', *Cambrian News*, 13 June 1890. Years later, in April 1934, Lloyd George described this speech as the best he ever made and claimed that Sir Henry Irving was one of the admiring audience (*Lloyd George: a Diary by Frances Stevenson*, p. 268).

[2] Alfred Thomas (1840–1927): Liberal member for East Glamorgan, 1885–1910; chairman of Welsh Parliamentary Party, 1898–1910; created Baron Pontypridd, 1910; like Lloyd George, a Baptist, unlike him, a bachelor.

can't stand this solitude much longer. It is unbearable. Here the House adjourns in a few minutes now, that is at 6, & I go to my lodgings like a hermit or a prisoner to his cell. Dark, gloomy dungeon my room is. I don't know what I would give now for an hour of your company. It would scatter all the gloom & make all the room so cheerful. I *will* come home soon.

14 June 1890

Shortly after I wrote my letter of yesterday to you I got up & spoke for the first time in the House of Commons. . . . There is no doubt I scored a success & a great one. The old man & Trevelyan,[1] Morley,[2] Harcourt appeared delighted. I saw Morley afterwards & he said it was a "capital speech—*first rate*" & he said so with marked emphasis. He is such a dry stick that he wouldn't have said anything unless he thoroughly believed it. I have been overwhelmed with congratulations both yesterday & today. . . . Tom Ellis who is genuinely delighted because one of his own men has succeeded—told me that several members had congratulated *Wales* upon my speech. Stuart Rendel said I had displayed "very distinguished powers". . . . There is hardly a London Liberal or even provincial paper which does not say something commendatory about it.

16 June 1890

There is a jolly row in the House. I heard it in the lobby when I was writing this letter & I rushed in. The Government it appears had just told the House that they would agree to the appointment of a Committee on the Compensation question.[3] This of course is a complete change of front. Formerly this Bill was considered as a recognition of the principle of compensation. . . .

. . . What does the hen langc [old boy] think about the Pall Mall [Gazette] & the general reception given to my

[1] George Otto Trevelyan (1838–1928), politician and historian; Liberal member for various constituencies, 1865–97; Chief Secretary for Ireland, 1882 and for Scotland, 1886 and 1892–5; joined Liberal Unionists in 1886 but rejoined the Liberals in 1887.

[2] John Morley (1838–1923): Chief Secretary for Ireland, 1886 and 1892–5; Secretary of State for India, 1905–10; Lord President, 1910–14; created Viscount Morley, 1908.

[3] i.e. the compensation fund in connection with the granting and suppressing of liquor licences.

maiden? I've had more compliments today. One Tory M.P. said he heard several on his side praising it.

19 June 1890

I propose making another speech in Parliament before the Bill is disposed of. But I must see that it is really good or the favourable impression made by my first speech will be blotted out. That's why I didn't speak on my own amendment on Monday. Tell uncle. Besides it is the greatest possible mistake a man can make to speak too frequently in the House. The seldomer you speak the greater the desire to hear you.

We came within 4 now of defeating the government. There was a jolly row.

23 June 1890

We had a very rowdy meeting in Birmingham. Joe's minions came there—a dirty, mangy pack of ruffians.[1] I withstood them better than anyone else although I was very hoarse. Still the meeting in spite of them was a success. The Chairman introduced me to the meeting as one who had made a very brilliant maiden speech. He was delighted with my comparison of Joe to the political contortionists at the Pavilion. . . .

6 p.m.

The Government after all have only abandoned a part of their Licensing Bill. The most objectionable portion perhaps but still we must fight as they recognise the principle of Compensation. I must remain here.

26 June 1890

For the sake of morality & the great influence of example moral monsters like William Humphreys must fail. Who can believe in the existence of a good God who has organised & fashioned the principles upon which the Universe is to be governed, if rascals of that calibre march over every rule of goodness to a triumph. He is a moral eunuch who is as deficient in honest impulse as any castrated colt in the stall is in another sort of impulse (equally elevating)—or as deficient as he himself appears to be in that line. Don't show this letter to anyone. . . . I read a good book of Thackeray's the other day where the virtues

[1] The *Birmingham Daily Post*, 23 June 1890, reported that this meeting was interrupted by 'a hundred resolute rowdies'.

necessary to the constituting of an excellent wife were set forth. I marked the passage & said again "That's my own little Maggie" every inch of her. He is contrasting the mere meretricious dazzle of a showy woman with the sterling qualities of a good wife. But I'll show it to you when I come down.

15 July 1890

I attended a meeting of Liberal workers at Bangor at 8. They were very enthusiastic about their member. Speakers said they had always a high opinion about my ability but that I had exceeded their highest anticipation & they said that was the general talk. They appeared highly delighted with my success. I explained my Tithe vote but it was hardly necessary—they were all satisfied upon the point.

29 July 1890

[He consoles his wife who is in the final stages of her pregnancy and has been feeling very depressed. He is uncertain about whether to speak with Sir Charles Russell at a demonstration in Buckinghamshire.]

In fact I never feel satisfied about going to any big meeting unless I have first of all submitted my speech to the criticism of my good angel at Criccieth & obtained her approval. I know that if she approves I am bound to succeed. Her judgement has invariably proved infallibly correct & she is too genuine a lover of my welfare to flatter me when she doesn't in her heart applaud my things. Next year you must be up with me here altogether. Then I shall never have to go to any meeting without first of all reciting it to you. Besides if you were here I would stick to work ever so much better. I ought last night to have gone at it to prepare my speech for tomorrow, instead of that I fool about, read newspapers, talk to Tom Ellis & sleep in the upper lobby. If you were here I should have paired for 2 or 3 hours, dined with you & then sat down to get my points together. How I hate going to Craven St. it is so lonely. I am sure I would attend to my business in the morning also ever so much better. All these points we'll manage better next session.

31 July 1890

The Government intend conferring a grant upon the Roman Catholic school at Carnarvon in spite of the strenuous opposition of the School Board. It places me in rather a tight corner as my best supporters are Roman Catholics.

Lloyd George now knew that Sir John Puleston, a popular Welsh landowner, had been nominated to fight him in Caernarvon Boroughs in the next election. He would clearly be a powerful opponent. In the meantime, Lloyd George was preparing his second speech in parliament, an attack on the funds paid on the installation of Prince Henry of Prussia as a Knight of the Garter.

7 August 1890

Sir John Puleston came to me just now in his usual fussy pseudo-frank manner to invite me to visit him at his Pwllheli house. The American minister President Lincoln's son is coming down there to spend a few days with Puleston & P. wants me to meet him. Simply bluster. Puleston is a great hypocrite & fraud. The only difference between his pharisaism & that of the canting methodistical psalm-singers whom I revile is that the latter affect religion & Puleston trades on an appearance of good-fellowship. But cunning as he is I shall see that he does not win the seat with the ease he imagines.

I am on the job Saturday or Monday. I have given notice of my intention to object to a vote of £2,000 for providing fill breeches or something of that sort to a fellow who happening to be Lord Lieutenant of Ireland imagines he ought to ape royalty. If I can summon up sufficient courage for the purpose I shall make a short speech which will not be particularly sweet to those who adore the Peacockism of Royalty.

S. T. Evans[1] & I intend objecting to making some Princeling of Royal Lineage a Knight of the Garter at an expense of £400 to the country. People are starving or what is worse dragging a miserable existence through penury, poverty & toil whilst these vile aristocratic & royal vagabonds are spending the nation's money in idle frippery of this sort. Don't you think old Maggie I ought to have a fling at them even if the Tories howl me down & brand me as a wild revolutionary fanatic. D— the whole brood (& that is damning a good lot for they are exceedingly numerous).

[1] Samuel Thomas Evans (1859–1918): Liberal member for Mid-Glamorgan, 1890–1910; the son of a Skewen grocer; Solicitor-General, 1908–10 and President of the Probate, Divorce and Admiralty division in 1910. Something of a rake and suspected by Mrs. Lloyd George of leading her husband into immoral ways.

9 August 1890

Well you cannot imagine how dull it is in this House of Commons. We have half-a-dozen superannuated old Colonels talking about musket and cannon bores. The most perfect bores are themselves & if the War Office would only take them as a model they would be above criticism. In the debating chamber, there are hardly a dozen members listening to these dry discussions. The remaining M.P.'s have either left for the session or are lounging about on the Terrace or in the tea-room. It is perfectly ghastly to listen to these army men complaining that the guns are not killing enough & that they would be more destructive to human life if certain improvements were effected in them & all this they talk about as coolly & as indifferently as if it were a matter of destroying vermin. They talk far more feelingly about shooting hares than men.

. . . Talking of Puleston a very interesting thing happened last night. Whilst I was listening to some dreary debate or other about 110 ton guns a Conservative M.P. called Mr. Henniker Heaton[1] with whom I am rather chummy, & a very decent fellow he is too, beckoned me to come over to sit by his side on the Conservative benches. This I did & I found by the aroma of his breath that he had imbibed just a sufficient quantity of the wine which maketh glad the heart of man to make him communicative. It was after dinner & that's the time to get at an Englishman's secrets. He told me that he was very sorry for what the Government had done with Carnarvon Castle.[2] That it was an act of gross jobbery & that all the members sitting around him on the Tory side were very disgusted over it. He said he hoped it would do me no harm for he went on to say "although I am a Tory I have a sneaking sort of regard for you". He then told me somethings [*sic*] about Puleston. He didn't think much of him.

11 August 1890

Hearing a big cheer at this point I rushed into the House & hear Sexton firing [?][3] into T. W. Russell[4] like fury. Russell

---

[1] Sir John Henniker Heaton (1848–1914): Conservative member for Canterbury, 1885–1910.

[2] i.e. they had appointed Sir John Puleston, the prospective Unionist candidate for Caernarvon Boroughs (see p. 25, n. 3 above) to be its constable.

[3] Thomas Sexton (1848–1932): Irish Nationalist member, 1880–96.

[4] Sir Thomas Wallace Russell (1841–1920): Unionist member for South Tyrone, 1886–1910 and for North Tyrone, 1911–18.

is the fellow who by his speeches at Carnarvon & Bangor very
nearly lost me my election & career. So I am rather glad to hear
him slanged and heckled. . . .

Healy didn't speak as well as usual. However his speech &
that of the other Irish members had had this effect at least, that
my motion can't come on tonight. I am jolly glad of it too. It
will give me more time to polish my speech & impress it deeper
on my memory. That is just what I want. When you get up in a
hostile House you must have your speech well rooted in your
mind or you will be upset.

12 August 1890

We were at it until 3 o'clock this morning. Healy spoke
about twenty times. On one occasion he held the House for an
hour and 3/4s but he delivered such a sparkling, savage speech
that scarcely one man dropped out of his place. It was a very
brilliant affair. He attacked the Government for sending some
General Lintorn Simmons to Rome to negotiate some mysterious business with the Pope. He was sent there presumably to
settle some difficulty about Maltese marriages but Healy would
have it that he was despatched there to induce the Pope to use
his influence with the Irish Catholics to abandon the Nationalist
leaders. He was frightfully biting. Lintorn Simmons he called
all sorts of hideous names, "this ecclesiastical horse soldier" was
one of the mildest of them. "This clumsy diplomatist" was
another. He broke the rules of propriety which are so stringent
in the House but it was very amusing. There is a psalm-singing
Wesleyan on the Tory side—the only Wesleyan on that side—a
fellow who is always at Church & missionary meetings.[1] Healy
called him the "honourable & *pious* member for Boston". The
Chairman very angrily pulled him up but the House roared
with delight at this impudent sally. He referred to the Under
Secretary, a sanctimonious-looking Scotch Protestant,[2] as
"sleeping with Foxe's Book of Martyrs under his pillow". A
more impudent, audacious speech has hardly been delivered
ever with impunity within these walls. The Celts are having
their revenge upon the brutal Saxon.

[1] This refers to H. J. Farmer-Atkinson (1828–1913), Conservative member for
Boston, 1886–92.
[2] i.e. Sir John Fergusson, under-secretary for Foreign Affairs.

13 August 1890

[He defends himself against his wife's attack on him for spending Sunday on the river with S. T. Evans, a convivial friend, instead of going to chapel.]

. . . There is a great deal of difference between the temptation to leave your work for the pleasure of being cramped up in a suffocating malodorous chapel listening to some superstitions I had heard thousands of times before & on the other hand the temptation to have a pleasant ride on the river in the fresh air with a terminus at one of the loveliest gardens in Europe. . . .

As for Sam Evans he is the only Welsh M.P. available. All the other except Bryn [Roberts][1] & one or two of the old chaps have gone. Besides S.T.E. & I have another bond of sympathy in our being both equally the butts of attacks of Vincent Evans's clique.

[1] John Bryn Roberts (1847–1931): Liberal member for Caernarvonshire (Eifion), 1885–1906; a county court judge from 1906; a fierce opponent of Lloyd George's Cymru Fydd policy, but like him, an ardent 'pro-Boer' in 1899.

CHAPTER 2

Backbench Rebel

(1890–92)

Lloyd George's first parliament was an exciting and satisfying period of his life. He and his family moved into a new flat in the Inns of Court, Verulam Buildings on the Gray's Inn Road, in January 1891. Their third child, another daughter, Olwen (now Lady Olwen Carey-Evans), was born on 3 April 1892: much fairer than the two older children, she was given the pet name, 'Llwydyn'. Although Mrs. Lloyd George felt uneasy in the vast, mysterious metropolis and was at times inclined to stay on in Criccieth rather than respond to her husband's entreaties that she and the children join him in London, their married life was a very happy one. Further, for the young backbencher it was a dramatic parliament. The political situation was thrown into turmoil in November 1890 when the Irish Nationalist leader, Parnell, was cited as co-respondent in the O'Shea divorce case. In the event, the Irish Party split fatally and was never able henceforth to recapture its former dominant role in the Commons. Lloyd George took a close interest in this crisis: he was friendly with Tim Healy, T. P. O'Connor, and other Irish members. He felt that the moral of the affair was that sex should always be kept subordinate to politics, and he was an unforgiving critic of Parnell.

The tide of radicalism was now flowing irresistibly through Wales in the aftermath of the tithe riots, with the Liberal Party there becoming increasingly nationalist in tone. A new generation of young Welsh radicals had emerged in the 1886–92 parliament—D. A. Thomas and Samuel Evans in industrial Glamorgan, Tom Ellis and, of course, Lloyd George in the rural north. Evans and Lloyd George spearheaded a fierce Welsh resistance in the Commons to the government's Tithe Bill in January and February 1891. Lloyd George intervened repeatedly in debates, using the tithe issue to focus attention on the grievance of the 'alien' Church of England in Wales, and linking it with the upsurge of democracy in Britain as a whole. It was testimony to the growing influence of the Welsh in the Liberal Party nationally that the Liberals' Newcastle Programme of October 1891 placed Welsh disestablishment second only to Irish Home Rule. Lloyd George's political methods now became more daring. Between March and June 1892 he led a prolonged campaign of obstruction during the committee stage of the Clergy Discipline Bill, a measure which he claimed symbolized the basic anomalies and injustices of a state church. It brought him into severe conflict not only with the Conservative government but also with his own party leader, Gladstone, a dedicated son of the Anglican church. Morley, Harcourt, and other senior Liberals also deplored the disruptive tactics of the Welsh rebels. Others were alarmed at the growing violence of Lloyd George's speeches, as when he denounced Balfour, the Irish Secretary, as 'the fiendish spirit of aristocracy incarnate' in a speech at St. Helen's, or when he claimed that the Church Congress at Rhyl had 'floated on barrels of beer' and had been spiced with 'Romish sauce and Burton ale'. But these rhetorical flights only added to his stature throughout Wales; while the great majority of Liberal newspapers and rank-and-file party activists there poured forth a torrent of congratulations for the young Welsh rebels against the Clergy Discipline Bill. Although Samuel Evans and Wynford Philipps, a Welshman who sat for a Scottish constituency, were also active in the fight, it was Lloyd George who gained most of the credit.

The general election of July 1892 brought another crisis. For some months, as his correspondence shows, Lloyd George had tried to raise local issues in the House which might reap electoral dividends—harbours and fisheries, railway rates, and slate royalties. But he had again a very difficult contest, this time against Sir John Puleston, a popular Welsh Conservative recently appointed constable of Caernarvon. After a very hard fight, Lloyd George was again returned, with an increased, though still narrow, majority of 196. But the Liberals' overall majority, as Gladstone took office for the fourth time, was only forty. The sharp decline in their popular support since the O'Shea divorce scandal (even though Parnell was now dead) was amply confirmed. Further, thirty-one Liberals had been returned in the thirty-four Welsh seats: for the first time, the Welsh Party theoretically held the balance of power in the House. The fate of disestablishment and the other Welsh issues would rest on how they seized their opportunity.

21 October 1890 (from Manchester)

[He is due to address a United Kingdom Alliance meeting in the evening.]

I am fearfully anxious about tonight & heartily wish it were over. There is something weighing heavily at my heart. I fear all sorts of results. Pictures of dismal, flat failure are conjuring themselves before my eyes and it is all the worse that I succeeded before. That aggravates matters. I never felt so apprehensive. There is Trevelyan & there is Sir Wilfrid Lawson, Caine, Pope, the lot of them fine speakers with a great reputation at Alliance meetings & I a poor unknown Welsh boy with his spirit scooped out of his body by neuralgia. O fervently have I wished myself at home with my dear old Maggie.

Never mind. I'll go there & talk fearlessly whatever about successfully. I am getting one of my spasms of courage now. Look out.

22 October 1890 (from Manchester)

Well I suppose your first concern is to find out how I got on last night. Wel campus yn ddiau. Dywedir yn gyffredin ei bod yn "best of the evening". Canmoliaeth mawr iddi gan Sir G. Trevelyan. Dywedodd wrthyf ar ol eistedd i lawr ei bod yn "beautiful speech" ac aeth i'r Alliance office heddyw a rhoddodd yr un ganmoliaeth iddi wrth y swyddogion yno.[1] Have sustained my reputation & enhanced it. Invitations poured upon me at the end of the meeting even from Scotland. There were people there from all parts of the country.

I feel much better today in all respects. Lewis Roberts' brother took me to the Wesleyan College where I lunched with the students & professors & got a great reception. Referred to by one of the professors as one who had already made a name as a public speaker.

Sir Wilfrid in his speech last night referred to me in very handsome terms. Said he wished they had more such 'boy members'. Got grand reception, equal if not better than Trevelyan.

In the autumn of 1890 the Liberals seemed to be in a strong position and likely to win a commanding majority at the next general election. Then the political situation was transformed by the sensational news of Parnell's involvement in the O'Shea divorce scandal.

25 November 1890

The Irish party are now upstairs discussing Parnell's[2] future. I saw him just now in the tea-room looking as calm & self-possessed as ever. But it is a serious business for him. Here he is quite a young man having attained the greatest career of this century, dashing it to pieces because he couldn't restrain a single passion. A thousand pities. It is a still worse business for some of his following holding doubtful seats. Parnell's fame is

---

[1] Well, excellent no doubt. It is generally said to be 'the best of the evening'. Great praise for it by Sir G. Trevelyan. He told me after sitting down it was a 'beautiful speech', and went to the Alliance office today and gave it the same praise to the officials there.

[2] The O'Shea divorce scandal, in which Parnell was cited as co-respondent, was first reported in the press on 17 November. At the National Liberal Federation at Sheffield on 20–21 November, there was widespread condemnation of Parnell. Gladstone's letter, urging Parnell to resign, was made known to the Irish Party on 26 November. Eventually on 5 December the Irish Party divided into 29 Parnellites and 44 anti-Parnellites.

Criccieth in the 1880s

Mrs. Lloyd George's chapel at Criccieth

Lloyd George and 'Uncle Lloyd', *c.* 1910

certain were he to resign this moment. Not so most of us. We have our spurs to win & this fellow by his idiotic misconduct ruins us all. There is much talk of a dissolution. I hope Parnell will resign before it comes off.

At the Welsh party meeting today we had a discussion as to Disestablishment. A suggestion of mine was strenuously backed up by Bryn Roberts & Bowen Rowlands[1] and found general acceptance.

27 November 1890

Everyone is preoccupied about Parnell. Well it appears that fellow persists in brazening it out. The situation is getting very serious & acute & no one knows what will become of it. If Parnell sticks & his party stick to him it is generally conceded that Home Rule is done for. Isn't he a rascal. He would sacrifice even the whole future of his country too.

28 November 1890

The situation here is unchanged. Parnell has appealed to the Irish people against Gladstone. He must be a base selfish wretch.

By sticking to his post he is doing incalculable injury to the Irish cause—whatever happens eventually. He is dividing the Irish people into two parties & the schism will not be bridged over in a hurry.

1 December 1890

Yesterday morning I stayed indoors. Afternoon I went to hear Hugh Price Hughes[2] who made another awful onslaught on Parnell. There were loud cheers for him. He also spoke on the Temperance question & his remarks on this question also were greeted with loud cheers, a quite unusual proceeding for a religious service.

In the evening I went with Alfred Thomas M.P. to the Baptist Chapel. After chapel I supped with D. H. Evans the wealthy Welsh Draper. I told you about him before. I somehow

[1] W. Bowen Rowlands (1837–1906): Liberal member for Cardiganshire, 1886–95; later a High Court judge; a High Churchman who turned Roman Catholic.
[2] Rev. Hugh Price Hughes (1847–1902): Wesleyan minister and director of the West London mission; self-appointed spokesman for the 'nonconformist conscience'.

D

don't care for either him or his wife. They talk with such contempt about all ideas which are not reasonably genteel that I absolutely loathe them. . . .

The Irishmen seem to be utterly unable to settle Parnell. They have been sitting in secret conclave for hours today but they have adjourned without arriving at any conclusion. Cunninghame Graham,[1] who is with the Parnell section of the Irish party, came to see me now & said that Parnell wiped his boots on them right & left at the meeting & that they sat there like a pack of dumb dogs. I can hardly credit that when I know that daredevils like Healy are in the opposition. I don't believe he would stand any of Parnell's insolence.

3 December 1890

Well we are getting through our work so rapidly, owing to the absence of the Irish fellows, who are upstairs wrangling with each other, that Parliament will by the time it rises have already gone through almost all—if not all—the work which it was reasonably expected it would go through before Christmas. So that you may expect Parliament will adjourn Monday or Tuesday next over the holidays. We disposed of the address to the Queen which formerly took a week, in one night & the Tithe Bill took one night instead of as last year *two*, & the Land Purchase will take a day and a half instead of three, which it took last year. So that unless the Irishmen patch up their differences in a day or two & unite in assailing Balfour upon some question of Irish policy I shall be down Tuesday. . . .

The Parnellites are still upstairs talking, with no prospect of an end to their stream of talk. Parnell still walks about the House as cool & as defiant as ever, puffing at his cigar "like blazes". He is a bad lot but undoubtedly clever.

22 January 1891

Lest I forget I want you to send me by tomorrow's post *without fail* a book or pamphlet called "Fabian Essays in Socialism".[2] In that book there are some notes I took of the attendance at the parish churches in England & I *want those*.

---

[1] R. B. Cunninghame-Graham (1852–1936): Liberal member for North Lanarkshire, 1886–92; a prominent radical, friendly with Keir Hardie.

[2] George Bernard Shaw's edition of the *Fabian Essays* appeared in 1889.

27 January 1891

Unfortunately the tone of the debate yesterday was too conciliatory altogether. It was impossible to give a kick to the Government or the parsons or the landowners. There was too much of the embracing & falling on each other's necks about the whole thing. . . . Never mind Ellis Griffith. He doesn't affect me in the slightest degree. . . .

Lloyd George first made his name as a backbench member during the lengthy resistance by himself and some other Welsh members towards the government's Tithe Bill. This was the third successive measure that had been introduced since 1889: the two previous bills had been withdrawn in the face of bitter Liberal opposition. Lloyd George played a dominant role in the committee stage of this final measure.

29 January 1891

About the Tithe Bill[1] neither of my amendments came on yesterday, an old amendment of Gray's[2] trying to reduce the tithe to $\frac{1}{2}$ in certain cases taking up almost the whole of the time. I didn't like speaking upon that as the Welsh members were far from being agreed upon it. My amendments, at least some of them, will come on for certain on Monday, so you may purchase Tuesday's Daily Post with some degree of assurance that you will read something of what your husband has said. Tell this to my good old uncle. He must not be impatient. I know my opportunity & what I can best do. About the trumpery little points we have been discussing I feel very little & did not really care one toss how matters went. On Monday I shall be speaking upon questions I care something for.

. . . If you come up I shall stick to preparing a good speech on the Disestablishment debate in the House on the 20th Febry. i.e. today 3 weeks. There is no time to lose if a fellow is to prepare carefully & that is just what one ought to do. I have today jotted down several very good points. At least I think they are.

3 February 1891

[He gives a detailed description of the furniture for their new flat in Gray's Inn.]

---

[1] The Tithe Bill, introduced in response to the Welsh tithe riots, aimed to make tithe payable by the landowner, not the tenant farmer.

[2] C. W. Gray, Unionist member for Maldon, a prominent Churchman.

Now as to the Tithe Bill. I scored a great success last night. S. T. E[vans] & myself bossed the whole show. I spoke 7 times. The Star today singles us both out as young men who showed ourselves to be not only "effective debaters but possessed of great dialectical skill". The Daily Graphic also couples us together as leading the Welsh M.P.'s. I am very satisfied with my achievements last night. I had the narrowest majority against me of the lot.

4 February 1891

I wanted to fight last night again but the whole of the Welsh & English party were against me on that point so in order not to appear "contrairy" which as you know I greatly dislike I withdrew my opposition or rather postponed it to another stage called "Report". I have however amply compensated myself for the pang of last night's act of complaisance by placing 9 amendments on the paper for tomorrow. Harcourt was not here last night, otherwise he would have backed up my desire to fight. I have just seen him & he agrees with me that we should throw it over tomorrow.

. . . The Grand Old Man has just delivered one of the finest orations he ever uttered on his Roman Catholic Disabilities Bill. Give the Old Chap an ecclesiastical topic & he is happy. He bounced, he whirled around, he flung his arms, he banged the brass box, he shouted until the corridors rang. Wonderful old boy. He was as agile as a child. Never heard his like.

24 July 1891

I have scored heavily today. The Government gave way on all my most important amendments with the exception of terminals & even on those we have been placed on the same footing as the English railways. This is glorious work I think because we have succeeded without wrecking the Bill. We didn't want that as it suited our purposes in other respects admirably.

26 July 1891 (from Crewe)

I think my good old uncle is quite right in advising me not to risk the loss of anything by returning home. The Tithe Bill is a lesson to me not to go home too soon. And after all the House of Lords may strike out the concessions I gained on Welsh

Railways. So I must return. Tom Ellis is up & Sam Evans has also returned.

27 July 1891

I find that I must remain to the last as I intend raising the question of Crown royalties. This is very important to me as Menzies has almost promised to support me in the next election if I succeed. I shall I think be able to persuade the Treasury into giving me what I want. At least I must try. I fancy that the last fortnight's work has done much more to establish me in the Boroughs than all the previous exertions of mine. Men who are not keen politicians must appreciate my successful attempt to reduce railway rates on slates & goods & also the attempt I now make to reduce slate quarry royalties.

30 July 1891

We had a little fight last night over a bill which is called the Clergy Discipline (Immorality) Bill. It is a bill to remove from the Church all clergymen who may be guilty of some crime or immorality. Sam Evans had a grave objection to this & he moved the adjournment of the debate. This was defeated on a division. The speaker was then about to put the bill when I jumped up & moved that the Bill be read that day three months. Then another debate which resulted in the Government being compelled to adjourn in spite of their teeth [*sic*]. It will probably come on tonight again. We will however defeat the concern by sheer obstruction. I don't see why we should be bothered with a confounded ecclesiastical bill when the session is already so late & there is so much essential work to be got rid of. Last night we had a rare time of it. Tom Ellis was in high feather over the postponement of the Clergy Discipline Bill. R. T. Williams—the Methodist minister—was an admirer of Bryn Roberts & defended it strenuously. This was too much for Tom & they disputed & discussed & shouted against & across each other until, I am positive, our neighbours must have thought there was a drunken row going on. At last I took out Carlyle & Victor Hugo & to the huge delight of Tom & J. T. pelted the fellow with the fearful denunciations from these books. . . . The Lords struck out part of my amendments to the Railway Rates Bills with the result that coal & lime will have exceptional charges put upon them. The Government fortunately steadily refused to reimpose exceptional rates on slates. I have wired to Robinson of Talysarn & Parry Bethesda as to further opposition. I shan't give in without a stiff fight altho' I am kept here another week.

I have today given Jackson notice that I shall call further attention to the Royalty question on the Appropriation Bill.

31 July 1891

Here I am preparing for another tussle. After writing you last Ellis, Evans & myself took it into our heads to fight the Education Bill & we kept them dancing for almost 3 hours until the Government squared us by accepting an amendment I suggested. Then the fight collapsed for the English members could not carry it on. About half past two in the morning, I raised another discussion on voting money to Church schools. We were of course beaten but we had our say & we prevented the Clergy Discipline Bill coming on. It was almost five this morning when we went home! Quite light when I trotted along the Strand with Tim Healy & Flynn. . . . Bryn Roberts I hope will stay at least. I've brought pressure to bear upon him on railways & royalties. I asked two or three questions about the latter today. Got a trifle more satisfactory answer today but won't do yet so will press it on. I must succeed in this matter.

25 September 1891 (from Wick)

Well now you'll want to hear how I got on. My reply is between ourselves that I got on magnificently. It was a very fine meeting. It contained all the elements of inspiration for me— not the least of which was the fact that I was interrupted by some bouncing, swaggering land-agent. I need not tell you how delighted I was. He had interrupted some previous speakers & before I got up I made enquiries about him—so I was prepared for him & I simply danced upon his carcase to the unbound joy of my Highland auditors. I fired up towards the end ac mi eis i dipyn o hwyl.[1] You should have seen the hush that fell upon them & when I sat down they shouted their applause. . . .

20 February 1892

What a small majority the Government had.[2] The Liberals

---

[1] And I got into a pretty rapturous mood.

[2] A motion by Lloyd George on 19 February 1892, seconded by D. A. Thomas, deploring the appointment of Judge Beresford, an Englishman unable to speak

cheered to the echo. Chamberlain voted against us. I shall never say another kind word of the old rascal. But it doesn't matter. The effect has been very good & I think the result is that Beresford[1] must go otherwise we'll fight the Estimates & waste some more time for them.

In February 1892 the second county council elections were held. In Caernarvonshire and other counties in Wales, the Liberals retained the overwhelming majorities they had gained in 1889.

8 March 1892

I do not think the County Council elections in the Boroughs are any criterion whatever of the strength of the two parties. Conway furnished a very good instance of this. There the whole thing turned on the question of School Bd. or no School Board. The Conway ratepayers happen to be opposed to the idea. Hence the Liberal defeat. Bangor did very well.

(Undated—early 1892)

When I went to Verulam on arriving in London last night I found the whole place in a topsy turvy condition—Mrs. Fox having evidently been cleaning. Under these conditions I accepted Sam Evans's hospitality & slept with him last night. I ran over to Verulam today & sent for Mrs. Fox & told her to get a fire in my bedroom & air the sheets.

I took the eggs out also today & found them all whole— not one cracked. We meet earlier now & have what they call morning sittings. That looks as if the Government intended to dissolve at an early stage, probably in June. In that case it would hardly be worthwhile keeping Verulam Buildings on— unless of course we met again in August. I have therefore had a mind unless it is a very expensive process to give up chambers & send furniture on to Criccieth. What do you say?

Did you see my onslaught on Puleston at Carnarvon? He is very annoyed about it. I met him just now in the Lobby & he seems to be much smashed by it. Confound him. Let him not

---

Welsh, to the Mid-Wales circuit, was defeated by only 23 votes. Several Conservatives, including Sir John Puleston (Devonport), spoke and voted in favour of the motion, while William Abraham, 'Mabon' (Liberal, Rhondda) startled the House by delivering a few sentences in Welsh (Hansard, *Parl. Deb.*, 4th ser., Vol. I, pp. 827–63).

[1] Cecil H. W. Beresford (1852–1912): County Court judge on the Mid-Wales Circuit, 1891, and on the Devon and Somerset Circuit, 1893.

tell these reckless lies then. Ynte yr hen gariad [Isn't that so, old darling].

For the next few months Lloyd George was much involved in prolonged obstruction of the Clergy Discipline Bill which facilitated the dismissal of clergy guilty of scandalous conduct. He felt that this measure symbolized the whole church–state connection and fought strenuously against both the government and his own party leadership. Stuart Rendel, chairman of the Welsh Party, was appalled 'by the madness of Wales in slapping John Morley and Mr. Gladstone in the face', but the episode undoubtedly added to Lloyd George's stature in Wales and in radical circles generally.

(undated—early 1892)

I am here spending Sunday with Mr. Wynford Philipps.[1] . . . As Philipps is on the Clergy Discipline Committee we propose going through the amendments together either tonight or tomorrow so as to be fully prepared for the fight. It is all the more important as Sam Evans will be absent & I am anxious to prove that we can get on well without him. In fact now I am rather glad of it because I generally do better when I am thrown entirely on my own resources.

30 March 1892

I do not think I shall leave tomorrow as the Clergy Discipline Bill is on the paper & I have also given notice of a question which I intend to ask Balfour on the point. I got a very long & interesting letter today from a prominent High Churchman cordially approving of my resolution & suggesting two or three good points in favour of it. He says that he prefers Disestablishment to legislation of this sort! Fancy High Churchmen approving of my conduct. Last night I received with Viscount Halifax's[2] compliments (he is President of the English Church Union) a long report prepared by the High Church party on the Bill. The next thing you will hear is that I have turned proselyte! For all that I think we are playing a very astute game as we are winning the support of the Ritualists.

The Times thinks that the Government will not proceed with the Bill until after Easter. If that is their decision we shall

---

[1] J. Wynford Philipps (1860–1938): Liberal member for mid-Lanark, 1888–94, and for Pembrokeshire, 1898–1908; created Baron St. David's in 1908 and Viscount in 1918; later chairman of the trustees of the Lloyd George fund and a valued adviser to Lloyd George; his papers have mysteriously disappeared.

[2] Second Viscount Halifax (1839–1934): president of the English Church Union, 1869–1919.

be able to kill it. That is my opinion. We'll overwhelm it with amendments.

31 March 1892

Balfour has replied to my question. Judging from the general purport of his reply I do not think that the second reading will come on before Easter. The whole of next week will be taken up with the Small Holdings Bill. It docs not directly affect the boroughs except in places like Nevin, Pwllheli & Criccieth perhaps which are semi-agricultural.

5 April 1892

This afternoon Tom Ellis & I, finding the House very hot & the debate very uninteresting, strolled out. We turned into Covent Garden on our way & there I bought for you & the chickens a box of very nice & *sweet* tamarinds or Tangiers. They are not the ordinary Tangiers oranges—at least they cost three times as much. They are better for you as there is no sourness at all in them. . . .

After packing those off we walked down as far as the "Magara in London" place. They have got a magnificent cycloramic view of ancient Egypt. They have Egyptian music there, Egyptian coffee rooms, Egyptian waiters, all of which Tom tells me are exactly like the Egypt of today.[1] In fact he was quite fascinated. There is a weird melancholy about the music which is singularly enchanting. We must go there & get a cup of Turkish coffee when you come up after Easter. I was thinking of how you would enjoy it when we get the opportunity.

6 April 1892

I forgot to tell you how delighted I was to learn of the great & surprising Nonconformist victory at Criccieth. . . . Well, last night we went to the theatre & on the whole enjoyed ourselves there. Ellen Terry's acting magnificent & the spectacular part of the performance—the processions, dresses &c.—was truly gorgeous. We must have a look at it again when you come up.

8 April 1892

I asked the Speaker about [the London & North Western

[1] Tom Ellis had visited Egypt in 1890 to help regain his strength after illness.

Railway Bill] last night & he told me it would not be in order. I must therefore seek another opportunity. I today saw the officials of the Company about it & told them that I would soon find another & better opportunity to fly at their throats. They assured me there was no necessity for it. My own impression is that there will be no further attempt to degrade Welshmen. It will serve as a warning to them.

I am now working up the Fisheries question. I am trying to get a loan for helping the Criccieth pier on. I have seen Mr. Arthur O'Connor M.P. who is a member of the Public Works Loan Board—a first class fellow—& he promises to do all in his power to assist me. Of course one must move cautiously with the Criccieth business as the Directors are pretty well all Pulestonians but I must endeavour to outwit them.

9 April 1892

Gladstone's crushing of Joe last night was very entertaining.[1] It was beautifully done. Both sides of the House shaking with laughter. The Tories seemed to be even more delighted than the Liberals were that possible. Joseph himself did not look particularly comfortable. He looked much greener than usual. He hasn't had it now for years & it was high time he should get a dressing. He was becoming too perky for anything.

27 April 1892

The Women's Franchise Bill is before the House & the Division is now taking place. As I am not in favour of enfranchising widows & spinsters without giving a vote to married women at the same time I take no part in trotting round the lobby at all. I am in favour of the general principle.

29 April 1892

I am sure you will be anxious to know how I got on last night. Eminently satisfactory—that is my honest & unbiassed opinion. Never got better in the House. Spoke for over 45 minutes in a full house which listened to me attentively especially the old man [Gladstone] who moved to the corner seat where Chamberlain usually sits in order the better to hear me. I was very cool—& I fancy even defiant. I didn't mind a button in [*sic*] the old boy and anybody else for the matter of that.

[1] In the debate on the Small Agricultural Holdings Bill.

He was very nice to me personally in his reply. Called me his "honourable friend" & credited me with "acuteness". Said that no one else could have put the case better but of course that it was a thoroughly bad one. I was congratulated on all hands even by opponents. We defied everybody all round & kept them dancing until at last they had to closure us & even then we divided the House five times. I never enjoyed myself anything like last night. We'll fight their confounded Bill in season & out of season, Gladstone or no Gladstone.

30 April 1892

I am glad to observe in the letters which I received from Criccieth that all my good people—the only persons for whose opinions I really care a toss—are quite as pugnacious as I feel myself about the Clergy Discipline Bill. We're making preparations for a stiff fight in the committee upstairs. Dr. Cameron[1] who is on the Committee of selection came yesterday to ask me whom I should like to be on the Clergy Discipline Committee. I named three or four of our fellows who will fight out & out. We will keep it going there as long as we can so that it will be late when it returns to the House. There will be a much better chance of killing it when the Session is old & members are anxious to go down to their constituencies to prepare for the election. That is our plan of campaign. Gladstone will also probably be on the Committee & that will guarantee some very keen fights. The old man is very anxious to pull it through & he will be exceedingly wrath [*sic*] with us.

2 May 1892

The great labour demonstration was to come off & I thought it would be more interesting & instructive to go to the Park to watch that. You recollect our being there last year observing it. It was an immense procession. The largest that has yet turned out. Sam & I went there together. We heard John Burns[2] deliver a very fine speech.

10 May 1892

[J. T. Roberts, his election agent, has resigned.]

[1] Dr. Charles Cameron (1841–1924): Liberal member for various Glasgow constituencies, 1874–95 and 1897–1900.
[2] John Burns (1858–1943): Labour leader, member for Battersea, 1892–1918; President of Local Government Board, 1905–14, and of Board of Trade, 1914.

Bother J. T. I am very anxious to get rid of him. He very nearly ruined me at the last election. He was a constant irritation & worry. One of my office boys—even Parry—would have done just as well without having the additional provocation of constantly bickering & quarrelling with me at every available opportunity. So I am gladly going to accept his resignation in a *very nice* letter which I have already written. I shall ask either Will or W. J. W. Caernarvon to accept the post.

12 May 1892

I have been hotly engaged all day in fighting the Clergy Discipline Bill in the Standing Committee on Law. We started at 12 & let off at three. Evans & I made some twenty speeches each—at least not far from it. We got very fair support from Wynford Phillips [*sic*] & the result was that when the Committee adjourned we had not disposed of the first subsection of the first clause of the Bill. Unfortunately Evans will be down in the country on Monday & as there are only two of us besides him who are prepared to oppose the Bill tooth & nail it will be most difficult to keep it going. . . .

16 May 1892

Well I am afraid they are getting on very slowly with their Clergy Discipline Bill. After three hours discussion today they have not yet got even through the first sub-section of the first clause of their bill. At this rate they wont get it for a month. I have two or three amendments upon this subsection & they have two more subsections before they get the first clause. So I should not be very much surprised if this week did not give them even the first clause. The Chairman[1] is very much amused. I saw him afterwards. I have shelled [*sic*] out two fresh amendments today—both of them capable of considerable discussion. Oh it is capital, upon my honour it is.

(undated—probably May 1892)

Now we are making preparations to fight more strenuously than ever over the carcase of this blackguardly Bill [the Clergy Discipline Bill]. The papers furnish very interesting reading today. The Standard has in the largest print on its placards "Welsh obstruction in Parliament". The rest seem to be more

---

[1] Sir Henry Campbell-Bannerman, later to be Liberal Prime Minister, 1905–8.

amused than angry. The Pall Mall foams a bit in its leading article. The Liberal Dailies are silent.

I do hope Will[1] can get on without me the coming week. If not it can't be helped. I must get down there by Monday night's mail & return by the evening mail, that is all. My blood is up & I am in for it. I care not for anything or anybody—except my pets of course—a thousand kisses to them all.

20 May 1892

[The Government has proposed that the Committee on the Clergy Discipline Bill should sit on every day of the week.] We kept them on for two hours discussing the motion, the House being crowded during the whole discussion. We shall go on fighting them line by line up to and after midnight if they really desire it. It furnishes capital exercise in the way of addressing the House.

23 May 1892

It is now 6.20 p.m. and they have decided to sit on until they get the whole of Clause 3. They have now only just started with it & if they go on as slowly as they do now they won't get on for another couple of hours. I feel very tired but I am going on. I have cooked three fresh amendments on the very first sub-section of this clause. We are talking at much greater length.

24 May 1892

Well we had the dickens of a row today. We kept them on last night until after seven and they gave it up in sheer disgust for the night. Today they ruled all our amendments practically out of order—would not allow more than two of us to speak on one amendment. We were not permitted to speak twice. At last seeing that at this rate they would get their bill through & beat us we thought we should make an effective protest & after three or four frightful scenes we got up & said that owing to the rulings of the Chair we had determined to retire from the Committee & move our amendments on what is known as the report stage in the House. Friends of mine tell me that there was an intense feeling growing up against us on our own side but that they were all forced to admit the great ability with which

---

[1] i.e. his brother, William.

we fought. . . . Gladstone has just delivered a superb speech on the Irish Bill. He is really a marvellous old man.

25 May 1892

Having washed our hands of the Standing Committee on Law I am free today. I am still convinced that we did the right thing under the circumstances. Bannerman's rulings made it impossible for us to go on for more than another day. If we had wasted another day it would not have been Government time, today being private members' time & even if we had wasted tomorrow I should simply have lost my opportunity of once more calling attention to the fisheries question without in the slightest degree hampering them. Now we have some excuse for moving these amendments in the House on the grounds that we were not allowed to speak in Committee. If I get a chance I'll talk about herring or harbours tomorrow. That ought to tell locally. And so Mari fach [little Mary] was in a great hurry to go to the "ffair" [fair]. Just at that moment her dada was squabbling & brawling with everybody all round.

A story appears in one of the Tory papers that "Sam Evans & I supplied the brains & Phillips [*sic*] the impudence" in the fight. Arthur O'Connor says we fought our battle much more skilfully than the Irishmen used to do it. Well look out for squalls next week.

26 May 1892

I have just been talking on the Birmingham Water Bill. Joe accepted one suggestion of mine. The greatest satisfaction about the matter is that we have wasted nearly two hours Government time. That means something taken from Clergy Discipline. Concerning this uncle need not fret a bit about this. We have undoubtedly done the right thing. We were not wasting Government time after Tuesday. Up to Friday last we were doing so. Afterwards it was not much good except as a protest. We wanted therefore a good & valid excuse for washing our hands of their committee & proposing our amendments wholesale in the House. This we got at last & we've used it. I think there are one or two Churchmen from the other side of the House who will help us.

30 May 1892

[He describes a large banquet he attended at the Mansion

House]. Sam Evans under some sudden impulse declined to get up with the rest of the company when the toast of the Queen was being given. It was utterly unpremeditated on his part & why he did it no one knows. There was quite a scene raging round him, Lascelles Carr, the editor of the Western Mail,[1] getting very excited & taking up a glass of wine to chuck it over Sam. He was stopped. One fellow threatened to chuck him out. The proper thing to be done was either not to go there at all or merely get up & not pledge the old lady by raising the glass. I adopt the latter course. Where you are a guest you have no right to tread on your hosts corns nor on those of your fellow guests. Sam got up last time we were there & even upon this occasion he stood up for the Prince of Wales.

31 May 1892

We had some fun last night. About midnight I raised the question of Welsh Fisheries on the Vote on recount. Courtney[2] was inclined to be nasty. He was anxious to help the Government to get their vote at the earliest hour. He ruled me out of order six times consecutively & still I persisted. I absolutely refused to sit down, getting up after each ruling & trying another tack. At last seeing Courtney would not allow me to discuss piers & harbours I resolved that rather than be sat upon by Courtney I would talk about any mortal thing so I snatched up the report of the Fishery Commissioners of the Board of Trade & began to comment upon that especially upon their refusal to sanction the reduction of the salmon license in South Carnarvonshire from five guineas to one. Upon this point I went on to the intense delight of "Tim" [Healy]. Immediately I sat down he shouted "Well done, Lloyd George, you circumnavigated the chair very cleverly". . . . I spoke about a dozen times last night after midnight. My blood was up. They did not get their vote until half past three.

(undated fragment—apparently 1 June 1892)

Just had a small score over the Government.[3] Last night I

---

[1] Henry Lascelles Carr (1841–1902): sub-editor, then editor and part proprietor of the Cardiff Conservative newspaper, the *Western Mail*, 1869–1901.

[2] Leonard Courtney (1832–1918): Liberal member for Liskeard, 1874–85, and then Unionist member for Bodmin to 1900; rejoined the Liberals in 1900; at this time, chairman of committees and deputy-speaker.

[3] Hansard, *Parl. Deb.*, 4th ser., Vol. V, p. 374 (31 May 1892).

pressed them to show me Forster Browne's report on the Slate Quarry Royalties. This they said they would give an answer upon on Thursday. I said No you must reply before you get supply. So I put a question on the paper today about it. They refused it absolutely. Then I got up & said I would call attention to the matter on report. Seeing I could stop report they sent Marjoribanks[1] our whip to me to press me not to proceed. I declined to withdraw unless they gave me a guarantee to show me the document. He went off to Balfour[2] immediately & got a favourable answer. I went afterwards to arrange an appointment with Balfour & Goschen.[3] Balfour was very nice to me—exceedingly pleasant. Dyna ydynt hwy [That's what they are]. It was simply spite on the part of the Crown officials against me for what I've done.

(undated—June 1892)

I am now waiting & watching for a motion I have placed on the paper with regard to fishing harbours on the Welsh coast. I've just got it over. Tom Ellis & I spoke. I referred to Cardigan Bay. It ought to do us good at the Election.

Clergy Discipline did not come on after all & I am glad of it in a way. Sam Evans' motion on the Bill had by a mistake on the part of the Clerks at the table got in before mine—so he might have moved its rejection. My resolution is much "cuter" so say they all. Next time the Clerks will have corrected the mistake & I'll come on naturally. The Government have placed it on the paper for Thursday. I was to be down at Carnarvon that day attending an important meeting on registration & preparatory for the Election but of course I must be here to move my amendment. I've just seen Illingworth[4] & he very

---

[1] Edward Marjoribanks (1849–1909): Liberal Chief Whip, 1892–4; Lord Privy Seal, 1894–5; First Lord of the Admiralty, 1905–8; Lord President of the Council, 1908–9; 2nd Baron Tweedmouth, 1894.

[2] Arthur James Balfour (1848–1930): in Conservative governments of 1885–6 and 1886–92, Leader of the House, 1891–2, later Leader of the House, 1895–1902; Prime Minister, 1902–5; First Lord of the Admiralty, 1915–16; Foreign Secretary, 1916–19; Lord President of the Council, 1919–22, and 1925–9; created Earl Balfour, 1922.

[3] George Joachim Goschen (1831–1907); Liberal, then Liberal Unionist member, 1863–1900; Chancellor of the Exchequer, 1887–92; first Lord of the Admiralty, 1895–1900; first Viscount Goschen, 1900.

[4] Alfred Illingworth (1827–1907): Liberal member for various Yorkshire constituencies, between 1868 and 1895; a Liberal whip.

Frank Edwards

Herbert Lewis

D. A. Thomas

Tom Ellis

Lloyd George at the time of the Education 'revolt', 1903

heartily approves of it. Says he thought it had been "most wisely drafted".

Last night I spoke for a few minutes. Labouchere[1] had asked [me] to prevent a bill coming on if he were not there. I moved the adjournment of the debate & they had to take three divisions in order to shut us up. So I am constantly at it. A member just told me that my speech on harbours just now was "very nicely delivered".

Parliament was dissolved in June 1892 and again Lloyd George found himself in a strenuous contest in the attempt to save his seat. His opponent now was Sir John Puleston.

9 June 1892 (from Bangor)

Been round through upper Bangor this morning visiting the brethren (in the political faith). They all seem to be hopeful whilst realising that it will be a very stiff contest.

10 June 1892 (from Caernarvon)

We had a capital meeting at Bangor last night. Looked business all over. Some of the best men of the town there. Think if Will keeps them up to the work that we'll show a good record in the cathedral city.

23 June 1892 (from Conway)

Just a word to tell you that I am alright in spite of the tremendous strain. Mary[2] will have told you what a magnificent meeting we had at Carnarvon last night. Scores standing in the street failing to get in. Little Dick got a big cheer on his own account. He was the only thoroughly cool head in the whole assembly. Poor little fellow, he slept before his dada got up & he did not see the great reception he met with.

2 July 1892 (from Conway)

Just seen D. P. Williams. Came over specially from Rathbone[3] to see me. Rathbone is afraid—or rather has been

---

[1] Henry Labouchere, 'Labby' (1831–1912): Liberal member between 1868 and 1906; an unorthodox radical and editor of *Truth*.

[2] His elder sister, Mary Ellen.

[3] William Rathbone (1819–1902): Liberal member for Caernarvonshire, 1880–5, and for Caernarvonshire (Arfon), 1885–95; a prominent Liverpool businessman, much out of sympathy with Lloyd George's Welsh nationalism.

specifically told by the Tories that if he speaks for me there will be a contest. So he offers me one of two alternatives.

(a) that he shall speak for me, or

(b) that R. D. W. & Abram of Conway should be placed *gratuitously* at my disposal. Of course. I had no hesitation in accepting the latter. Abram is a very experienced worker & R. D. is of course an old hand & R. O. Roberts is a novice & requires assistance. . . .

. . . I am very anxious you should come to Nevin.

5 July 1892 (from Caernarvon)

Sitting up to write address & for results. Liberals won nett 7 seats—that is won 9 seats from the Tories & lost 2 so far. Campus [Excellent]. Canvass Cricth for me tomorrow *thoroughly*, that's a pet. We must keep it up. If we get a good majority there we win. Visit every house, go at it. I implore you.

Polling day was on 10 July. This time Lloyd George held his seat with an increased majority of 196. He and his fellow Welsh members now concentrated on securing guarantees from Gladstone about the place of Welsh disestablishment in the programme of the next government.

11 August 1892

Tell uncle that Gladstone has given us better pledges on Disestablishment than even we ventured to anticipate.[1]

To recover from the intense physical and nervous strain of the election, Lloyd George went on holiday with some Welsh friends to Switzerland in August and early September. Gladstone had now taken office as Prime Minister for the fourth time. One promising omen for Wales was that Tom Ellis was a junior whip. In the autumn session, the various Welsh issues made some progress. A royal commission to inquire into the Welsh land question was accepted on 14 December; preparations were made for the drafting of a charter for the new University of Wales; and a Welsh Church Suspensory Bill was announced, presumably a preparation for disestablishment and disendowment. Welsh Liberalism, which increasingly saw Lloyd George as its tribune, now reached a new peak of national enthusiasm.

[1] On 8 August 1892, the Welsh Party unanimously passed a motion that Welsh disestablishment be placed second on the programme of the new government, next to Irish home rule. Gladstone gave a series of evasive replies.

CHAPTER 3

Revolt of 'The Four'

(1893–94)

For most politicians, the overriding public issue now was the second Irish Home Rule Bill which Gladstone introduced and which eventually was rejected by the Lords in September 1893 after a marathon session. For the Welsh Party, however, the supreme question of the day was whether the government would introduce a Welsh Disestablishment Bill, as foreshadowed in the Newcastle programme. In the summer of 1893 the Welsh members, Lloyd George prominent among them, sought firm guarantees from Gladstone but received only evasive replies which gave no pledge as to the priority of the Welsh measure in the government's programme. Some South Wales members, headed by D. A. Thomas, the coal owner who represented the radical stronghold of Merthyr Tydfil, now urged that the Welsh form themselves into an independent party, on the lines of the Irish. But at this stage Lloyd George was opposed to such a move, not so much on grounds of party loyalism as because he suspected that it arose from the private ambitions of the South Wales members concerned. At a crucial meeting of the Welsh Party on 1 September 1893 Lloyd George acted closely with Tom Ellis in out-manœuvring the rebels and securing the passage of a compromise motion. It was Lloyd George's last appearance in the guise of a party loyalist for quite some time.

In the 1894 session Lloyd George was again apprehensive that the tottering Liberal government might go back on its pledge to introduce a Welsh Disestablishment Bill. At this critical moment, Gladstone resigned on 3 March 1894 after long differences with his colleagues over the naval estimates and on whether to call an election on the Irish question. After a savage struggle with Harcourt, Lord Rosebery succeeded as Prime Minister. Tom Ellis became Chief Whip and had the thankless task of trying to keep afloat a Liberal ministry whose majority had shrunk in by-elections to not much more than twenty, and which faced interminable sniping from the Welsh and other backbenchers. Lloyd George at first welcomed the advent of Rosebery, whatever his penchant for the turf. For the new premier, unlike Gladstone, was far from being solely preoccupied with the Irish question, and the prospects for Welsh disestablishment seemed momentarily brighter. However, to immense radical disappointment, the Welsh measure had only a very lowly place in the government's programme announced for the 1894 session. On 14 April, Lloyd George, Frank Edwards, and D. A. Thomas declared that they were rejecting the Liberal whip as a protest. A few days later they were joined by Herbert Lewis and 'the Four' toured North Wales proclaiming their dismay with their own government and justifying their 'revolt' on nationalist grounds. Nonconformist leaders in England also warmly applauded Lloyd George's stand. Some of the impetus left the revolt when Asquith introduced the new Welsh Disestablishment Bill on 26 April. However, Lloyd George and his allies were skilful enough to avoid direct censure by their parliamentary colleagues. Even so, the affair increased ill-feeling among the Welsh members; in particular, relations between Lloyd George and Tom Ellis, the Chief Whip, inevitably became more distant. But Lloyd George's wider standing in Welsh politics was not seriously impaired, while on 30 August he persuaded his own constituency Liberal Association to set up a new election expenses fund on his behalf. His local critics were swept aside.

Lloyd George's increasing absorption in politics inevitably took some toll of his family life. His London home now (and until 1900) was at Palace Mansions, Kensington. But his wife and children remained at Criccieth for long periods; when Lloyd George went on holiday to Switzerland in August 1894 it was with the rebel Welsh M.P.s, Frank Edwards and Herbert Lewis, but without his wife. However, the bonds between them were still very close, notably after their fourth child, another son, named Gwilym, was born on 4 December 1894.

At the start of 1893 Lloyd George was much preoccupied with a scheme to promote a Welsh gold-mining syndicate in Patagonia.

5 January 1893

I am ready for any action in the matter. In fact the prospect of a rumpus rather pleases me. I am parched for lack of a good fight. Things are too dull altogether for my palate. The Patagonian meeting passed exceedingly well. T. C. Lewis and R. O. Davies were there—& Vincent Evans! We reduced the number of directors to 5 & decided to give them £3–3–0 for each meeting they attend. That looks like business—don't you think so. We made T. C. Lewis chairman—at my special request. He is a good blind for the public. Myself they made deputy chairman.

7 January 1893

I am still at it re Patagonian Syndicate. At this very moment I am supposed to be discussing the question of issuing debentures in order to raise money at some future moment.

I am sorry for your accident. Sincerely hope it isn't a bad one. . . .

I am now enjoying the supreme satisfaction of feeling that I am earning £5–5–0 for attending this meeting. As a country member of the Board I get £5–5–0. When I move up here I get only three guineas. I have just received my cheque for £10–10–0 for yesterday's meeting & the present one. So don't despair. I shall bring a crust home with me for the pets.

8 January 1893

It has been a cruelly cold day to travel in—a dirty thaw in London & a heavy fall of snow in the country. A racking toothache kept me awake a good part of last night & I get a spasm of it now & again all day long. This last journey in the frost, snow & fogs has knocked me up. So you must be good to me when I arrive.

28 January 1893 (from Cardiff)

Well last night was an *immense* success. Place crowded to the bung with a highly intelligent audience. Splendid reception when I rose—all the audience rose & cheered & still finer reception when I sat down, they rose again & cheered frantically. There is a leading article upon it in the South Wales Daily News about the impression I made. How I raised the audience to a high level &c. Highly eulogistic. The editor was present.

4 February 1893

I am very grieved that Mari bach [little Mary, presumably a dog] behaves so badly. I do hope that she has left no mark on the little darling's cheek. If she has then I will have to thrash her very severely. In any event I fear it must be done. This trick must be whipped out of her. The little Grasgarth pet is so thoroughly goodnatured that I am surprised it could have happened. I feel very angry indeed about it.

By the summer Lloyd George was deeply involved in attempts to put pressure on Gladstone over Welsh disestablishment.

3 July 1893

We had a splendid meeting on Saturday night. Never spoke better. People excited beyond measure. It was very amusing. I turned up in my little grey coat & the people wouldn't believe I was "Lloyd George". They were fully convinced I think before the thing was over.

5 July 1893

Gladstone has replied to our letter.[1] He pleads the Home Rule Bill as an excuse for not giving a definite answer just now. He promises to give a further reply after it is substantially through. I don't care for the nature of the reply & we must press him hard. He will try to get out of it if he can.

But we must not allow him to do it.

7 July 1893

[His son, Richard, has been unwell.]
This recurrence of sultry weather is very bad for the little chap but perhaps you will be able to remove him to a more airy room. That little back room must be very stuffy for him when there are so many passing in & out of the room constantly & lapping up all the fresh air. I know very well that in the country these ideas are regarded as fads & that there is a notion prevalent that fresh air is more or less of an evil & that the weaker a man happens to be the more foul ought to be the condition of the atmosphere he inhales. But really I do wish you would set aside this silly superstition for once.

We had an immense scene last night—well worth being in. Directly it was over I sallied out with T. C. Lewis & Lewis Jones & Jenkyn Thomas through the streets to see the illuminations [for a royal wedding]. The crowd was a more inspiring spectacle than the lights. . . .

Today I lunched with the Welsh Land Commissioners.[2]

27 July 1893

I meant to run down to Wales tomorrow but we have decided to have a meeting of the Welsh party to consider whether we should have any further communication sent to Gladstone before he replies. We had a meeting of the Emergency Committee today but although at first they were all against me they came round to my way of thinking at last.

[1] On 26 June, Rendel, on behalf of the Welsh Party, wrote to Gladstone, inquiring about the prospects for a Welsh Disestablishment Bill and pointing out that the issue had been placed second in the Newcastle Programme in 1891. In fact, a Disestablishment Bill was prepared by the government in the autumn of 1893.

[2] A royal commission to inquire into the Welsh land question was appointed by Gladstone and held its first session on 25 May 1893.

28 July 1893

I have been for two hours and a half fighting for my letter to Gladstone at a meeting of the Welsh party. Rathbone & Sam Evans did their very utmost to wreck it but failed most conspicuously. I stuck to my point & I was supported by Rendel & Ellis & the Major.[1] I have been since told that I fought very tenaciously & with good tact.

7 August 1893

Gladstone has replied. Rendel showed me letter *very confidentially*. He has not shown it to anyone else, not even to Ellis. The old boy refused to pledge himself. I am half inclined to send my letter to [the] Independent. If uncle thinks so tell him to wire me. . . .

8 August 1893

Ellis told me last night that he thought the old man would give in after all. He'll give us a vague promise in his next letter & something more definite still if we press him still further. Well, we shall see the very text of the letter tomorrow & Ellis & I are going to keep ourselves free tomorrow evening so as to discuss it together.

16 August 1893
Confidential

Patagonia is, I fear, a failure. *Don't let uncle or anyone else* know a word. Hoefer wires that "the property falls short of representations". He will be here in a month & will let us know whether it is worthwhile going on with the matter any further. Will & I may be able to save ourselves to a great extent by a stiff lawyers' bill but we must of course lose a lot of money. Just like our luck.

29 August 1893

I have been for 3 hours listening to a debate in the House of Lords on the Welsh University Charter.[2] By a majority of 9

---

[1] Major Evan Rowlands Jones (1840–1920): Liberal member for Carmarthen Boroughs, 1892–5; gained the rank of major during the American civil war.

[2] The Lords carried the Bishop of Chester's motion that the University charter be withheld as St. David's College, Lampeter, an Anglican institution, was excluded from it. Bryn Roberts, the Liberal member for Eifion, had opposed the charter in the Commons on the grounds that the university should be an examining rather

they have thrown the Charter out or rather condemned because they have no power to reject it fortunately. Tonight it comes on in the House of Commons & there the order will be reversed. The Charter will be carried in spite of Bryn Roberts & the Tories. So there will be a conflict between Lords & Commons & I am glad of it.

31 August 1893

You know that D. A. Thomas had been forming a 'cave' with five or six other fellows about this Disestablishment question. Alfred [Thomas] with his usual impetuousness rushed into it without thinking quite blindly. When he saw me he repented his hurry & has been ever since trying to get out of it best way he can. Now I drafted a kind of "compromise" resolution for him. This he has distributed to the David Thomasites & he has already got three of them besides himself to agree. So D.A. is almost alone now & Alfred is in a great state of delight with what he calls *my* resolution. He is quite excited about it. Our meeting comes off tomorrow. Sam [Evans] can't be there.

(undated—1 September 1893)

I am now upstairs at a meeting of Welsh members discussing what we shall do. Bryn [Roberts] is at it now firing away against every proposition to do anything. There is one resolution moved in favour of breaking off at once from the Liberal party. There is another resolution—mine—in favour of warning the government that unless they pass the Bill next session we shall take an independent course. Opinion now is very much divided. Ellis &—curiously enough—Sam [Evans] are both with me. So is Herbert Lewis.[2] But at the present

---

than a teaching body. The government ignored the Lords' motion, and the University charter received the royal assent on 30 November 1893. Lloyd George took scant interest in the university thereafter.

[1] David Alfred Thomas (1856–1918): Liberal member for Merthyr Tydfil, 1888–1910 and for Cardiff, 1910; quarrelled violently with Lloyd George over Cymru Fydd in 1896 but was reconciled with him twenty years later and, as Lord Rhondda, served in his wartime government as President of the Local Government Board in 1916 and as Food Controller in 1917; a millionaire, he owned the Cambrian Collieries (including those at Tonypandy).

[2] Sir Herbert Lewis (1858–1933): Liberal member for Flint Boroughs, 1892–1906, for Flintshire, 1906–18, and for the University of Wales, 1918–22; a junior whip, 1905–9, and parliamentary secretary to the Local Government Board and the Board of Education, 1909–22; a close colleague of Lloyd George for over forty years and a highly dedicated public servant.

moment it is very doubtful which way things are likely to go.

Dr. Clarke has just been looking into my throat. He says there is an irritation at the base of the uvula & he advises me to gargle it with port wine.

Meeting adjourned.

1 September 1893 (later)

Well we have had our meeting & it has been a very long one—three hours in all. I have carried my resolution by an overwhelming majority. We beat all sections all round—the extremists & the Bryn Robertsites together. Ellis & I stuck together all through, Ellis ostentatiously associating himself with me from beginning to end. . . . Rendel was also with us.

7 September 1893

I am now in the House of Lords listening to Lord Selborne droning through what threatens to be a long & dismal harangue on the Irish Home Rule Bill. I am doing it not because I am particularly enamoured of Lord Selborne's oratory or specially desirous of becoming acquainted with his views upon the question but because I know Lord Rosebery is expected to come on immediately after him. Rosebery is a casual dog. Although he is supposed to reply to Selborne he did not turn up at all until half-an-hour after Ld. Selborne had been speaking. Even then he got so tired of this drivel that he has walked out once or twice since. He looks quite bored now.

13 September 1893

Your explanation as to Dick is complete. It is a triumph of feminine logic. First of all he can't bend his foot just yet. In the second place he may be able to do so but he won't & in the third he can do it, he will do it & as a matter of fact does it now. I understand. It is all right hen gariad [old darling]. I could kiss you for so womanly a letter.

14 September 1893

I had some hopes that I should be able to run down to Criccieth today & I had arranged to do so but when I got the parliamentary papers I found that Sir Francis Powell of Wigan had a notice on the paper to call attention to the Bangor College scandal. I had therefore to abandon all idea of leaving this place. It cannot come on today but Ellis thinks it very likely that it will come on tomorrow & he has wired Bryn Roberts to come up for it. Bryn is on the Council of the College & knows all about this wretched business. He will therefore take part in the debate. I also may say a word. It all depends upon the way in which Powell presents the question to the House. If he assumes an aggressive attitude & attacks the Non-conformists then I shall be in the fray with all my heart.

I spoke last night on Pritchard Morgan's[1] motion as to his gold mine. I only said a few words but I have heard from all sorts of people that I made quite an impression in a small way on the House. They were all as still as mice & listened as if I had a great message to deliver. I think I did very well. Last night I went to Loughs & we had a little dinner party of seven M.P.'s. Two or three of them referred to "the melody of my voice". There is an advantage in making oneself scarce in this House. They listen to you with all the greater interest when you do talk.

28 September 1893

We met today to consider an offer from the Andes Exploring Co. . . . to take a 1,000 shares at 10/– premium in our coy. We have wired them to come up in order to consider the matter. If this can be arranged & we manage to raise another £1,000 somewhere we propose sending Hoefer or somebody else out to prospect the country around. Hoefer says it is certainly gold bearing & the question is to locate the gold. You may rely upon it that I am not going to risk another penny piece.

26 December 1893

. . . lo! there was a telegram from Chance since Saturday night offering to put £5,000 in the Company & another letter which arrived yesterday morning confirming telegram & taking 3,300 shares at 30/– each that would [? mean] £4,950. Now isn't that glorious for a Xmas present? It means a present of £120 at the least to me for it will keep the affair going for 18 months even if we get no further funds. But we'll have no difficulty now in raising another £2,000. People are much more apt to take shares if they know that you don't particularly care

[1] W. Pritchard Morgan (1844–1924): Liberal member for Merthyr Tydfil, 1888–1900, losing the seat to Keir Hardie; mined for gold in Australia, Korea, and Merioneth.

whether they do or not. With £5,000 behind us & 50 per cent premiums there will be a boom in these shares.

28 December 1893

As to [the] new dress. Don't you think you had better leave that until you can select the material yourself & get the whole thing done up here. It strikes me that fitting has more to do with a bodice & a skirt. And besides I don't quite see how I am to get the right size & length for the latter. However you say the word & *wire me* early tomorrow to Palace Mansions.

(undated fragment, perhaps 1893 or 1894)

Am y [About the] reception. I behaved very modestly. I am sure Mrs. Gwynoro[1] hardly saw me *speaking* even to any ladies—at least very casually. It was very crowded. I dined that evening at Wynford Phillips & took his wife, a black thin skinny bony Jewess whom you could not squeeze without hurting yourself. This lady I took to the reception & left her there directly he arrived. I then joined myself to Tom Ellis & Dalziel,[2] the young M.P. for Kirkcaldy. It was a very foolish affair. There was a good proportion of Welsh delegates. I met Mrs. Evans of Llanelly (formerly Miss Hughes) Belle Vue, Miss Griffith Springfield, Miss Jones (hogan goch & spectols)[3] Plasyracna & Mrs. Dr. Price, Mrs. Dr. Parry & a few more whose names even I do not recollect.

Although the government was now known to be preparing a Welsh Disestablishment Bill for introduction when parliament re-assembled early in 1894, Lloyd George was alarmed that all Liberal candidates might not share the enthusiasm of the Welsh for disestablishment.

1 January 1894 (misdated 1893)

Torr, the Liberal candidate for Horncastle is against Disestablishment or rather Disendowment & as I consider his victory would be a disaster for Wales I have taken in hand the matter of either bringing him round or punishing him. I attended a meeting of the Liberation Society[4] today & proposed

---

[1] i.e. the wife of Rev. J. Gwynoro Davies (1855–1935), minister of Caersalem Calvinistic Methodist chapel, Barmouth, Merioneth.

[2] Henry Dalziel (1868–1935): Liberal member for Kirkcaldy Burghs, 1892–1921; a newspaper proprietor and one of Lloyd George's main contacts with the press.

[3] A girl with red hair and spectacles.

[4] The society which advocated the disestablishment of the Church of England. Lloyd George served on its executive.

that Fisher should be sent down to interview him & tell him that unless he voted for Welsh Disestab. the Liberationists in the constituency would be asked not to support him. The meeting was adjourned until Thursday to receive Fisher's report. I fought hard for Wednesday but Fisher said he couldn't guarantee to be back by then. Now that I have taken it in hand I mean to see it thro' at all costs. I don't see why these snob Churchmen should be allowed to ride on Nonconformist votes into the House of Commons to oppose Noncon. principles. Do you approve of my staying for that?

3 January 1894 (misdated 1893)

There will be a row tomorrow at the Liberation Society. That fellow Torr the Liberal candidate has positively refused to have anything to do with Disestablishment. I am going to propose a manifesto to the electors of Horncastle—from the Society of course—appealing to them to abstain. I am very wild about it.

4 January 1894 (misdated 1893)

We induced [the Liberation Society] to carry a resolution appealing to the electors [of Horncastle] to withhold their support from Torr. I also, with much greater difficulty, persuaded them to pass a resolution to send that to each elector. I guaranteed the expense. I have since seen Dilke[1] & Labouchere & they have undertaken to find the money. I knew I would get it. The Liberation Society folk are quite terrified at their daring. There is a great flutter about it here.[2]

6 January 1894 (misdated 1893)

And so old Sion Prisiart has flickered out at last. Well he is better off than leading the miserable existence he dragged in this world. Let us hope that he will find more mercy than he dispensed himself. If not he is dead & damned. I know not of a single wretch who deserves the latter fate if he does not. He led

[1] Sir Charles Dilke (1843–1911): Liberal member for Chelsea, 1868–86, and for the Forest of Dean, 1892–1911; President of the Local Government Board, 1882–5; led campaign over the 'sweated trades'; career ruined by divorce scandal, 1886.

[2] The outcome was that the Conservatives retained Horncastle with an increased majority of 838. The Liberation Society's proclamation doesn't seem to have made much difference to the outcome.

a purely selfish existence & is an awful warning to all men of his kidney. May Heaven preserve us from his failings. I don't care a brass button what becomes of his money. No good can come of it. It was coined out of his manhood & there was nothing left. It is all the price of a lost soul.

Uncle Lloyd is alright as long as W. & I have a crust between us & I think my little wife would also consent to share the last crumb with so dear & devoted a friend as Uncle Lloyd is.

I am not going to Cardiff. I have been engaged in sending out the Liberationist resolution & a reprint of an article in the Independent to the electors of Horncastle.

Gladstone resigned on 3 March and Lord Rosebery followed him as Prime Minister. One of the attendant changes was that Gladstone's close friend, Stuart Rendel, chairman of the Welsh Party, went to the House of Lords. This caused a vacancy in the marginal constituency of Montgomeryshire and Lloyd George was the leading Liberal speaker in this critical contest.

21 March 1894 (from Machynlleth, Montgomeryshire)

Magnificent meeting last night. I never delivered a better speech. Spoke for an hour and a half. C. R. Jones said it was "the most eloquent speech he had ever heard". Said so publicly & repeated it. Mrs. Henry Leslie— of Dwyfor Villa—was there & listened with apparent delight although I roasted landlords & parsons. Some fellow got up to question me & I sat upon him to the immense satisfaction of everybody. I spoke in English.

(undated, March 1894) (from Llanfair Careinion, Montgomeryshire)

I came here last night from Glansevern[1] intending to return but the good folk of this town were so importunate & I was so hot after my speech in a packed room that I stayed here after all. . . .

We had a magnificent meeting—too packed if anything. The atmosphere was simply poisonous & I felt its depressing influences even to this house. I have been suffering from neuralgia at least up till now. But after dinner I had a dose of some neuralgia cure prescribed for one of the family. I took a

---

[1] The home of Arthur Humphreys-Owen, the Liberal candidate for Montgomeryshire, and its member, 1894–1905. As an Anglican and a landowner, he was not *persona grata* with Lloyd George at this period.

snooze & woke pretty clear of it. I sat upon some parson at the meeting last night. He had been making insulting observations upon the Irish members & I dressed him down with a good deal of vitriol. When I arrived at Newtown yesterday there was a huge crowd in the road opposite the Bear's Hotel & when I mounted the balcony they raised a tremendous cheer.

2 April 1894

The Montgomery election was a narrow shave wasn't it? I had calculated upon a reduction in the majority—but not to that extent.[1] Owen roused no enthusiasm anywhere & they all told me that had I not gone down it would have lost for a certainty. These respectable moderate men who never make mistakes, they are not liked at all. People as a rule prefer harem scarem chaps who occasionally say & do wild things.

4 April 1894

One of the Tory members for Shropshire—Jasper More[2]— who had been down to Montgomery told me that everybody said I was the member & not Humphreys Owen as I was the man who had carried the seat. Carr, the lobby representative of the Western Mail, said the same thing to me just now.

(undated—apparently 6 April 1894)

The difficulty of leaving this place now is that the Government don't seem to be getting on at all. We were beaten yesterday by a majority of one[3] & later in the evening our majority was reduced to 18 & 15. I am afraid that Ellis is not getting on at all. He has fallen on bad times. He is sometimes compelled to submit to the grossest personal insults. There is a fellow called Captain Fenwick,[4] a brewer who got in as a Liberal for a Durham constituency. Ellis stopped him the other day as he was walking into the Tory lobby. He turned round & said "Don't you think I know how to vote without your telling me, you damned Welshman". Isn't that abominable? I think he ought to have been knocked down. I am exceedingly sorry for Ellis all round.

[1] The Liberal majority slumped to 225, a drop of 600.
[2] R. Jasper More, Conservative member for Ludlow, 1885–1903.
[3] On the East London Water Bill, 5 April 1894.
[4] Capt. H. T. Fenwick, Liberal member for Houghton-le-Spring, 1892–5.

*When the government's programme for the 1894 session gave Welsh Disestablishment
a low priority, below the budget and Registration and Evicted Tenants Bills, Lloyd
George, with D. A. Thomas and Frank Edwards, declared his independence of the
Liberal whip at a widely-publicized meeting at Caernarvon an 14 April. The
government majority was now barely twenty.*

23 April 1894

Frank[1] is a "sticker". He was delighted to see me. He is
fully satisfied with the situation & feels that we are standing on
a rock. . . . The Major [E. R. Jones] is quite miserable about his
attitude. He is thoroughly ashamed of himself—that is my
opinion. Frank made him look very foolish this afternoon in a
talk with him. Rathbone thinks that we are alone consistent. He
says the others have no backbone. That is also Bryn's view.
Bryn [Roberts] will join in repudiating life interests to parsons
if the Govt. Bill is so framed. Saw Ellis and had a talk with
him. He is very "euog" [guilty].

24 April 1894

We have had a meeting of Welsh members this afternoon.
Frank Edwards as whip made an explanation of why he took
action without consulting the party & challenged them to
express their approval or disapproval of our conduct. They all
funked it & said we had a perfect right to act on our own
initiative without consulting the party. The country I think is
coming round to us.

*Lloyd George prepared a major speech on the second reading of the Welsh Disestablish-
ment Bill.*

27 April 1894

Well I am in possession of the House so that when the
debate is resumed on Thursday I lead off. The Speaker called
upon me at once. I am very glad I didn't speak yesterday now
that I am certain to be called. It will give me more time for
preparation & also more time to thoroughly study the scheme. I
shall strongly criticise the life interests part of the measure but
of course I shall avoid anything in the nature of an attack on
the Government.

---

[1] Frank Edwards (1852–1927): Liberal member for Radnorshire, 1892–5,
1900–Jan. 1910 and Dec. 1910–18; although a cousin of the Bishop of St. Asaph,
he was a passionate advocate of Welsh disestablishment.

30 April 1894

Got it over. Think I succeeded wonderfully. Held house much better than Balfour who followed me—& it was a much better House. Heaps of members trooped out after I sat down but they stuck there for me all thro'.

3 May 1894

I receive daily resolutions from different parts of Wales in support of my action. The feeling is evidently growing & some of the details of the Govt. Bill will assist us greatly in converting the country. Our game now is an independent party at the next election. Tonight I dined with Labouchere. . . . Herbert Lewis is anxious to make up his mind to come with us. His wife is a sturdy 'independent'. Humphreys Owen is wavering but both the Liberal papers in the County of Montgomery are for us.

5 May 1894

Herbert [Lewis] has finally declared himself with us. He is accompanying us to Bangor & we will between us set the heather on fire. Mrs. Herbert Lewis had been an independent from the morning I breakfasted with them when I left for Wales.

8 May 1894

[He describes a highly successful meeting at the Congregational Union.] I hit out straight—never did I hit straighter. I gave Guinness Rogers[1] one in the eye & he felt it. The Welsh ministers crowded around me after it was over to congratulate me on "my splendid speech" and to thank me. The Chairman referred to me as "the very eloquent speaker we have just listened to". It was a tremendous score. Hirst Hollowell[2] said "Go on, Young Dissent in England is with you".

9 May 1894

I must be here tomorrow evening to support the Government on a very critical division over the Budget. You saw my row with the Guardian had told—they inserted a lengthy screed from me in today's paper. The Major has been given his

---

[1] Rev. James Guinness Rogers (1822–1911): minister of Clapham Congregational Church.
[2] Rev. James Hirst Hollowell, a leading Congregationalist; a fierce advocate of passive resistance.

'dimittis' from that paper & I am glad of it. He was down speaking in South Wales yesterday & Monday. D. A. Thomas hearing of it went to the meetings. The result was that the little Major had to shut up on Disestablishment & to talk about something else.

We'll have a big meeting at Bangor but don't expect to get it all our own way.

17 May 1894 (from Caernarvon)

Mag—nificent meetings. Immense—swept all before us. Made many converts by my speech last night. I was in fine form & carried them step by step completely with me. This afternoon we had also the same measure of success attendant on our efforts. Bryn candidly confesses that the meeting last night was a great surprise to him. He thought all along I would get a vote but he thought also that the opposition would be much more formidable than it has turned out to be. But it was simply a pitiable collapse. T. C. Lewis' father was against us before the meeting—strongly & angrily so—but he told T.C. that my speech was a "very powerful one" & changed his mind. Mrs. Price College [*sic*] also among the converts.

I haven't a brush & comb.

18 May 1894 (from Rhyl)

Well we are winning hands down. Last night we had a magnificent meeting at Conway. I never spoke better in my life. The Conway people were completely carried away. It was I think one of the finest things I have ever done. They were perfectly unanimous & enthusiastic. Today Mrs. Herbert Lewis, Kate Jenkins & Frank [Edwards] formed a Women's Liberal Association at Conway & they made a very good start I believe. Herbert, D. A. Thomas & I came on here to the North Wales Federation.[1] We got hold of some of the leading members before the meeting & set them right. We then decided that it would be better not to go in ourselves. Resolution carried with only one hand held up against it.

"Cebol" was there & a very amusing incident occurred in connection with him. As usual he hadn't the remotest idea what was going on & when the resolution was put to the meeting he held up his hand for it; altho' he was really against it & had

[1] i.e. the North Wales Liberal Federation which supported the 'revolt'.

F

come all the way from Criccieth to vote against it he will now appear as having voted for it. What an ass he is. The meeting was the most numerous & representative yet held. Gwynoro [Davies] spoke strongly for us. He said that he had been talking with Ellis for hours yesterday & that Ellis had utterly failed to convince him that the government were in earnest in their intentions to push the Bill through.

Herbert & the women have gone to St. Asaph. We have a meeting here tonight. Of course it is in Samuel Smith's constituency [i.e. Flintshire] & there may be opposition. But I don't care. If we carry a meeting outside our own constituency it will be very significant.

19 May 1894

We had a first rate meeting last night—altho' barely a few hours' notice had been given we had a full house—scores were even standing at the end of the Hall. I had the very amusing experience of receiving an encore. I had spoken for about three quarters of an hour & then sat down but the audience insisted on my getting up again—cheered & cheered again until I got up & went on for another quarter. Resolution—strong— carried with but four dissensions. Daily Post today admits we have carried North Wales.

21 May 1894

I wonder what kind of meeting Ellis had at Blaenau Ffestiniog on Saturday. He made a very dishonest speech.

23 May 1894 (from Rhyl)

After breakfast this morning in came Miss Gee with a story that the Welsh M.P.'s had met & condemned us. We got the papers at once & discovered that about a dozen of them had met "informally" & after censuring us determined upon summoning a meeting of the Welsh Party for Friday afternoon to discuss our conduct. I then decided at once that my place was in London to face the cowards who would not even criticise our action in our presence when we challenged them but who condemn us when our backs are turned. We'll fight it out if they want to. This is that little rascal the Major's business.

We had a magnificent meeting yesterday. Denbigh was very striking & at Mold the meeting was most enthusiastic. Gee is with us *heart & soul*. He is not in favour of giving in whether we get assurances or not. Go on with the formation of an independent party—that is his & my idea. He is incensed at Herbert Roberts[1] for not coming down. So were the farmers. That pecksniffian young gent will have to climb down a peg or two.

25 May 1894

Well we had a meeting of our party today & it was a beautiful collapse. Last night the other fellows—headed by Bryn [Roberts] & Sam [Evans]—met in odd corners to put their heads together & concoct thunder against us. They framed a resolution but were very secret about it—wouldn't allow us even to see it. Today Alfred showed me a letter from Herbert Roberts asking him to move it & the Major to second it. The Major was not there—for he *got another spree last night*!!! He was stupidly drunk about the House & Alfred had once more to take him home. So the general was wounded & hors de combat. Well I got hold of Alfred & persuaded him not to lend himself to the others as a catspaw. Alfred had not seen the resolution. Subsequently I saw him. He had a copy of it then & didn't like it. It was too extreme so he said & implied censure upon us. Well to the meeting we went—Alfred moved a very feeble resolution—blank dismay on the faces of Bryn & Sam. He had left out everything which looked like a censure upon us. He made no speech. Warmington[2] seconded without a speech. I moved an amendment declaring my position. Frank seconded. Sam Smith[3] got up & admitted our action had done good. The Four voted for my amendment. The rest had to vote for Alfred's but they were terribly disgusted & abused him. What a tremendous sell for them.

26 May 1894

The more I think of yesterday's affair the more delighted am I with its outcome. There was certainly a Providence in the Major's spree. It enabled me to get at Alfred. Bryn roundly accuses poor Alfred of being "under my influence". It is too

[1] John Herbert Roberts (1863–1955): Liberal member for West Denbighshire, 1892–1918; created Baron Clwyd, 1919; a temperance advocate.

[2] C. M. Warmington (1842–1908): Liberal member for Monmouthshire, 1880–5, and for West Monmouthshire, 1885–95; an English barrister.

[3] Samuel Smith (1836–1908): Liberal member for Flintshire, 1886–1906; a Scots Presbyterian, obsessed by the menace of Romanism.

delightful for anything. The other fellows are more afraid of us than they are even of the ministry. They are a wretched crowd.

29 May 1894 (from Newport station)

This afternoon I went over—having only received a *private* invitation—to the Annual meeting of the Baptist Association for Monmouthshire. Y gymanfa flynyddol [the annual assembly]. By the time I got there the word had gone abroad that I was coming & several ministers & deacons were at the station to escort me to the meeting. A big chapel full of ministers & deacons awaited me. I declined to speak then as I was anxious to have a hand in drafting the resolution. I heard that two or three leading men intended moving a resolution calling us *now* to return to our allegiance owing to Lord Rosebery's assurances & the fact that the Govt. had placed our Bill second on the programme. You know why they have done that now. I talked them over & got a resolution drafted in favour of an independent party. I spoke, with considerable effect I think, carried them comfortably with me. Pedr Hir[1] got up to move a resolution—seconded by somebody. Then a minister got up & moved a rider "That we tender our thanks to Messrs. Lloyd George & Co. for their independent stand", seconded by somebody & carried with only one hand against it. The one was an Englishman from Newport. I have won over Principal Edwards late of Pontypool.

Magnificent meeting at Llandrindod last night. I was never in better form. Frank delighted. . . .

3 June 1894 (from Cardiff)

The Goleuad[2] is a scurrilous, lying Methodistical rag. I mean to go for it.

Lloyd George was now turning the revolt against the government on Welsh disestablishment into a campaign for a Welsh national party on the lines of the Irish.

4 June 1894 (from Cardiff)

Been engaged all day with the editor & subsequently with the proprietor of the S.W.D. News.[3] They have as you know

[1] Peter Williams, 'Pedr Hir' (1847–1922): Baptist minister and writer; began life as a policeman.
[2] The leading Calvinistic Methodist weekly, published at Dolgellau.
[3] The major Liberal daily newspaper in Wales, published at Cardiff.

been fiercely opposed to us. Of course I couldn't expect them to confess that they have been wrong but I tried to induce them to drop the past & go in on general grounds for the formation of a Welsh National party. *I have succeeded* with Alfred's help. They intended boycotting our meeting tonight but after my talk it has been arranged to send up the chief reporter & the editor up to the meeting tonight. Now what do you think of that for a triumph?

5 *June 1894* (from Aberdare)

We had a magnificent meeting last night—about 4,000 people in all. The South Wales Daily News editor & chief reporter were there & were very much impressed. They give my speech an exceedingly prominent position & type—dividing it into sections with flaming head-lines. They refer to it in the leading article as "the eloquent speech etc.". Their articles today are very different in their tone. They go in for a Welsh party. We are winning hands down. The Major may be writing notes in the Guardian against us but it doesn't matter. We have already captured South Wales & I am the chap who did it yesterday.

7 *June 1894*

Had two hours talk with the editor of the South Wales Daily News this morning. Was engaged with manager two hours last night. He interviewed me on the question of a National party.

5 *July 1894* (from Caernarvon)

The Executive[1] passed off very well this afternoon. I told them that I could not afford to pay any more election expenses as elections were coming on so frequently & so I placed my resignation in the hands of the Association. They were quite dumbfounded & two or three men who were strongly opposed to my later tactics—Dr. Price, Henry Owen & John Jones—they got up & made very touching little speeches as to the "love" felt for me by everyone & that no one could carry the boroughs except me although I had gone wrong. They then determined to consult the local leaders at each of their boroughs & get a meeting soon. I think it will be alright.

[1] Of the Caernarvon Boroughs Liberal Association.

Lloyd George went on holiday to Switzerland in August with Frank Edwards and Herbert Lewis. He then devoted his major efforts throughout the autumn to attempting to form a Welsh national party, basing it on the controversial Cymru Fydd League.

19 November 1894 (from Caerwys, Flintshire)

Ralli, a wealthy Greek gentleman living at Rhyl, was at our meeting at Rhyl Friday last. On Saturday Herbert [Lewis] met him & he was in ecstasies over my speech. Said some passages in it reminded him of Gladstone! He prophecies [*sic*] that I would be a Cabinet Minister soon. He evidently doesn't know me.

CHAPTER 4

The Struggle for Cymru Fydd

(1895–96)

The year 1895 brought intense strain and bitter controversy for Lloyd George. It led to the first major crisis of his career, one which he barely survived. In the spring, his major preoccupation was to help exert pressure on the Rosebery government so that the Welsh Disestablishment Bill would be carried through all its stages in the Commons before the dissolution. On 1 April the Bill passed its second reading by the surprisingly large majority of 44.

But Lloyd George was now intent on a wider objective, that of home rule for Wales. Until the 'revolt' of 1894 he had remained an adherent of the view that disestablishment and other Welsh objectives could be realized only through the British Liberal Party. But the events of 1894 largely disillusioned him about the effectiveness of working through the central political system. He now argued that the various claims of Wales ought to be subsumed in a national crusade for self-government. Indeed, only through a Welsh legislature could disestablishment, land reform, and other measures receive the priority they had so conspicuously failed to obtain from Westminster and the British government. To this end, he formed a Cymru Fydd (Young Wales) League with which he hoped that the Liberal Federations of North and South Wales would be merged. In April 1895 the North Wales organization formally agreed to a merger. Lloyd George was half-way there. But the South Wales Liberal Federation, presided over by D. A. Thomas, so recently one of Lloyd George's associates in the 1894 'revolt', showed persistent hostility towards the Cymru Fydd League. Dominated as it was by the mercantile and industrial bourgeoisie of Cardiff, Barry, Newport, and Swansea, the great ports of the south coast, the S.W.L.F. was suspicious of a body originating from the Welsh-speaking rural and mining hinterland. The Cymru Fydd dispute played some part in the fall of the Rosebery government. During the committee stage of the Welsh Disestablishment Bill in May, Lloyd George sponsored an amendment to set up an elected Welsh council to administer the endowments of the Church after disestablishment. There was considerable doubt as to whether Asquith, the Home Secretary, did in fact accept this amendment. On 20 June the government's majority fell to only seven in the committee stage on the Welsh Bill. Shattered in morale, the government was defeated on the trivial 'cordite vote' a few hours later, and Rosebery immediately resigned. The episode did not serve to endear Asquith towards Welshmen in general or Lloyd George in particular.

In the ensuing general election in July, Lloyd George was yet again a figure of acrimonious controversy after his tactics during the committee stage of the Welsh Bill, tactics which some Liberals felt to have been disruptive and disloyal. Lloyd George again faced Ellis Nanney, his opponent of 1890, at the polls, and many observers predicted his defeat this time. Remarkably enough, he held on to his seat by a majority of 194, virtually identical to that of 1892. But the Liberal Party as a whole fared disastrously at the polls. The Unionists were returned with a majority of 152; for once, they even gained several seats in Wales. Lloyd George thus returned again to the calmer waters of opposition.

In the autumn of 1895 Lloyd George resumed his attempt to build up the Cymru Fydd League. His object now was to capture the South Wales Liberal Federation as he had done that of the north. To this end, he undertook an ambitious lecture tour in the mining valleys. Partly designed to help his finances, it was also a Cymru Fydd propaganda exercise, under the pretence of being an historical tour concerned with Llewelyn, the last prince of an independent Wales who had perished in the reign of Edward I and an established folk-hero for nationalists. Lloyd George now faced a bitter onslaught from a Welsh newspaper, the Methodist *Goleuad*, which alleged that his conspiracies with the Unionists and the Parnellites the previous June had actually brought about the fall of the Liberal government. Although Tom Ellis defended Lloyd George in the press, with exemplary loyalty towards a former rebel, Lloyd George's ambiguous reputation was amply confirmed. The climax of the Cymru Fydd movement came with a disastrous meeting of the South Wales Liberal Federation at Newport on 16 January 1896. Here Lloyd George, who attended the meeting under spurious credentials, was howled down. A packed meeting (in both senses) cheered a Cardiff Englishman who declaimed that the cosmopolitan population of the South Wales seaports would never submit to Welsh domination. Although it took several years for Lloyd George fully to absorb the point, his dream of a Welsh national movement under his personal direction had vanished overnight. Cymru Fydd's fragile structure collapsed in the face of official Liberalism, its press support petered out, and nothing like it ever emerged again. At the cost of violent controversy and intense physical strain, Lloyd George had suffered a decisive defeat, his only major setback between 1890 and his fall from office in 1922. Reluctantly he had learnt that Wales could not be preserved as his own private fief. There were limits there even to his own authority. Henceforth his future was to lie as a British Liberal not as a Welsh nationalist.

17 January 1895 (from National Liberal Federation meeting, Cardiff)

Llwyddiant mwyaf erioed [greatest success ever]. The meeting was a failure up to my speech. As somebody said, & several said in fact, I saved the meeting. I got a magnificent reception & when I sat down it was simply fine. They would not stop. The Welshmen were besides themselves that I had licked all the Englishmen. Poor Scott of the Guardian couldn't obtain a decent hearing & at last they beat him down, tired of him altho' he was barely 10 minutes. You will see tomorrow's S.W. Daily News.

5 February 1895

I sat on Osborne Morgan[1] at today's Welsh [members] meeting. He had got some foolish motion about the Duke of Westminster's[2] election fund & he was as big & excited about it as if he had found a gold mine. I ripped the whole thing up at the Welsh meeting. Old Osborne is very pleasant & profuse to me personally. Y mae arno ofn yn ei galon.[3]

7 February 1895

Things are warming up here today. The House is much more excited than it has been up to the present moment. There is nothing being done & I might as well have been down to be nursed by my kind & affectionate little wife. The only point I have gained is that I have secured the Guardian at the very outset of the Session. That is a great thing in itself & I console myself by thinking that it was worth coming up for, even if there were nothing else in view. The little Major [E. R. Jones] seems to have retired out of the contest—for the moment at all events.

8 February 1895

This afternoon I read up last year's debate on Disestablish- ment so as to be well up in their arguments. There is an old copy of the Geninen—it contains an article by Edwin Jones on "Yr Eglwys a Cenedlaetholdeb Cymreig" or something to that effect.[4] I am not sure of the wording. Send it hen gariad [old

---

[1] Sir George Osborne Morgan (1826–97): Liberal member for Denbighshire, 1868–85, and for East Denbighshire, 1885–97; chairman of the Welsh Parliamen- tary Party, 1894–7.

[2] The Duke, chairman of the Central Church Committee, owned considerable land in north-west Wales, part of it in Osborne Morgan's constituency.

[3] There's fear in his heart.

[4] The *Geninen* was a literary quarterly founded in 1883. The article referred to here is actually 'Yr Eglwys yng Nghymru a'r deffroad cenedlaethol' (The Church in Wales and the national awakening), *Y Geninen*, January 1893, pp. 15 ff. The Rev. Edwin Jones, vicar of Bangor, was a nationally-minded Churchman who advocated Welsh disestablishment.

darling]. Please also send Bishop of St. Asaph's Book on the Church—a thin brown book—also Pryce's ancient Brit. Church & the Extracts from Y Llan sent me by that parson chap.

10 February 1895

Our majority last night was dangerously small but good enough I think to pull us through. At the beginning of the week there were all sorts of rumours about a dissolution but it rather looks as if we were going to weather the storm in spite of Higgins & a few such rats.

Tomorrow I have promised to go with Alfred [Thomas] in the evening to Castle Street Baptist Church. I don't know whether I can pluck up sufficient courage to face them after being absent from their services for something like eighteen months.

At this time Lloyd George entered into secret but abortive discussions with some nationally-minded Churchmen who had proposed a compromise 'Bangor scheme' for disestablishment and disendowment. Lloyd George hoped that a settlement of the Church question might enable him to by-pass the nonconformist clerisy and open up the way to inter-denominational co-operation on behalf of Welsh home rule. It all came to nothing.

14 February 1895

Magnificent meeting last night. Very enthusiastic. I got a fine reception & delivered, I think, a speech which stirred them. The Church party was there in strong force & moved an amendment. A certain Canon Hall proposed it & went for me —taking no notice at all of Carvell Williams.[1] I sat upon him in reply. Got up early this morning so as to be in Court.

Today a "Churchman & Conservative" from Bangor sent me Edwin Jones' article in the Geninen with a very interesting letter accompanying it.

15 February 1895

We have just been listening to a fine duel between Chamberlain & Asquith.[2] Chamberlain delivered a tremendous

---

[1] John Carvell Williams (1821–1907): secretary and vice-president of the Liberation Society.

[2] Herbert Henry Asquith (1852–1928): Home Secretary, 1892–5; Chancellor of the Exchequer, 1905–8; Prime Minister, 1908–16; created 1st Earl of Oxford and Asquith, 1925.

onslaught on the Government. . . . Asquith simply smashed Chamberlain up. He was all Welsh Disestablishment & tripped Joe up fairly over that. Joseph looked abashed & sat upon.

17 February 1895

We had a magnificent meeting last night [in the Colchester by-election] & I think I did well. At any rate the people seemed pleased. I was announced as "the leader of the Welsh party", as if it were a recognised fact. I rather believe that we are going to win that seat.[1] If we do it will set the Government up for some time. The Tories are much discouraged by Joe's helpless failure on Friday. The debate was a very lifeless affair—only just a handful of people in the House after the two first speeches. The Tories ran away & our people paired with them.

19 February 1895

Here I am at a Committee meeting where I have just carried a resolution on the unemployed question in the teeth of a good deal of opposition. Osborne Morgan is rambling about something or other. He is a most effete & ineffective old man.

Last night we had a very narrow squeak. We were very nearly beaten & the Government would have gone out & Welsh Disestablishment would have been done for, at any rate for the next 10 years.

20 February 1895

Do you know that it is quite on the cards that we may be beaten tomorrow & have to dissolve. Sir Henry James[2] is going to move the adjournment of the House on the question of the Indian Cotton Duties. The Lancashire members, Liberal & Tory, *must* vote for it as their constituents insist upon it. In that case the Government are beaten & will have to resign. A very serious state of things for us. It simply justifies the revolt up to the hilt. We said all along that we should have to run all these risks in the last session of Parliament & that our Bill might be consequently lost.

---

[1] In fact, the Liberal candidate, Sir Weetman Pearson, gained Colchester with a 263 majority.

[2] Sir Henry James (1828–1911): Liberal, then Liberal Unionist member, 1869–95; Chancellor of the Duchy of Lancaster, 1895–1902; created 1st Baron James of Hereford, 1902.

21 February 1895

We are now in the midst of the exciting Indian Debate which may end in Dissolution. Now things look well. Some of the Tories are themselves doubtful as to the judiciousness of their move & if many of those take that view & support us then we are safe—if not then we shall be beaten straight & we shall all have to go to the country tomorrow to fight for our seats.[1] . . . I shd. like to know when the election is on. If it does not come on until week after next then I should prefer staying here until Disestablishment debate is over. . . .

22 February 1895

Things took a very unexpected turn last night. The Tories completely funked it. They drove right up to the ditch & then seeing Colchester on the other side they sheered off. That is really what it means. They are afraid of a dissolution.

25 February 1895

The Tories have been wasting 2 hours' time over a private Bill in order to postpone our Church Bill. It is an ill wind that blows no good. Their obstruction will have the effect of throwing the debate over tonight & by Thursday one can have more time to prepare. I have got my points arranged, all my facts & figures but the filling up is not complete. I want to know more about Pennant chapel. (1) When it was built? (2) Had they a chapel there before? (3) Have they to come to it from a long distance? (4) How did they pay for it? (5) What did they collect amongst themselves on or for the opening day? I want to show the great efforts they put forth. (6) Are the farmers there a poor lot?

16 March 1895

And you really think I haven't been such a bad husband after all. Well Ellis Griffith & I were comparing notes the other day & we both said that if we were asked on a future great occasion in what capacity we would like to be tried before the Judgement seat we would answer "As a husband if you don't mind". We both thought we would fare pretty well if we had to stand or fall by our merits or demerits as husbands.

[1] In fact the government was saved by a superb speech by Sir Henry Fowler.

23 March 1895

I hope my notes were in today's Guardian. I gave a good word for Sam [Evans]. I want to show myself above the petty meanness & jealousies of such fellows as he. I have nothing to fear from him or his rivalry. He made an effective lawyer's speech but when he attempted to rise above that level he was a dismal failure. He read out his peroration.

Lloyd George spoke on the second reading of the Welsh Disestablishment Bill.

27 March 1895

I spoke last night for over an hour starting about 10.25. Unmistakable success. Chronicle says it is the best I have ever delivered in the House. That is my opinion also. . . . I discovered afterwards that [Balfour] had gone up to the Bishop of St. Asaph[1] in the Press Gallery to ask him is that what everybody thinks, some question about what I was saying. . . . I have got my sea legs in the House. They now listen to me with deference & I manage to draw a parliamentary audience. One or two more speeches like that & my position here is secured. I am not sure that it isn't now. This debate has—rhyngo'n ni a'n gilydd [between ourselves]—been a revelation to me of the position I have already gained in the House. Gorst[2] said I spoke with authority on behalf of Wales. It was gratifying to see how members trooped out when I sat down & Sir John Gorst got up.

30 March 1895

Biggest parliamentary stroke. I spoke tonight on Home Rule all round, seconding Dalziel's motion. Never spoke better in the House of Commons in my life. . . . We have beaten the Tories over our motion by 26. But you'll see all in tomorrow's papers.

With his associate, Beriah Gwynfe Evans, Lloyd George was now mainly absorbed in building up the Cymru Fydd League. Already there were clear indications that the South Wales Liberals opposed it.

[1] Alfred George Edwards (1848–1937): Bishop of St. Asaph, 1889–1934; first Archbishop of Wales, 1920–34; at first a strong opponent of Lloyd George, but subsequently associated with him over the Prince of Wales's Investiture in 1911 and other episodes.
[2] Sir John Eldon Gorst (1835–1916): Unionist member for various constituencies, 1866–1906; vice-president of Committee of Council on Education, 1895–1900.

8 April 1895

I am very busily engaged with Beriah[1]—whom I got up to arrange a counterplot to D. A. Thomas' little plans in connection with Cymru Fydd.

20 April 1895 (from Cardiff)

I am off now to a place called Pontlottyn[2] to address a Cymru Fydd meeting in order to keep the ball rolling. We must smash up the remnants of this South Wales Federation[3] & we shall do it. . . . The Western Mail has a strong article in our favour today. It was written by a strong Nationalist who happens to be on the staff.

3 June 1895 (from Cardiff)

Yesterday was a smashing triumph. We beat them on all points. Ffoulkes of the Cymro[4] had come there to witness our discomfiture. He is the most bitter and spiteful opponent we've got. I called attention to his presence & had him turned out. We had a fight about it. Cebol was particularly anxious he should be in but we beat them. They then proposed quite a series of resolutions but were beaten at every turn. Bryn moved one in which he alleged that the proceedings at Aberystwyth were irregular & that we could not consequently recognise them, & then calling upon us not to touch the organisation until after the general election. For this he got so little support that he had to withdraw it. He then moved a resolution that we should appoint delegates to meet the South Wales Federation to confer with them. This looked so plausible that Gee was for a moment taken in. It really meant recognising the continued existence of the North Wales Federation. Luckily Bryn was beaten on it. Then Herbert Lewis moved a resolution in favour of replying to the invitation of the South Wales people to enter into a conference with them, by stating that we had already amalgamated with Cymru Fydd. This was carried by 15 to 7.

[1] Beriah Gwynfe Evans (1848–1927): a leading Welsh journalist, managing editor of the Caernarvon Welsh National Press Company; secretary of the Cymru Fydd League, 1895–6; later somewhat estranged from Lloyd George (see Evans to David Lloyd George, 25 May 1905, Lloyd George Papers, A/1/5/2).
[2] In the Rhymney valley, western Monmouthshire.
[3] The South Wales Liberal Federation, of which D. A. Thomas was president.
[4] Isaac Ffoulkes (1836–1904): founder of the weekly *Cymro* in 1890.

We licked them on several other points. When Bryn's resolution was beaten poor Gee lost control over himself & flinging up his hand he with a voice half choked with emotion shouted "Hooray—Hooray". The poor old man was very excited. He was beside himself with joy at the triumph of Cymru Fydd. What made it all the more significant was the fact that the majority of those present were not Cymru Fyddites at all.

. . . When I got to Cardiff another victory awaited me. You know why I went to the Amman Valley on Thursday. There was a meeting of the East Carmarthen Liberal Association to be held on Saturday & Towyn[1] had given notice of his intention to move that the Association should join the Aberystwyth Federation, i.e. the Cymru Fydd. Amman Valley sends up 50 delegates so it was the key of the situation. I appealed to them to attend. By the time I got to Bronwydd there was a wire from Towyn: "East Carmarthen enthusiastically joined the New Federation".

So there's another slap in the eye for the Bryn party.

7 June 1895

Just as I was off to the station for Tregaron a number of people rushed out of the Gwalia to ask me to see poor Herbert Lewis as he had just recd. the news that his wife was dead. His grief was appalling. The poor boy was trying to pack. He was distracted. I couldn't leave him in that state, so I took charge of him. By degrees I quieted him down. I have now come from the House where poor Mrs. Lewis' corpse lies.

Lloyd George was busily engaged in trying to get the government to accept his amendment to the ninth clause of the Welsh Disestablishment Bill.

'*Sunday*' (15 June 1895)

Asquith was not in the House as far as I could see last night. I shall tackle him sometime next week when I get the chance. My amendment[2] won't come on for a few days.

[1] Rev. Josiah Towyn Jones (1858–1925): Independent minister at Cwmamman, Carmarthenshire; later Liberal member for East Carmarthenshire, 1912–18 and for Llanelli, 1918–22; junior whip, 1917–22; a famous performer in the pulpit.
[2] This was an attempt by Lloyd George to set up a Welsh national council to administer the Church endowments after disendowment. There was great doubt as to whether Asquith in fact accepted the amendment, and it later led to violent controversy sparked off by the journal *Y Goleuad*, the following November (see below, p. 89).

On 21 June the government resigned after being defeated on a snap vote on the question of supplies of cordite to the army. The new Salisbury government then dissolved parliament. Lloyd George now faced his third hard contest at the polls in five years. His opponent once again was Ellis Nanney, the squire he had defeated in 1890.

William George to David Lloyd George, 3 July 1895

I tho^t I might drop you a word or 2 to say how things are getting on hereabouts. I have not yet quite completed my analysis of the Criccieth Reg^n. but on the whole I think we shall maintain our strength fairly well. I don't believe there will be a difference of ten in the majority.

Pwllheli one hears various Reports about but I have met none very despondent. Roberts Llanfyllin told me last night that a big man in Pwllheli had told him "I was one of those who did not agree with George but after hearing him at Pwllheli Monday I am as hot for him as ever & so are all I have seen." The spokesman as I afterwards found out was Rowlands, Commercial Traveller. Da onide? [Good, isn't it?]

The canvass is already nearly complete I believe & the party generally in good heart.

All therefore depends on that part of the County. Llwyddiant mawr! [Great success].

5 July 1895 (from Caernarvon)

[He describes a very successful election meeting at Bangor. He urges his wife to join him.] Come over by the 10 train & bring Mr. Thomas with you. They are expecting him there. They say that there are a few voters at Nevin whom he alone can influence. Beg him to come, will you. See him tonight.

12 July 1895 (from Deganwy)

Here I am after a very hard but successful day's canvass. I've got to address a meeting in about an hour's time. We shall at the very least hold our own in this borough. That is satisfactory because I feared all along Conway was going to the bad.

14 July 1895 (from Rhyl)

Canvass returns for the different boroughs not yet complete, so I have no idea—except from meetings—how things are going. W^{ms}. the Chronicle says I shall be out by 30 & he is prepared to bet on it. He also says that Herbert will be out for a certainty—also the little Major & Humphreys Owen.

Reed[1] loses Cardiff & Allen[2] the Pembroke Boroughs. That's his reckoning. His calculation for the Carnarvon Boroughs is very fine as you see. Everything depends on the next week's work. Unluckily the elections elsewhere are going against us. The first results came in last night. We have lost 5 & gained 1. Harcourt who got 2,000 last time is now out by 300.[3] That is of course a staggering blow. It will have the effect of putting heart into the Tories & of depressing our people. I must apply myself next week to rousing them to a final effort. If I succeed then we win. If not—then I shall apply myself for the next six years to Criccieth & business.

Write per mail tomorrow, if you have anything for me, to Liberal Com[ee] Rooms Carnarvon. I shall be there for the nomination. Tuesday I shall also be at Carnarvon. I return tomorrow afternoon to Bangor to speak & complete the canvass.

I shall want collars & cuffs for Tuesday. Can't you come with me to Nevin on Wednesday & bring baby?

16 July 1895

Bangor was very backward up till last night. I then summoned a meeting of the canvassers & told them straight how things stood. I said "All the others are building up a majority for us—with much care, trouble & anxiety & here with one sweep Bangor wipes it all out. Now I said I simply want you to realise that the entire responsibility rests with you for any possible disaster". They were quite stunned. I then told them that as I had a meeting in Upper Bangor they had better put their heads together and see what could be done—that they had better stick there as they were not wanted at the meeting. They did so loyally. I then went up & had a grand meeting. Wheldon[4] delivered a fine speech & so did Towyn [Jones]. I was also in my best form. . . .

24 July 1895 (from Wrexham)

[Sir George Osborne Morgan has appealed to him

[1] Sir Edward Reed (1830–1906): Liberal member for Pembroke District, 1874–80, and for Cardiff, 1880–95 and 1900–6 (crossing the floor over tariff reform in 1904); a prominent naval constructor.

[2] C. F. Egerton Allen (1847–1926): Liberal member for Pembroke District, 1892–5.

[3] At Derby. He was given a new seat in West Monmouthshire.

[4] Rev. Thomas J. Wheldon (1841–1916): Calvinistic Methodist minister at Tabernacle chapel, Bangor.

for assistance during the election in East Denbighshire.]

There is a certain irony of fate in the fact that the leader of the Welsh party has to send hysterical telegrams to the rebel chief for his assistance. At the commencement of the struggle he gave me a nasty stab under the rib which, had he any strength at all, would have finished me. Now I am having my revenge in rushing to the rescue of the man who tried to drown me.

Lloyd George was again victorious at the polls by a majority of 194. After the election he was prostrated by nervous exhaustion. However, once back in the House his growing stature among radical backbenchers was confirmed.

16 August 1895

I have just been elected a member of the Radical Committee[1] for the Session.

22 August 1895

I am at it busily obstructing. I have already spoken twice on the Salaries of the officials of the House of Lords. I made one motion & divided the House upon it. & for the first time reduced the Government majority under 100.

27 August 1895 (from York)

Storey[2] and I have been too much occupied in discussing our case.[3] We have also been into a project I submitted to him for starting a daily newspaper in South Wales. Storey is a large speculator in that line. He has started several newspapers & he is very disposed to go into this thing. Of course I wouldn't put anything in myself even if I had it nor does he want it. He has the money & he is prepared to dump it down provided I can prove the idea can be worked. All he asks for is that the local men shall fund say £10 to £15,000—he'll find the rest which would mean another £40 or £50,000. He has instructed me to get all the particulars as to population of districts, local trains &c. If he finds it is any good he'll run down with me to Swansea. Well if it goes I shall ask for the London letter at any rate. But I am counting chickens before they are hatched—just like me. But I am anxious to pay the S.W.D.N. out.

[1] An unofficial committee of left-wing Liberal backbenchers.
[2] Samuel Storey (1840–1925): Liberal member for Cleveland, 1881–95.
[3] Lloyd George was representing Samuel Storey in an election petition case.

Newspaper attacks now claimed that Lloyd George's disloyal tactics had caused the downfall of the Rosebery government the previous June. Tom Ellis defended him.

7 November 1895

Ellis has written a capital letter. He has one or two very effective digs at Bryn & D. A. Thomas.[1]

8 November 1895

We had a most successful conference at Shrewsbury yesterday & arranged for our South Wales campaign. Herbert Lewis & Wm. Jones[2] will take the lead. There is a distinct advantage in that. It will strip the movement bare of any sectarian appearance. The Baptists who are a mighty power in So. Wales are with us. But I am anxious the Methodists should come in. The Independents, especially the younger sort, are also with us. . . .

One good result of this South Wales tour is that I am overcoming my nervousness completely. The first night I was for the first quarter of an hour painfully nervous & really thought I must sit down. I however stuck to it—for an hour & twenty minutes. At Brynmawr I spoke for an hour & a half.

11 November 1895

I was rather surprised & disappointed that you did not make any kind of allusion to Tom Ellis' letter in the Guardian. Neither you nor Uncle say a word about it. I should have expected you both to be burning with impatience to see it. The Western Mail had three columns about it, but the S.W. Daily News wouldn't give a line of it! Although they published columns of the other side. I am going for that paper tonight so as to let people know what to expect in future from it. If you can't get a paper frankly to give you fair play, it is better to prejudice men's minds against it so that whatever it says about me will henceforth be taken with a grain of salt. I am

[1] On 5 November Ellis wrote to the press to refute allegations by Bryn Roberts, D. A. Thomas and the *Goleuad* newspaper that the fall of Rosebery government in June had been caused by Lloyd George's disloyalty during the committee stage of the Welsh Disestablishment Bill (Kenneth O. Morgan, *Wales in British Politics, 1868–1922*, Cardiff, 2nd edn., 1970, pp. 155–8).

[2] William Jones (1857–1915): Liberal member for Caernarvonshire (Arfon), 1895–1915; junior whip, 1911–15; his 'silvery tones' won the admiration of *Punch*. The point here is that both Lewis and Jones were Calvinistic Methodists.

sending a note to the Western Mail people so that they may have a reporter present.

Oh yes, Miss Jones. She is lovely. Twenty-one, charming & so jolly. It is a perfect delight to spend Sunday in the same house. Dyna i ti rhen Fagi! [There you are, old Maggie!]

Love, fond & warm from
Your sweetheart.

Lloyd George spent most of November campaigning on behalf of Cymru Fydd throughout South Wales. He was anxious to secure a majority of sympathetic delegates to the meeting of the South Wales Liberal Federation in January. He also spent much time in trying to win over the editors of local newspapers.

12 November 1895 (from Ferndale, Rhondda)

Today we had a most successful Cymru Fydd conference at the Café, the best men of the town being present. Elfed[1] & I spoke. Elfed is with us heart & soul. I made the best speech I ever made in my life. The only man who spoke in favour of postponement was the Methodist minister. I adroitly hinted that Herbert Lewis would come down to address their demonstration. This chap then subsided & was instantly put on the Committee.

13 November 1895

Last night I went hot and strong for the S.W. Daily News —there is a column in the Western Mail. You'll get it in a day or two. The meeting passed a strong resolution condemning the S.W. Daily News for its action. They have a short article today denying that they received Tom Ellis' letter. I wired Beriah—he made enquiries at the Post Office & there he was told that the letters were wired to the S.W.D.N. So I am going for them tonight again. There is a great feeling against the News. South Wales is just in the state of mind which would make a new paper successful. I'll press Storey to take it in hand. That will bring the News to its knees.

14 November 1895 (written in the train to Paddington)

I had a most successful meeting last night. Went for the South Wales D[aily] N[ews] again & got a vote of censure

---

[1] Rev. H. Elvet Lewis (1860–1953): leading Independent minister and a distinguished poet and hymn-writer.

passed in spite of the protests of an unfrocked Baptist minister who happened to be there. He only got two votes against the resolution. Even these condemned the South Wales—the three of them. The S.W. today climbs down.

16 November 1895

Ellis G[riffiths] is a wobbly, weak sort of creature—doesn't know his own mind about anything. He promised at last under pressure from Vincent[1] (whom we subsequently saw at the Club) to address one meeting for us in South Wales. Vincent is now & has been for some time a violent rebel. Griffiths thought I had been exceptionally lucky both with Goleuad & South Wales Daily News, both papers having committed such egregious follies.

I met Pitt, the parliamentary representative of the Times, who came up to me to congratulate me on shifting the quarrel on to Tom Ellis, Bryn & Thomas. Cleverest thing I have done for a long time, so he said. Thomas' attack on Ellis in the papers is a very bitter one & will do us all the good in the world as it will force Ellis' friends into our camp.

19 November 1895 (from Tredegar)

You have more brains than you give yourself credit for. Mrs Freeman was telling Towyn Jones on Monday that you were the very essence of commonsense. She never met anyone so thoroughly sensible. That is exactly my opinion. You have the most valuable intellectual faculty—sound judgement & if you have transmitted it to the children I shall be more content than if they have inherited all the troublesome powers I may be endowed with. Got a capital meeting last night altho' the audience in these semi-English districts are not comparable to those I get in the Welsh districts. Here the people have sunk into a morbid footballism.

20 November 1895 (from Tonypandy)

The Rhondda is coming over to us bodily. Mabon[2] who

---

[1] i.e. Vincent Evans (see above, p. 25, n. 5).
[2] William Abraham, 'Mabon' (1842–1922): miners' agent in the Rhondda valleys, from 1870, first president of the South Wales Miners' Federation, 1899–1911; Liberal, then Labour member for the Rhondda, 1885–1918, and for Rhondda West, 1918–22.

started with the Federation has been compelled to throw them over.

21 November 1895 (from Swansea)

Last night's demonstration was simply *immense*—that is the word. Nothing like it in the Rhondda—not in the memory of the oldest inhabitant has anything to equal it been seen. Crowds from all parts of the Rhondda came down. Hundreds of D. A. Thomas' own colliers amongst them. Mabon looked blue. I talked Home Rule for Wales & all the nationalist stuff which the Mabon crew so detest—but the people cheered to the echo. The Rhondda has been captured.

22 November 1895 (from Landore, Swansea)

This morning I walked over the hill from Landore to Morriston with Towyn Jones & the Rev. W. P. Williams of Seren.[1] Williams has been won over completely on Welsh Home Rule. That will be a great advantage because his paper has a circulation of 7,000 amongst the leaders of the Baptist denomination. I have also got Richards Tonypandy to promise that he'll write to the Tyst[2] so that we may remove misapprehension in that quarter. Tom John, the editor of the Glamorgan Free Press won over. Ap Ffarmwr[3] who is editor of the Merthyr Times I've asked to meet me tonight. One of the editors of the Celt I converted last week. So that I hope to more than counteract the baneful influence of the S.W.D.N.

25 November 1895 (from Newport station)

Last night I went to Merthyr with Mr. Gibbon to see ap Ffarmwr. . . . I have won him over on Home Rule for Wales. He had started on the wrong tack.

29 November 1895

I saw Llew's[4] article. It is very fine. An excellent piece of

---

[1] *Seren Cymru*, the main Baptist periodical.

[2] *Y Tyst a'r Dydd*, the Independents' Welsh-language weekly.

[3] John Owen Thomas, 'ap Ffarmwr' (1861–99): editor of the *Merthyr Times*, 1895–6, and leader-writer on the *Nottingham Express*, 1897; a pioneer socialist. The interview with Lloyd George appeared in the *Merthyr Times* on 28 November.

[4] W. Llewelyn Williams (1867–1922): barrister and author, editor of the *South Wales Star* (Barry) and the *South Wales Post* (Swansea) in the 1890s; Liberal member for Carmarthen District, 1906–18; for years, one of Lloyd George's closest Welsh friends, but quarrelled violently with him over conscription in 1916.

writing, full of spirit and vivacity. And I fancy it is rather true what he says about my being repeatedly on the brink of political extinction to all appearance & suddenly bobbing up higher than ever. Willie Lewis Jones[1] always says that & compares me to a cork which always comes to the surface.

6 December 1895

Sat on Ellis Griffith last night at a Cymru Fydd meeting. He made one of his usual "sitting on the fence" speeches & I went for him out & out. Saw Bryn today. Bryn was delighted beyond measure as he has a great contempt for Griffith. Griffith was white with anger and chagrin.

17 December 1895 (from Sunderland)

I am surprised at Uncle Lloyd's criticism of Ellis' speech. I thought it admirable. He went as far as he dare go & it will do the cause of Welsh Home Rule incalculable good. Fair play— the gaffer is out of all reason. He is too impatient. He must restrain himself.

Lloyd George spent December and early January in Sunderland, appearing on behalf of Samuel Storey, the former Liberal member for Sunderland, in an election petition. He was also still trying to persuade Storey to finance a new Liberal newspaper in South Wales to counteract the influence of the South Wales Daily News *which was hostile to Cymru Fydd. Then Lloyd George returned to South Wales for the decisive meeting of the South Wales Liberal Federation at Newport on 16 January.*

12 January 1896

We have decided to swamp the Rhondda with letters for the meeting of delegates which is coming off there tomorrow. A good deal will depend on it. I wrote two letters yesterday on the point. If we carry Rhondda it will mean the turning of the scale at Newport on Thursday. Dyma fi etto yn nghanol y rhyfel.[2]

13 January 1896

Beriah wires me that I am duly elected a delegate for the S. Wales Lib. Fedn. on Thursday.

---

[1] William Lewis Jones (1866–1922), lecturer, then professor in English at University College, Bangor; at this time, a Welsh correspondent for the *Manchester Guardian*.

[2] Here I am again in the midst of the conflict.

14 January 1896

[He attended a preaching meeting at Falmouth Road Methodist Chapel.] Cynddylan [Jones][1] was in great form. He was delighted to see me. Came to me & said he was with me absolutely in the "Goleuad" business. Even if its charges were true "it was a fine thing for Wales that a Welshman could upset a Government".

15 January 1896

Heard from Rhondda that the Cymru Fyddites scored "a grand victory" there last night & that all the delegates are to vote for us tomorrow at Newport. That cripples Mabon's mischievousness.

16 January 1896 (from Newport)

The meeting of the Federation was a packed one.[2] Associations supposed to be favourable to us were refused representation & men not elected at all received tickets. There were two points of dispute between us. By some oversight they allowed me to speak on one & we carried it—as it turned out not because the majority of the meeting was with us but because they went to the vote immediately after my speech & I can assure you the impression made could be felt. I simply danced upon them. So they refused to allow me to speak on the second point. The majority present were Englishmen from the Newport district. The next step is that we mean to summon a Conference of South Wales & to fight it out. I am in bellicose form & don't know when I can get home.

18 January 1896 (from Neath)

Welsh Wales is with us to the fore. We have simply got to stir it up. I went to Swansea today & saw a number of our friends. They are delighted we should have chosen Swansea. I told them that we had asked the S.W. Federation to do so but that the Cardiff chaps were jealous of Swansea—there is a

---

[1] Rev. J. Cynddylan Jones (1840–1930): moderator of the South Wales Calvinistic Methodist Association and a noted 'new theologian'.

[2] At an uproarious meeting of the South Wales Federation at Newport, Lloyd George was howled down and his attempt to merge the Federation with the Cymru Fydd League failed (see *South Wales Daily News* and *Western Mail*, 17 January 1896).

deadly rivalry as you know between the two towns. Just fel Bangor a Carnarvon.[1]

(undated—some time in the 1890s)

Fancy Mari[2] going off to Sir Fon [Anglesey]. She is the most worthless of the lot. I would prefer being a scapegrace in a family to being its idler. She ought to be ashamed of herself. I am surprised at Will providing her with funds. I shouldn't without a stiff quarrel. If Will gets married I should like to know what will become of her then. She spends more in dresses & holidays than my old Maggie will do in housekeeping &— God help her—she is so devout & puritanical. Just like the whole d—d pack of puritans.

[1] Just like Bangor and Caernarvon.
[2] i.e. his elder sister, Mary Ellen. It should be added that the account in this letter is very unfair to Mary Ellen George, who was immensely kind to all the Lloyd George children and a warm champion of Mrs. Lloyd George. She married Captain Philip Davies, an uncle of Professor Seaborn Davies (who succeeded Lloyd George briefly as Liberal member for the Caernarvon Boroughs in 1945). Her death in her early forties brought great sorrow to the Lloyd George family at Criccieth. (Private information.)

CHAPTER 5

Parliamentary Opposition and Personal Crisis

(1896–99)

Lloyd George wasted little time in repairing his reputation after the débâcle of Cymru Fydd. At first he was reluctant to admit that it was a defeat. He tried to persuade his Welsh colleagues to found a new Federation to succeed the old League, now virtually defunct. He also used the backbench Radical Committee as a forum for promoting the cause of 'home rule all round', devolution for England, Wales, and Scotland as well as for Ireland. But by the end of March 1896 it was clear that neither move had much chance of success. The Welsh members were anxious to bury the bitter conflicts that Cymru Fydd had unleashed, while the parliamentary Liberal Party had no wish to revive the issue of home rule 'separatism', even in modified form, after it had cost them so dear at the polls. The Irish Nationalists were also discouraging. It was, therefore, a wider issue, the Agricultural Land Rating Bill of 1896, that again brought Lloyd George to the fore. At a time when the Liberals were still dazed and divided over Irish and imperial questions, Lloyd George gave them new heart by his fierce attacks on the Bill during its passage. He alleged that it amounted to a present to the landlords by the taxpayers to the tune of £1,500,000. He was a supremely skilful opponent in committee, while he achieved the further accolade in radical circles of being suspended by the Speaker. The Land Rating Bill, together with his onslaught on the Education Bill in 1897, because of its increased grants to Church schools, suggested that his reputation was now becoming nation-wide.

In addition to these assaults on the squires and the clergy, the traditional targets of rural radicalism, he was for the first time now involved with organized labour. In 1896 a savage strike erupted in the Penrhyn slate quarries in Caernarvonshire; it was to drag on intermittently for seven years. On the platform, in parliament and ultimately in the courts, Lloyd George championed the quarrymen and denounced the feudal pretensions of the autocratic Lord Penrhyn. This quarry strike gave Lloyd George a new concern with labour and with industrial questions. The Welsh radical was making his first tentative acquaintance with the New Liberalism of social reform.

In 1897 the even tenor of his personal life was severely disturbed. Catherine Edwards, the wife of a Montgomeryshire doctor, alleged that Lloyd

George was the father of her illegitimate child. Rumours of this scandal had circulated while Lloyd George was away on a carefree business trip to Argentina in the autumn of 1896; in July 1897 the Edwards case appeared in the divorce list. Tales about Lloyd George's relations with women had been heard before, but there was hitherto no evidence to suggest that his behaviour had lapsed from conventional standards, nor that it had caused any strain between him and his somewhat puritanical wife. But this new crisis threatened his entire future. Lloyd George's devoted brother, William, was now his closest counsellor. Largely through his efforts, it was established that Mrs. Edwards's accusation was wholly false, and made under duress in order to protect another man. Lloyd George's name was therefore completely cleared. But the incident lingered on in the minds of his enemies—and apparently within his own family circle. There is no doubt that this agonizing crisis severely upset the hitherto happy and placid relations of David and Mrs. Lloyd George. But by the end of 1897 the harmony of their domestic life was fully restored, and there are no grounds for claiming that the Edwards case created any permanent rift.

This trial overcome, Lloyd George resumed his role as a leading voice for radical dissent and little Englandism. While he was still much involved in the labyrinthine complexities of Welsh politics, his political interests were now much more wide-ranging than three years earlier. He took a prominent part in debates on Old Age Pensions which the government had failed to introduce. He led further attacks on increased spending on armaments. Above all, as a fierce adherent of the anti-imperialist wing of the Liberal Party (now under the leadership of Sir Henry Campbell-Bannerman) he kept a critical eye on the crisis brewing between the British government and two Boer republics in South Africa.

9 February 1896

[He has again been discussing the project of a new South Wales newspaper with Storey.] Storey is now inclined to start at Merthyr. That will suit me just as well. It will cut down the circulation of the S.W. Daily News evening edition by thousands. Those chaps are getting rather timid about their quarrel with me. Their manager wrote to Llew a letter evidently intending he shd. show it to me. It contained an admission that they had committed an "error of judgment". But their halting apology came rather too late. It will cost a few thousands a year before I am done with them.

11 February 1896

It is quite true what you say about one getting accustomed even to these periodic separations from one's family—but all the same I get spasms of hiraeth [longing]. You know very well that the pressure to bring us together invariably comes from me. I have led a very strenuous & anxious life for the past five years & it is beginning to tell upon me. That has had a good deal to do with my apparent indifference to my home. Other interests have absorbed my mind but I always come back with a sensation of restful delight to Brynawelon. I only wish I could get such a fortnight there as I enjoyed immediately after my election collapse. In spite of my complete physical prostration I never enjoyed my life as I did then. I felt perfectly happy. It is such a fortnight as that I want now to set me up for the Session.

11 February 1896 (later)

Poor W. J. [William Jones] He made an ass of himself at today's meeting of Welsh M.P.'s, E. J. G[riffith] moved a resolution that we should be bound in future by the decisions of the party. I have no doubt it was directed against me & those who act with me. But I knew that Bryn & D. A. [Thomas] would never accept it so here was an opportunity of putting them in the wrong. Bryn was not there but D. A. opposed it fiercely. W. J. rushed up & suggested some foolish compromise. I made a strong speech for Griffith & it had such an effect that altho' the majority present were prepared to vote against Griffith they got quite funky & begged for an adjournment of the debate. Ellis ran out. I went for them hot & strong. You could feel the impression. I don't care much whether it is carried or not. The great point is that it puts D. A. & Bryn in the wrong. I stand as the man who is prepared to abide by the vote of the majority. Won't I make use of that. I sat on Brynmor Jones[1] who made one of his opportunist-pleasing both parties speech [*sic*].

13 February 1896

There was a lying report in the Mercury as to what I had said at the Welsh members meeting on Tuesday. I simply placed the matter before them today—there was a good deal of indignation expressed all round & they passed unanimously a resolution that it shd. be officially denied in the Press. Old Sir George [Osborne Morgan] called it "a downright lie". The beauty of it is that Willie Lewis Jones' friend who writes

[1] Sir David Brynmor Jones (1852–1921): Liberal member for Stroud, 1892–5, and for Swansea District, 1895–1914; a barrister.

articles against me in the Liverpool Mercury had based a nasty
article today on the report.

14 February 1896

The Govt. have had a snub from old Kruger the Boer &
Chamberlain has had his first reverse as a Minister[1]. . . . Herbert
Lewis has had a correspondence with Willie Lewis Jones in the
course of which he complained bitterly of the treatment he
meted out to me. The little pimp replied that he had always
the friendliest feelings towards me personally &c. We'll see.
If he makes another of his vile misrepresentations I shall com-
plain to Scott[2] about him.

*Defeated over Cymru Fydd, Lloyd George tried, through the Radical Committee, to
get the Liberal Party to commit itself to 'home rule all round'.*

18 February 1896

You are a jealous little creature! Miss May is not there.
As a matter of fact I have not seen her for months. . . . Today
I raised the question of Home Rule All Round at the Radical
Com[ee]. They asked me to bring it on formally at their next
meeting. Labouchere & Dilke are strongly in favour of my
motion. Tell uncle.

19 February 1896

We secured excellent places in the ballot today for three
or four Welsh questions but now I hear Balfour means to take
the whole time of the House for Govt. business. That shuts us
out. I wish the Liberals almost would make up their minds just
to leave half a dozen men in charge here & then plant the rest
of their men in the constituencies to educate the electors. They
would win the next election for us & turn these fellows out
bag & baggage. That policy would suit me down to the ground.
All this is a farce. The real work is to be done in the country
& perhaps in Committees up here.

---

[1] This refers to the collapse of the Jameson Raid. On 2 January 1896 Dr. Jameson
surrendered with 500 men to the Boers at Krugersdorp. Chamberlain, the Colonial
Secretary, was guilty of complicity (J. S. Marais, *The Fall of Kruger's Republic*,
Oxford, 1961, pp. 64–95).

[2] Charles Prestwich Scott (1846–1932): editor and eventually governing director
of the *Manchester Guardian*, 1872–1929; also Liberal member for Leigh, 1895–1906;
a warm supporter of Lloyd George for almost all of his career.

21 February 1896

Welsh debate on Museums Grants been on. A very good one. Division brought the govt. majority down to 68. So we have done excellently.

23 February 1896

[He has dined at Ellis Griffith's home]. It is such a pity that he has so many qualities 'sal' [bad] for he possesses much amiability of character. I sincerely wish to get on well with him because we can do so much more & better work for Wales if we are [*sic*] cordial relations with each other. Besides it is so much more pleasant for one.

28 February 1896

I spoke twice last night & on the wire I sent you I used the word "today" unintentionally. I got on remarkably well. The House was anxious for a division & they would not listen to Atherley Jones[1] who came before me but I got a remarkably good hearing. I spoke I think with effect for 18 minutes. Repeatedly cheered. Good report in Times. I spoke about 3 o'clock this morning mewn hwyl fawr [in great form]— cheered tremendously by the Radicals. Tell uncle all about it as I may not have time to write him. I distinctly scored under the most difficult circumstances. I triumphed by sheer force of will & clear emphatic speaking. I'll soon seek out another opportunity of having a fling.

Griffith is very annoyed about his defeat yesterday. It has done him good by driving him over to our side for the time at any rate.

(undated—probably early 1896)

Had a long talk first with Scott of the Guardian & afterwards with "Tim" [Healy] about Home Rule All Round. Scott does not now object to Welsh Home Rule but thinks Ireland ought to come first. Edwards of Nottingham, formerly of the Genedl, was with me when Tim came up. Edwards strongly in favour of my scheme. I complained to Scott about Willie Lewis Jones—told him I had remonstrated privately

[1] L. A. Atherley-Jones (1851–1929): Liberal member for North West Durham, 1885–1914.

with him & that Ellis Griffith had also done the same thing. Told him that he was good fellow enough but that he buried himself behind academy walk & thought he could see further through a brick wall what was going on outside than others could.

3 March 1896

The Radical Committee today fixed Tuesday week for the general meeting of their members to consider my motion on Home Rule all round. That is very important for me to carry & it will not be easy as it will change the policy of the Liberal party. It would lift the question at once to the very front rank of the programme.

4 March 1896

I am so sorry to have to disappoint you. But it is one of the incidents of the campaign & once one is in it one can only grin & bear. Don't you forget that it is very much worse for me than for you. You've got the youngsters around you. Every little one I see toddling around reminds me of one or other of the hen byttia bach [little tots]. I get quite depressed about it occasionally. However after the Radical meeting next Tuesday I hope to be able to get down. I have already got 35 members to promise to be present to support me. Herbert Lewis is coming up tomorrow & he'll help me to whip up members. I do hope we'll carry it.

6 March 1896

I have been consulting Tim Healy about the Home Rule all Round resolution. It was rumoured last night that the Irish were likely to make a disagreeable fuss about it. I therefore consulted Dillon[1] & arranged to leave out all the words to which he took exception. Tim also agrees. So that stile has been crossed. It is beginning to create a stir. . . .

9 March 1896

I hear that that young sneak—Willie Lewis Jones—has actually written Bryn Roberts to find someone who can write the work from Westminster "as an M.P. is quite impracticable". . . . I gave him a dig in the ribs in today's notes when I said that

[1] John Dillon (1851–1927): Irish Nationalist member, 1880–1918.

in English literature Bangor is hopelessly outstripped by Aberystwyth. That will make him wince a little. No harm giving him a taste of what he been administering to me. I wonder how he'll like it.

24 March 1896

The Radical meeting is just over. We had a very lengthy discussion but at length the debate was adjourned to a future date. There was a question of great importance being discussed down below in the House & as we had been on for a couple of hours they thought we had better adjourn. Bryn was sat upon by the Chairman for rambling wide of the question. He was very nearly beaten down. The general sense of the meeting was in favour of Home Rule All Round. Some excellent speeches were delivered in favour it.

In fact, this meeting of the Radical Committee marked a permanent defeat for the cause of 'Home Rule All Round'. However, Lloyd George was soon very active in the Liberal attack on the government's Agricultural Land Rating Bill, introduced in April.

14 May 1896

I have just done what is generally regarded as a smart thing. The Chairman ruled out of order two or three amendments which were supposed to be good for 2 or 3 hours. The next amendment stood in the name of D. A. Thomas but he was not there to move it. As the Chairman was about to move on to the next I jumped up & said I would take charge of it. But as I had not the remotest idea what it was I read it out to the Committee, then I began to talk & got hold of a very good argument. Chaplin[1] made a very weak defence. Then Sir John Dorington[2] got up. He is a very respectable old Tory country gentleman & supposed to be great authority on rating. But he made a glaring blunder in law. I jumped up & tackled him. He still denied but I went & got the authority & floored him. He got up & admitted it. I then went for Chaplin. Did well I think.

[1] Henry Chaplin (1840–1923): Unionist member for Sleaford, 1868–1906 and for Wimbledon, 1907–16; President of the Board of Agriculture, 1886–92, and of the Local Government Board, 1895–1900; the spokesman of the squires.

[2] Sir John Dorington (1832–1911): Unionist member for Tewkesbury, 1886–1906; described himself in *Who's Who* as 'a busy country gentleman'.

Lloyd George's eldest daughter, Mair

Lloyd George playing with Megan in the garden

22 May 1896

I wired you this morning informing you of our suspension.[1] You will have had full particulars in evening papers. All the Radicals are delighted beyond measure. Say it is best thing yet happened for [the] cause. It has had one effect which will please you—the ensuring of a longer holiday. First thing that occurred to me when sentence was pronounced.

Lloyd George used his free time after his suspension from the House to campaign for Barlow, the Liberal candidate in the Frome by-election.

(undated—evidently May 1896) (from Bath)

Broadhurst[2] and I chief speakers. They were fairly roused. I think we have helped Barlow not a little towards the top of the poll.[3] It is the outvoters alone who can beat us now. There are 600 of them of which only 100 are Liberals. There are 1,100 freehold voters in Bath who have votes for both town & County in respect of the same property. These are mostly Unionist. If the constituency were free to express its opinion we should win by a huge majority.

Tonight we go with Broadhurst to the Wesleyan Chapel. He is a fine genial & kindly old man. He has given me much good counsel.

4 June 1896

Introduced Barlow. I am very glad that was done. I ascribe it to Broadhurst & to Ellis who was keen about it. . . . The Central Liberal Federation per Ellis gave me £12/12/– for my ex[pens]es & time at Frome. They ask me to spend it in recruiting myself so as to be fit for [the] Education Bill.[4]

4 June 1896 (later)

I am on the job once more. The justification of my wasting

[1] Lloyd George, Herbert Lewis and three Irishmen were suspended by the Speaker for a week on 21 May 1896, after refusing to leave the chamber when the closure was moved.

[2] Henry Broadhurst (1840–1911): Lib.-Lab. member for various constituencies, 1880–1906; former secretary of the Parliamentary Committee of the T.U.C.

[3] In the Frome by-election, the Liberal candidate, J. E. Barlow, recaptured the seat by 299 votes. He retained it until 1918.

[4] Gorst introduced an Education Bill which would set up new education authorities in each county, and would also make additional financial grants to Church schools. After fierce opposition from the Liberals, the Bill was withdrawn on 22 June.

of time on small bills is to be found in today's Times. I have said all along that the Education Bill ought to be fought on the Rating Bill, the Light Railways Bill &c. so as to drive them into a corner as regards time. Now the Times says that they cannot carry it in its entirety without an autumn session & suggest that part of it should be thrown overboard.

Most amusing estimate of me today in the Daily Mail, a Tory paper with an enormous circulation.

11 June 1896

I rather think I shall run over with Herbert [Lewis] to Boulogne on Saturday so as to be fit for the Education Bill fight. Today there are no amendments on so far which I can see my way to support. We are now in the only good part of the bill & I am lying low until we come to something I can fight for. Tell Uncle not to be at all fidgetty about it. He'll hear quite enough of me before this Bill is out of Committee. I cannot honestly fight for a thing I don't believe in & some of the amendments moved on our side are contrary to the principles we have all been fighting for in Wales. I am not going to say so in the House as I do not wish to be at loggerheads with the men on our side of the House.

24 June 1896

It is a good thing that I came here for they were rushing through the Bill at a tremendous rate & they all said as Robson Q.C.[1] told me just now "That is what comes of having no Lloyd George here". I got one amendment in & have spoken three times. The Speaker does his very best to rule everything out of order. He was very nasty to poor old Harcourt but I "circumnavigated" him today once & he had to admit it. I have put three or four fresh amendments tonight for tomorrow

26 June 1896

Tonight I am applying myself to the manufacture of a few more amendments. The papers are full of my fight yesterday. The Tories were very angry & did their best once or twice to howl me down but that is just the way to set my teeth on edge & to harden my heart. I'll pay them out for every howl

[1] Sir William Robson (1852–1918): Liberal member, 1885–6 and 1895–1910; Solicitor-General, 1908–10.

by keeping them longer at it. If they go on all night we must try & arrange relays of members to take up the fight. I can't keep on all night.

30 June 1896

The last speech I made was about seven o'clock this morning. Completely cornered the Government. Our own fellows quite excited—including Harcourt who beamed with pleasure at the roasting I gave the Government. Balfour & Sir Michael Hicks-Beach[1] looked, as Sir Wilfrid [Lawson][2] put it, like a row of slaughtered pigs. One of the most successful speeches I have yet made in the House. Congratulated all round. Harcourt so delighted that he wanted to drop all further fight at that very point so as to leave off with a discomfiture for the Ministry. He has written me a very nice letter today on my "eminent services". There was a scene of much excitement.

Let the Garth[celyn] folk see this. The Bill is coming up for third reading tomorrow & Harcourt wants me to speak so I must prepare.

1st July 1896

I spoke for five minutes this afternoon on the third reading of the Agricultural Rating Bill. Harcourt paid me a public compliment in his speech this afternoon, amid great cheers. Dyna i ti hen gariad [There you are, old darling]. It is lucky in a way that the Education Bill has been withdrawn for it has made this the most important measure of the Session & I scored very heavily on it. Harcourt said the whole House recognised the eminent services I had rendered in connection with the Bill.

31 July 1896

I am very annoyed with Uncle Lloyd. He has upset me tremendously. He might have trusted me when to shut up seeing what I have done. Tell him that if I hear he fumes again I shall apply for the Chiltern Hundreds. I am quite serious.

[1] Sir Michael Hicks-Beach (1837–1916): Conservative member, 1864–1906; Chief Secretary for Ireland, 1874–8, Secretary for the Colonies, 1878–80, Chancellor of the Exchequer, 1885–6 and 1895–1902, President of the Board of Trade, 1888–92; created 1st Viscount St. Aldwyn, 1906 and Earl, 1916.

[2] Sir Wilfrid Lawson (1829–1906): Liberal member, 1859–1906; a 'little Englander' and a fervent advocate of temperance.

1 August 1896

I was so very vexed about Uncle Lloyd's unreasonable conduct that I could not restrain myself & so I wrote Will about it. It is high time he should be kept within bounds. Would he have me kill myself? What gratification would that afford him?

I went for the Government last night on prison-made goods—made a tremendous attack upon them amid loud cheers from our side of the House.

2 August 1896

[He will try not to intervene in the debate on the Scottish Rating Bill.] I must not throw away my reputation by needlessly rushing into debate when I can do no possible good. Sir Charles Dilke says I am popular on the other side whilst Dalziel is detested. They think I know what I am about & that I am in earnest.

3 August 1896

Scottish Rating Bill on. They are doing very badly & it is a matter of general comment what a contrast between their fight & mine. They are now begging me to assist. Morley said either Harcourt or I or both of us ought to step into the arena. He told me just now in the Lobby. But I don't think it would be wise unless there were an exceptional opportunity—for this I shall watch. I mean to speak on the Local Government Board vote & on the Appropriation Bill before we separate. That will be my final kick.

6 August 1896

I have important Welsh questions to raise. I mean to cling to them like a leech. One of them threatened to pass a steamroller over me yesterday. I said I am made of india rubber & shall be none the worse for it. But no doubt the challenge has been thrown out to us & I mean to kill the Military Lands Bill & to discuss Wales so that the last word they hear will be Welsh.

Digalon [Dejected]. Yes, I get fits of uncontrollable despondency. I do so want to see you. . . .

Killed the Military Lands Bill. Just heard from Balfour. That's their steamroller.

15 August 1896 (from Carmarthen)

We had the most magnificent meeting you ever saw. Place crammed long before doors opened. I was in great form. You saw the [word omitted] today in my telegram. It was fully justified. The people frantic. Never got such a reception. Elfed & all the ministers there. A truly great gathering.

I have already met some warm friends here. This morning I spent with Tom John the editor of the Glamorgan Free Press, a warm Cymru Fyddite. I am now off to tea with the leading Liberals of the place. Very anxious I should address a meeting here. Pressed the moment they discovered I was here. I can't walk the village streets but that they say "Dyna [there's] Lloyd George".

30 November 1896

Who do you think I had supper with last night? Lascelles Carr the proprietor of the [Western] Mail. He was delighted to see me here when I paid him a call in passing the morning & he would have me turn in for supper & so I did. He may be useful. He is an amusing old chap. I must say his paper has always treated me uncommonly handsomely—especially considering it is on the other side.

Between August and November Lloyd George had been with Henry Dalziel and Herbert Lewis on a business visit to Argentina. During his absence, Harcourt succeeded Rosebery as leader of the Liberal Party. At this time also, the first news of the Edwards paternity case reached William George.

1 December 1896 (from Aberystwyth)

I'll tell you about the Bangor letter. There is nothing that you need feel ashamed of your old Dafydd. But the scoundrels have attacked me more viciously than ever in a sneakish, underhanded sort of way. Since my return I have endured tortures on account of it. I never liked to trouble you as I know you would feel hurt. But I shan't be sorry now you have found out. I have repeatedly been on the brink of telling you. W. knows—in fact everybody knows. You can ask W. if you like if he calls in the morning.

7 December 1896 (from Kirkcaldy)

Dalziel disappointed me very much on the platform. I thought he was a much better speaker than he has turned out to be. Unfortunately he has devoted such a time to City affairs that he has taken no heed of politics at all. So he is out of it. And even from the point of delivery he is monstrous. Just fel Ellis heblaw fod Ellis a gwell stwff gando yn ei areithiau o lawer.[1]

21 December 1896 (from Cardiff)

I mean to talk Labour politics to them tonight. There are excellent reports in the Mail & S.W. Daily News of Saturday's meeting at Barry. Both acknowledge the crowded & enthusiastic character of the meeting & the warmth of the reception.

5 January 1897 (from Rhyl)

Today at Conference I sat effectually on the proposal to resuscitate the North Wales [Liberal] Federation. Carried a resolution calling upon the Welsh members to summon a conference for the *whole* of Wales to consider the question of organisation.

19 January 1897

The Queen's speech is not a very sensational one but still I have [no] doubt we can raise a fight on some of the questions included in it when the time comes.

The Welsh members decided to move an amendment to the address on Welsh land today. Brynmor [Jones] is to do it. I moved that it should be done. Wm. Jones is to move the adjournment of the House on the Penrhyn business.[2] I am afraid of him.

25 January 1897

Prysur iawn gyda'r chwarelwyr [very busy with the quarrymen]. Adjournment not to be moved until Thursday. I am so glad of that as I am far from prepared. They are waiting for me now in the lobby. The choir sang magnificently yesterday. I went round with them. Ellis & R. A. Hudson (National Liberal Federation)[3] & I took them to the Club & gave them

[1] Just like Ellis, except that Ellis has better stuff in his speeches by far.

[2] The first of the two lengthy strikes in the Penrhyn Quarries, Bethesda (1896–8 and 1900–3). The basic cause of the dispute lay in Lord Penrhyn's refusal to recognize the Quarrymen's Committee. Lloyd George attacked Penrhyn fiercely over this, and later successfully defended some Bethesda quarrymen in court cases.

[3] Sir Robert Arundell Hudson (1864–1927): secretary of the Liberal Central Federation from 1893; a close colleague of Tom Ellis.

tea. We all then went to Dr. Clifford's Chapel to hear them. We spoke at the overflow meeting. Then Ellis & I took Mrs. Llew[elyn Williams] & Miss Annie Davies (Cwrtmawr) (!)[1] to supper at Frascati. Ellis touched with the fever. Y fo fynnau dalu [He insisted on paying].

26 January 1897

Penrhyn Quarry. Engaged with W. H. Williams, the quarrymen's leader,[2] & Massingham[3] & Acland in Ellis' room for some time. Money flowing steadily for the men.

29 January 1897

You will have heard from William's letter written late last night how I got on in the Penrhyn debate. Never made a more effective debating speech in the House of Commons. Spoke for 50 minutes in all & roasted Penrhyn. W. J. [William] Jones] did well as I told you already. The discussion has done good.

11 May 1897

Welsh meeting over.[4] Great fight. Bryn smashed. Even his own friends deserted him. . . . Ellis Griffith completely lost his temper but dare not vote against us. In fact he raised his hand for the scheme when I could see that he was burning with spiteful anger against it. Sam [Evans] ditto. Ellis stood like a brick. So did Brynmor & Alfred Thomas.

12 May 1897

D. A. Thomas & Bryn are both furious about yesterday's meeting of the Welsh party. D. A. threatens to secede altogether from the party. He says he won't attend the adjourned meeting on Friday. He "nobbled" the Press Association last night and

---

[1] Miss Annie Davies, Cwrt-Mawr, Llangeitho, was the sister of J. H. Davies, later registrar and then principal of the University College of Wales in Aberystwyth. Tom Ellis married her in 1898.

[2] Williams was secretary of the North Wales Quarrymen's Union, founded in 1874.

[3] Henry William Massingham (1860–1924): journalist, editor of the *Daily Chronicle*, 1895–9, and of the *Nation*, 1907–23.

[4] At a meeting of the Welsh Party on 11 May, Albert Spicer's scheme for an autumn convention which would create a Welsh Liberal Federation was carried 11 to one ('Our London Welsh correspondent', *South Wales Daily News*, 12 May 1897).

got a very mendacious account into some of the papers. Today I saw the Press Association lobbyist—you know Shaw, Palace Mansions—& told him the report was inaccurate but as I did not wish him to take my version of it I would speak to Osborne Morgan about it & let him know. I got Osborne to see him & tomorrow the report will be corrected. Shaw was very sorry. They got a big headline in the Western Mail 'The hand of Spicer[1] but the voice of George'. They think I am at the bottom of it altogether.

25 May 1897

I am now at a meeting of the Welsh party upstairs to complete the arrangements for sending off the Scheme. [D. A.] Thomas has now formally sent in his resignation. I moved formally a vote regretting that he should do so & asking him to reconsider his decision. I thought it the right thing to do & it will serve a good purpose in the country. The scheme was *unanimously* adopted, Sam moving that the Chairman & secretaries sign on our behalf. This commits him.

27 May 1897

[He rebuts a charge that he has been unduly friendly with Mrs. Timothy Davies, the wife of a London Welsh draper.]

You say I have done nothing & might as well have been down at Criccieth. Well I was under the delusion until I received your letter that I had accomplished a good deal. I have put through the scheme for organising Wales. D. A. [Thomas] is also under that impression—that I have done it. For all that you may be right & I may have nothing to do with it after all.

Lloyd George was now very anxious to persuade his wife that they should acquire a new home nearer to London, perhaps in the London suburbs or Brighton, and that she should join him there. He had now begun a new solicitors' practice with Arthur Rhys Roberts, a Welsh friend, at 13 Walbrook, London E.C.

28 May 1897

You say you would rather have less money & live in a healthy place. Well, hen gariad [old darling], you will not

---

[1] Sir Albert Spicer (1847–1934): Liberal member for Monmouth Boroughs, 1892–1900 and for Central Hackney, 1906–18; Congregationalist and director of a paper-making firm.

forget that you were as keen about my starting as I was myself. Then you must bear in mind that we are spending more than we earn. I draw far more than my share of the profits though I don't attend to 1/10th of the work. This is neither fair nor honourable & feel sure you do not wish it to continue. Now you can't make omelettes without breaking eggs & unless I retire from politics altogether & content myself with returning to the position of a country attorney, we must give up the comforts of Criccieth for life in England. As to attending to the business during sessions & running away from it afterwards your good sense will show you on reflection that is impossible. No business could be conducted successfully on those terms. You are not right, however, that it presupposed living in London. If you prefer, we can take a home in the suburbs—say Ealing or Acton, Ealing for choice. There the air is quite as good as anything you can get in Wales as it is free from the smoke of the great city. Or if you prefer we could go still further out & live say in Brighton as Clifton does. . . . Think of it, old pet, & think of it with all the courage of which I know you are capable.

3 June 1897

Last night I dined at Dilke's. We further considered the question of Home Rule all Round. Sam [Evans] tried to hedge but I spoke out quite straight.

6 August 1897

How infinite your self pity is! Poor lonely *wife*. You are surrounded by all who love you best, father, mother, children, Uncle Lloyd & all. But can't you spare some sympathy & compassion for the poor lonely husband who is surrounded by wolves who would tear him—did they not fear his claws? . . . So sorry to hear you have a bad cold. You must be careful of it.

11 August 1897

Llew [Williams] & I were talking about our respective wives last night & we both said that the affection of a man for his wife was a much tenderer & deeper feeling than any passing fancy of the hour. I said that I had discovered that when you were ill.

19 August 1897

[He fiercely attacks his wife for wilful disobedience of

her husband.] You threaten me with a public scandal. All right expose me if that suits you. One scandal the more will but kill me the earlier. But you will not alter my resolution to have neither correspondence nor communication of any sort with you until it is more clearly understood how you propose to guide your course for the future. I have borne it for years & have suffered in health and character. I'll stand it no longer come what may.

21 August 1897

[He urges her again to come up to London.] Be candid with yourself—drop that infernal Methodism which is the curse of your better nature & reflect whether you have not rather neglected your husband. I have more than once gone without breakfast. I have scores of times come home in the dead of night to a cold, dark & comfortless flat without a soul to greet me. I am not the nature either physically or morally that I ought to have been left like this. . . . You have been a good mother. You have not—& I say this now not in anger— not always been a good wife. I can point you even amongst those whom you affect to look down upon much better wives. You may be a blessing to your children. Oh, Maggie anwyl [dear], beware lest you be a curse to your husband. My soul as well as my body has been committed to your charge & in many respects I am as helpless as a child.

9 September 1897

Saw Massingham (Daily Chronicle) last night. He is anxious I should take in hand the resurrecting of the Liberal party & do what Lord Randolph Churchill did for the Tory party. He says I am the man to do it & he'll back me up through thick & thin. I told him I would do it provided we could agree on a definite line of policy. Tell Uncle Lloyd.

13 September 1897

I went to Castle Street[1] last night ac mi siaredais yn y Seiat nes oedd pobpeth un clecian.[2] The preacher had said that he sometimes thought he would have liked to have lived in Palestine when Christ visited it. I told them how much better

---

[1] Lloyd George's Baptist chapel, near Oxford Circus, London.
[2] And I spoke at the Fellowship meeting until everything rattled.

off they were to see Christ in the perspective—that the ages
enhanced & proved his greatness. I really got into the hwyl
[rapture].

*Lloyd George took an active part in the East Denbighshire by-election, which the
Liberal candidate, Samuel Moss, won easily.*

26 September 1897 (from Wrexham)

Three very successful meetings yesterday at Cefn, Ruabon
& Rhos. The last meeting was immense. Ellis & I were the
lions. No one looked at Ellis Griffith or took the slightest notice
of him. He was so disgusted that he left the Ruabon meeting in
high dudgeon without speaking at all.

29 September 1897

Moss' victory is quite startling. I expected a big victory
but nothing so sweeping. I have seen Massingham about it just
now. He was quite taken aback.

20 December 1897

[W. T. Howell][1] told me that the Government meant to
redistribute seats before they went to the country. He thought
6,000 votes would be the minimum. In that case I shall be
wiped out & so will he. I don't mind in the least.

29 December 1897 (from Rome)

[He is on holiday in Rome with Dalziel and some Welsh
friends.]
Today Dalziel and I went to the Vatican to see the pictures.
Some of them are remarkable. "The last communion of St.
Jerome", "The burial of Christ" & "The Transfiguration"
impressed me most. The last named is supposed to be the finest
picture in the world but I prefer the other two. That may be
attributable to the fact that we had no time to enter into its
hidden meanings & beauties. The pens here are execrable &
I can assure you that I am writing under enormous difficulties.

13 August 1898

I know you would stick up for me—on all occasions. I
would trust you with my life & honour. There is no one—except

[1] William T. Howell: Unionist member for Denbigh District, 1895–1900.

my dear old uncle—whom I place such implicit unquestioning confidence in. You will, I feel certain, pardon my placing him on a level even with my hen Faggie [old Maggie]. Won't you hen gariad [old darling].

17 August 1898

Price brought my newspaper cuttings from Mansions. Here is one—Newcastle Daily Leader. "Mr. Lloyd George has distanced all competitors. He delivered some of the more daring speeches of the session, & his attack on the financial clauses of the Irish Local Government Bill was admirably sustained. The member for Carnarvon has strenuously repudiated the idea that the Liberal party is bound to support any Irish legislation which may appear good to the Nationalists. He has earned himself enemies but he has laid the foundations of a big Parliamentary reputation." Go dda ynte [Pretty good, isn't it]? The N. Wales Observer ought to print these things. I send you Baner. Vide London letter.

18 August 1898

Have been to the Daily News office with [David] Edwards. We have been concocting an article or rather a series of articles on 'Is Nonconformity a declining force?' Edwards wrote it although I supplied most of the ideas.

22 August 1898 (from Dunbar)

We passed this afternoon past the ground on which Cromwell fought the battle of Dunbar. You can see the hills on which the Scots were posted, the house where Cromwell had his headquarters, the place where the Scots came down the hill intending to form the battle array, the place where Cromwell led his troops, the brook he crossed to attack them. It is all intensely interesting.

23 August 1898 (from Edinburgh)

Have you seen today's Daily News—the second article? I supplied Edwards with *all* the ideas for this. The attack on the Front Opposition Bench as a preserve for churchmen & perverts will do good. This sort of thing for which Gladstone is mainly responsible must come to an end & I have made up my mind to back up this Anglican regime in the Liberal party. Dissenters have too long been the doormats of snobs yr Eglwys [Church snobs].

30 August 1898 (from Stirling)

Whether I am offered a seat in the next Liberal Cabinet or not—or whether I live to see another Liberal Cabinet formed or not, it is not without satisfaction to feel that a great number of keen, intelligent politicians assume that I must needs be in. Isn't that so, hen gariad [old darling].

12 September 1898

I am very disappointed with your letter. I had been thinking very fondly of you all day yesterday. I had been drawing pictures of your coming to the office to fetch me at 4, of our going to tea together, then spending the evening either in the Parks or some place of amusement & this morning as I woke I looked forward with a sense of anticipatory joy to receiving an affectionate warm letter from my old Maggie. But when I read it! How it chilled me. "If you wish me to come" let me know—I'll obey if you command. I thought in my foolish heart that you might not be displeased at the idea of having any excuse for seeing your Dei after five weeks of separation. I am to go here but not there. I am to see these people but not those. This is the tenor of my recent correspondence. It won't do. I should have thought bitter experience had taught you I am not to be directed by letter. However as you will.

What arrant stupidity not to forward me the Warminster poster. . . .

19 September 1898

[He has returned from speaking on behalf of the Liberal candidate, Owen Philipps, in Darlington.]

Darlington we had a great defeat. Majority against us 688. I knew we should be beaten. Everybody wore Pease colours, especially the young people. Philipps[1] expected to be beaten

[1] Sir Owen Cosby Philipps (1863–1937): Liberal member for Pembroke District, 1906–10 and Chester, 1916–22; created Baron Kylsant, 1923; a shipowner and financier; brother of Wynford Philipps (see above, p. 46, n. 1) and of General Sir Ivor Philipps (see p. 175, n. 2).

by 400. Met Mrs. Wynford [Philipps] there—she was very gushing as usual. Wanted me to call on her in town. May do so today.

29 September 1898 (*'Yn y trên'* [in the train])

I am now on my way to Nottingham. On taking up a newspaper this morning at the breakfast table I was staggered by the news of Mr. Gee's sudden death. Only a few days ago I received a most cheery letter from him to which it will always be my regret that I never replied. It is now for ever too late.

If his funeral is a public one, I must attend at all cost, business or no business. He treated me always as a father would his child—affectionately.

Lloyd George spent Christmas 1898 on a Mediterranean cruise.

'Nos Nadolig' [Christmas night] (from S.Y. Argonaut, in the Mediterranean)

Amongst the strangers my biggest chum is Miss Hughes (Cambridge), Price Hughes' sister. She is church but a strong Radical. We have had several sets to over church matters & female suffrage & we hit without sparing. She heard me at Ipswich & was proud of the way I at last after a hard struggle 'lit up a dull East Anglian audience'. Although she was quite angry with the bitter things I said about the the church she still very nearly cried, so she told me.

7 January 1899 (from S.Y. Argonaut)

You have more brains than all those women put together, but you don't always think it worth your while to exert them. T. [Timothy Davies] was telling me the other day "I always consider Mrs. George a woman of very strong common sense". . . . You are worth a luggage train packed full of the women you mention. And especially *for me* if you only knew it. You are just fitted.

12 April 1899 (from Shrewsbury)

The last thing that Ellis ever read was a letter from me.[1] He got it the Monday before he died. He insisted on reading it himself & he laughed outright at the joke I had in it.

[1] Tom Ellis died on 5 April 1899, aged 40.

21 July 1899

I trust all will be well at Cardiff tomorrow.[1] It is weighing a little on my mind. What I am concerned about is the possibility that the North Wales & other Welsh delegates may not turn up & that the Cosmopolitans may have it all their own way.

In July a Select Committee, under the chairmanship of Henry Chaplin, reported in favour of a limited scheme for Old Age Pensions to be financed partly out of the poor rate and partly by the Exchequer. Lloyd George had been a member of this committee.

21 July 1899

Old Age Pensions has reached the most critical stage. We are now considering the report & if we carry our point we can place the Government in a most awkward fix.

22 July 1899

I am so sorry to find that you are down once more with a bad cold. You must be careless I fear. Don't you think a course of *cold* baths would do you good? Your baths as you know are either hot or tepid. This is bound to make you tender & more amenable to colds. Don't you really think so yourself? What you want is to harden yourself against sudden changes & I know of no surer remedy than a series of cold baths. That is what I am doing every morning with excellent results.

26 July 1899

I may go to Cardiff tomorrow. Up to the present I have refused because I disapprove strongly of the nature of the resolutions moved. I am dead against these Church Discipline Acts. Disestablishment is the only answer. They want the former.

26 July 1899

I dropped Llew[elyn Williams] a note to ask him to come somewhere tonight—either to a theatre or a restaurant, but he has not even condescended to reply altho' I told him I was very lonely. He can be mean when he likes. It won't pay him I can assure him. I have not quite forgiven him & his wife the shabby trick they played with you last Sunday. I've got to tell him about that yet. . . .

[1] At a meeting of the Welsh National Liberal Council.

I told you in my other letter that Old Age Pensions is through. We sat on until 6 & carried it. I have added some millions on to this Bill for them. I am sure I put on 2 or 3 millions yesterday & a similar sum today. Never mind, it goes all to the poor who really need it. It has the additional advantage of putting these bandits who are now in power in a nice fix. They can neither carry out these recommendations nor drop them—not without discredit.

Chaplin told me today that the Chancellor of the Exchequer is already swearing at him. The curious thing is that the Tory members of the Committee are very pleased with me & the Liberals are equally pleased. Sir Walter Foster[1] said today that it was a very good thing for us that I was there to force the running as I did. Good Heavens, what would have happened if poor Alfred [Thomas] had been put on instead!

26 July 1899

Dalziel & I have rather fallen out. He brings that woman to the House & he insists on my going to the Ladies Gallery to see her as she wants to talk to me about her case. As you know, I have my own opinion about her. She is a most unscrupulous & selfish creature & she will ruin poor D. So I declined peremptorily to go. Told him I would see her in the Central Lobby where all visitors are seen. There was a row & now he doesn't talk to me. Dim odds [It doesn't matter]. I have been a true friend to him in this business & he'll find it out by & by. . . . He is a perfect child & he drinks too much. This has made him quite nervous & irritable. He constantly sips whiskey, liqueurs & the like. It is a pity. His sudden access of fortune has become a curse to him.

27 July 1899

I am now engaged in a protest in the House against the Naval Works Bill. They are proposing to take £23,000,000 to build docks for the navy & I moved an amendment against the Bill by way of protesting against these increased armaments.

6 August 1899 (from Warminster)

I am now at the Congregational Chapel Warminster with my host. He is a fine sturdy old nonconformist & it is much to

---

[1] Sir Walter Foster, Liberal member for Ilkeston; created Baron Ilkeston, 1910.

Lloyd George, Mrs. Lloyd George, and Megan, *c.* 1910

Lloyd George, Sir Rufus Isaacs, and C. F. G. Masterman, Criccieth, 1911

Lloyd George and Churchill, October 1915

his credit that in spite of all social blandishments he stuck to his Dissent. Hen Fachgen yn sefyll yn syth ben ac y mae yr un fath efo'i grefydd ai wleidyddiaeth. . . .[1]

We had a very fine meeting in his grounds, Lord Edmond Fitzmaurice[2] in the chair, the candidate & I speaking. Owen Philipps was also there. His father was the late rector of the Parish. He is a baronet as you know—Sir James Philipps. The old chap has retired now & he was at our meeting. He has always been a Liberal. After the service Mr. Morgan & I lunch with the Liberal candidate. Dydw'i ddim yn credu fawr iawn ynddo fo.[3] He is no more of a Liberal than is absolutely necessary to secure for him the Liberal vote in the district. Still he is a pleasant spoken chap enough.

[1] An old boy standing upright, as he does with his religion and his politics.
[2] Lord Edmond Fitzmaurice (1846–1935): Liberal member for Cricklade, 1898–1905; created Baron Fitzmaurice of Leigh, 1906.
[3] I don't have much faith in him.

I

CHAPTER 6

Boer War and Radical Revival

(1899–1905)

When negotiations between the Boers and the British High Commissioner, Milner, broke down in September 1899, Lloyd George was in Canada on a mission to investigate the prospects for Welsh emigrants there. But as soon as the news reached him of the crisis in South Africa, he reacted with utter certainty. When war broke out with the Transvaal and the Orange Free State early in October, he was from the start an uncompromising opponent and an advocate of a negotiated peace. Lloyd George was no pacifist. He had condemned Salisbury's government for a humiliating surrender to the United States during the Venezuelan crisis in 1896. Nor was he necessarily an opponent of imperial expansion: during the Fashoda crisis in 1898 he had upheld the British government's resistance to the French in the upper Nile valley. But in South Africa he was convinced that aggressive and clumsy British diplomacy had landed the nation in an unnecessary and expensive war. In belligerent speeches in parliament and in the country, he concentrated mainly on the inept way in which the war was being fought—and on those, including Joseph Chamberlain, the Colonial Secretary, whom he alleged were making money out of it during its course. Indeed, his private correspondence indicates that as the war dragged on, Lloyd George felt a more than fleeting sympathy with the audacious Boer commandos, and viewed with grim relish the growing record of British failure in the field.

His anti-war stand required considerable courage. Until the end of 1900 the 'little Englanders' were in a small minority in the House. Most Liberals followed their leader, Campbell-Bannerman, in a qualified endorsement of the war. The Liberal Party, indeed, was deeply permeated by imperialism, even in Wales. Lloyd George's native land was very far from being the bastion of pro-Boer sentiment that some historians used to claim. He faced violent opposition there throughout the first year of the war. At a riotous meeting at Bangor in his own constituency in April 1900, he barely escaped with his life. He again faced a stern fight to hold his seat in the 'khaki election' of October 1900. The Unionist declared that a vote cast for Lloyd George was one cast for the Boers, His campaign, as ever, was uncompromising. It gained its reward with an increased, though still narrow, majority of 296. In Britain as a whole, however, the Unionists were again returned with a majority of 132. Thereafter, the tide of opinion began to turn, as the long-drawn-out guerrilla warfare against de Wet's commandos undermined the imperialist mood. It lent new authority to critics like Lloyd George. In fact, the Liberal leader, Campbell-Bannerman, virtually went over to the 'pro-Boers' in his party in June 1901 with an outspoken attack on the 'methods of barbarism' adopted by the British army in concentration camps on the Rand. The Boer War had another result closer to Lloyd George's heart. It strengthened the bonds of affection with his family in Criccieth as never before. Uncle Lloyd was an ardent pro-Boer, as was brother William. And relations with Mrs. Lloyd George became as serene as at any time in the past. When Lloyd George's fifth child, another daughter named Megan, was born on 22 April 1902, it marked a climax of private happiness in his domestic life.

During the Boer War, Lloyd George had become a national figure. The years which followed the peace of Vereeniging in 1902, years which brought a dramatic revival of the Liberals' fortunes after their internecine divisions during the war years, confirmed his new stature. He greatly added to it by his skilful response to the Education Act of 1902. Although his initial reaction to Balfour's measure was a favourable one, he was soon in the forefront of a nonconformist campaign which condemned, with the fervour of a latter-day John Knox, a bill which put Church schools, not to mention Rome, on the rates. Throughout 1902 Lloyd George dominated debates on the bill. But whereas English nonconformists preferred a nihilistic policy of individual passive resistance, in Wales Lloyd George offered a more coherent response. He persuaded the Welsh county councils to propose operating the Act if certain basic terms were met. With the aid of a Liberal landslide in the Welsh county council elections in February 1904, he was able to inspire a nation-wide revolt against the Balfour Act. By the end of 1905 there was a virtual mass abdication by the local authorities. The operation of the Act in Wales was largely at a standstill.

All this added enormously to Lloyd George's standing in the Liberal Party. He was already among the leaders of its radical, 'little England' wing. Now his constructive attitude towards the Education Act (which included an imaginative, though abortive, attempt to set up a national council of education for Wales) forged new links with Liberal imperialists like Rosebery, Asquith, and Grey. He was now finding support in all sections of the party. He was prominent in the Liberal defence of free trade when Joseph Chamberlain raised the banner of tariff reform in May 1903; in crusading against the 1904 Licensing Act; and in denouncing the evils of 'Chinese slavery' on the Rand. In many ways, he was a symbol of the new radical upsurge of 1903–5, a symbol of the union of the Old Liberalism of the chapels and the Celtic fringe, with the New Liberalism of social reform. Suddenly, the Unionist Prime Minister, Balfour, resigned on 4 December 1905. Contrary to expectations, Campbell-Bannerman was able to create a powerful and united Cabinet. It contained few of the younger Liberals, but one significant new recruit, unexpectedly appointed to the presidency of the Board of Trade and thus in the front line in the defence of free trade, was Lloyd George.

In September 1899 Lloyd George was on a visit to Canada. But he kept a watchful eye on the crisis building up in South Africa.

24 September 1899 (from Winnipeg)

I felt proud of my old Mag & her speech in the Guardian was so pat, sensible & to the point. Just fel hi ei hunan [Just like her]. C. & D. [Carnarvon & Denbigh] Herald & Genedl not arrived. Got Guardian. I am already preparing a speech on Transvaal. Worst of it is I have no material here. But I am full of it.

25 September 1899 (from Winnipeg)

Wish I had been at Carnarvon. Would have given anything to be there. My blood boiled when I read a report of the proceedings. I am all on fire to be back. Today I read in the Canadian papers that those London chipmunks have been screeching out for war. I wonder how many of them would face a Boer rifle. . . .[1]

27 September 1899 (from Winnipeg)

Hope you judiciously selected your extracts of my views on the Transvaal for the press. They were not intended for publication but I don't object so long as my hopes that the English will get a black eye are omitted. I am still at boiling point over it. It is wicked.

William George to David Lloyd George 29 September 1899

I have got at loggerheads with the Genedl[2] people over the Transvaal business. Vide. I am sending a stinger in reply. I also wrote the Directors & Pritchard to me just now that they passed a resol^n yest^y to support the Morley policy henceforth! I think Beriah [Evans] is the root of the evil there now & a childish wish to be independent of the Herald![3]

We are not yet in blood but it looks as if we were on the brink. I send you the Guard^n wh. contains an account of S.W. Convent^n. The London papers are sickening reading & I don't get them.

2 October 1899 (from Toronto)

Read the Duke of Devonshire's[4] speech in the American

---

[1] The British government broke off negotiations with the Boers on 22 September.

[2] *Y Genedl Gymreig*, A Welsh-language weekly published at Caernarvon, founded in 1877; the main Liberal rival to the *Faner*.

[3] *Yr Herald Cymraeg*, another Welsh-language weekly published at Caernarvon.

[4] Eighth Duke of Devonshire (1833–1908): Liberal minister under Gladstone (as the Marquess of Hartington), 1870–4 and 1880–5; became Liberal Unionist and served as Lord President of the Council, 1895–1903.

papers today. It looks like drawing back on the brink of war. It reminds you rather of the waters of the Niagara. They rush along madly in reckless confusion until they come to the edge of the fall—then they seem suddenly to calm down & to be hesitating when they see the terrible abyss they are plunging into. But it is too late. I don't think it matters much what they do now. I believe their downfall is assured. If they go on the war will be so costly in blood and treasure as to sicken the land. If they withdraw they will be laughed out of power.

War with the Transvaal and the Orange Free State broke out on 10–11 October.

22 October 1899

I have just left D^d. Edwards (Daily News). He is furiously opposed to the war & we are having an argument about it with some other fellows.

23 October 1899

There is news of another British victory against a 1,000 Boers. Their position stormed—camp captured with all equipment.[1] It is official. No news so far of cavalry who went in pursuit of the Boers at Glencoe. There is some anxiety about them here. Hope they all supped comfortably with Joubert.[2]

23 October 1899 (later)

I have never loved you so deeply and truly as I have during the past few years & you know that hen gariad anwyl [dear old darling]. You know that I am fond of you & of your society. I never get tired of it. On the contrary the longer I am with you the less do I wish to part with you. . . .

News from the Transvaal not so bright. Our losses in Saturday's battle were very heavy—especially in officers & we have been driven from Dundee leaving our wounded in the hands of the Boers.

24 October 1899

News from the Transvaal not so desperate as yesterday.

[1] At Elandslaagte, near Ladysmith. Glencoe was another Boer position to the north.
[2] General Piet Joubert, commandant-general of the Boer forces until his death in 1900.

We seem to have fought another successful engagement with the Orange Free State men this time. Joubert has not yet attacked General Yule & the two sections of the British army are endeavouring to join.

27 October 1899

I spoke in the House today a chefais hwyl anarferol.[1] Glad I did it. Was a bit ashamed of my silence but I could not break the ice for first time. You have no idea what a feeling it is. I pitched into them as they have not been pitched into before. Hit straight from the shoulder. Wish you had been there. I got my chance & used it. The Government had published a false translation of one of the Transvaal documents! Just think of that. I bullied the Speaker almost. Joe got him to call me to order for saying it was done deliberately. I retorted that if it was not done deliberately then the negligence was a criminal one seeing that it had sent hundreds of brave men already to their death. Either criminal negligence or forgery. I leave it to the right honorable gentleman to elect. It doesn't matter to me which. The Radicals cheered. Of course I said Chamberlain personally could not have been guilty of such a thing. But I said someone has & I want to know who. I have never uttered such home truths in that House & no one replied to me. They seemed quite flabbergasted for the moment.

30 October 1899

They are fighting at Ladysmith, but nothing has arrived as to the progress of the battle. It is too early for that. They will shell & manœuvre maybe for days, that is my opinion, before they get at each other's throats, & then there will be hell. The Boers have a month in which to do the job & they won't risk the event by undue precipitation. If they fail now it is over with them. But if they succeed in this battle I shouldn't like to bet that the war will be over this day twelvemonth. Poor fellows.

2 November 1899

Last night I went to the Haymarket with Llew to see the Black Tulip—Pretty & harmless. Afterwards we went to the

[1] And was in unusually good form. (For Lloyd George's speech, see *Parl. Deb.*, 4th ser., Vol. 77, pp. 782–3.)

Cafe Monico & smoked two cigars. That is the sort of life I am leading in your absence.

I wish this war were over. I cannot without the greatest difficulty get my mind on to anything else. Bad headaches trouble me the last 2 or 3 days. Can't get my mind on to Cardiff meetings at all. Can't get hold of a single idea. Must do something as I dare not disappoint them this time. It would be the fourth this year.

3 *November 1899*

Our losses on Monday were great & I fear the Boers must have lost heavily.

There is a gap in the correspondence between December 1899 and August 1900, during which period the Lloyd Georges purchased a new house in Wandsworth.

3 *August 1900*

Cefais hwyl iawn ddoe. Ar bwnc railway Nevin.[1] Trust the Carnarvon papers will give a decent report as it will be a most useful electioneering move. Unfortunately some of these reporters have no gumption at all. . . .

Got a letter this morning from Morley enclosing some cuttings from a South African paper which he wishes me to put a question about. He then cracks up my speeches & asks me if I can supply him with full copies of them. He then adds "I cannot say how much I admire both your brains & your pluck". . Isn't that fine?

7 *August 1900*

I carried through the Carnarvon Waterworks business & thus saved to the town some thousands of pounds. T. W. Russell did it for me. . . .

Rumour here that Parliament will be dissolved on the 11th Sept. One of the Tory Whips said today they knew nothing about it. He wouldn't lie to me as he is a straight chap. Still it is well to be ready.

9 *August 1900*

I am thoroughly prostrate & suffer greatly today & yesterday from a fluttering at the heart. You know I get these attacks but this is the worst & most persistent I have ever had. Don't

[1] I was in good form yesterday. On the question of Nevin railway.

tell Uncle Lloyd, otherwise he'll exaggerate it. There is nothing to alarm anybody. It is simply that the heart is very irritated with the wear & tear & greatly needs rest.

20 August 1900

Today I am still busy over the newspaper.[1] I have another meeting here at 6.30 with Lough & Fisher Unwin. . . . I meant to send you yesterday's Reynolds. There is a photo of your sweetheart with a most interesting note encircling it. T. P. [O'Connor][2] has something in today's Mail. He is discussing probabilities of return of "prominent" M.P.'s. He concludes by saying, after alluding to the dangers owing to the war tide "Still, as one Welshman told me, to get between Lloyd George & his countrymen is like getting between the tree & its bark." That's rather true. They'll abuse me themselves to their hearts' content but won't allow anybody else to do it. Send me Herald Cymraeg.

23 August 1900

But who came after me to Clapham but poor Spender[3] in a great state of perturbation & anxiety to consult me as to what he should do in the face of Transvaal Consul's use of his name in the letters found at Pretoria. He had been hunting for me at the Club—luckily he caught Roberts late at the office & came along with him. His brother, the editor of the Westminster, thought he had better see me. I helped him to cook[?] a letter which I think is a useful one. He couldn't go for Joe. It might be regarded as presumptuous in a man of his position. Have you read the letter?

I got another from Labby yesterday morning. Very amusing. I enclose copy. I want original to show Spender & my Pro Boer friends.

31 August 1900

We have just arranged terms for the purchase of the Echo —very favourable they are. Dd. Edwards has been my adviser

---

[1] The purchase of the *Echo*.

[2] T. P. O'Connor (1848–1929): Irish Nationalist member for Liverpool (Scotland), 1885–1929; founded the *Star* and *T.P.'s Weekly*.

[3] Harold Spender (1864–1926): journalist, serving successively on the *Pall Mall Gazette*, the *Manchester Guardian*, and the *Daily News* (1900–14); a warm admirer of Lloyd George, in contrast to his brother, J. A. Spender.

throughout. He knows all about this kind of business & he thinks we have got a very good bargain. Unwin is quite delighted with it. Now I've got to put it through—a very big job indeed. We've taken the first step. As I have told you all along it is well worth £300 a year to our office & it brings us into contact with people who can put a lot in our way. . . . Edwards thinks that if we are fairly successful in getting our capital we may be able to come to term with Daily News. That would be a tremendous deal.

With the imperialist hysteria at its height, the Salisbury government dissolved parliament in September 1900. Lloyd George's opponent in Caernarvon Boroughs, in another desperate contest, was Colonel Platt.

11 October 1900 (from Knighton, Radnorshire)

Looks as if Frank [Edwards] were going to win & Humphreys Owen to lose. Latter told me he would lose by 100. Am off now to help him.[1]

18 October 1900

The Carnarvon news is very gratifying. I have always told you that there is more real loyalty there at all times than in Bangor. Spender was with me last night. Scott is sending him on Saturday to Canada to do the elections there. He doesn't like it at all.

Lloyd George retained his seat in Caernarvon Boroughs by an increased majority of 296. Very little correspondence for 1901 has survived.

13 August 1901

[In a train travelling along the Sussex coast.] Down below lies Lewes & beyond the valley is the hill on which the great battle was fought 700 years ago—hundreds of poor Welshmen fell in it.

5 March 1902

Last night a clean 'foozle'. Had we resolute leaders on the Front Bench the Speaker would not have closured but they were as anxious as anyone that the Debate should come to an end fearing a 'rumpus' with the Liberal Imperialists. . . .

[1] Frank Edwards and Humphreys-Owen were both 'pro-Boers'. In fact, Edwards did recapture Radnorshire while Humphreys-Owen held on to Montgomeryshire. Wales was the one part of Britain to swing decisively to the Liberals in this election but it would be an error to attribute this mainly to the Boer War.

You tell Uncle Lloyd that I will soon make another Parliamentary opportunity pretty soon. I don't think I'll talk on meat & remnants Monday next. I do not care a scrap how much they are swindled by the Jews. Serves them right.

6 March 1902

Did you see the amusing interruption by a Liberal Imperialist to Bannerman's speech last night.[1] C.B. said "What cause is there to start the new League?" and one of them shouted out "Lloyd George". It is evidently a league started to keep me down. As usual they are enhancing my power by exaggerating it.

7 March 1902

Stori i [Story for] Uncle Lloyd. The Master of Elibank M.P. for Midlothian—he is the son of a Scotch Tory Peer—told me last night he had met Cecil Rhodes in Egypt. The latter told him "Botha & Delarey are winning. They have held up the British Empire."

8 March 1902

Ar y ffordd adre gyda Burns—wedi siarad yn y Ty. Hwyl campus.[2] You will have had the report before this reaches you. The House in fits over my exposure of the War Office Estimates as to duration of the war. I fear the reporters had not returned to the Gallery. Still there was a full House.

10 March 1902

After the concert Edwards, Griffith & I went to the Cafe Monico & had a good old talk there. Edwards thinks they are ruining the D. News. They have dismissed the foreign correspondents.[3] Edwards had been told that Spender is not now on the staff but simply an outside contributor. Serve him right if it is true. He growled & grumbled quite plenty altho' he had

[1] In a speech at the National Liberal Club. *The Times*, 6 March 1902, p. 7, reports the interruption.

[2] On the way home with Burns—after speaking in the House. Excellent fun. (John Burns, an ardent pro-Boer, was a near neighbour of Lloyd George in Clapham.)

[3] Lloyd George had persuaded the cocoa magnate, George Cadbury, to buy up the *Daily News* and to run it as a 'little England' newspaper. Lloyd George became one of its directors.

obtained a better position than any he had ever previously reached. He is too greedy. D. E. says Ritzema is bound to fail. All these changes for the worse in the character of the paper are a great personal triumph for Edwards. He thinks that gradually Ritzema will get rid of all the first class men & rely entirely on third raters.

11 March 1902

Very dull. The House presents a thoroughly dejected appearance. The disaster has depressed members. They are beginning to realise in a dim sort of way that things are not all right in Africa. It has caused a good deal of surprise which shows how ignorant even well informed & trained politicians are as to the course of events.

11 March 1902 (later)

Here comes Frank Edwards to take me downstairs to a Committee upon his Local Government Bill. Rhaid mynd [Must go]. What a speech Rosebery made on Gladstone. I hear half his audience was Liberal Unionist. Robson has quite given him up as a bad job (Dyna Irish cheer am rywbeth neu gilydd.[1] They are great boys. They have excited deep resentment by their savage exaltation over the British disaster). Y mae'r Sacson yma fel pethau wedi tori ei cynffonau.[2]

12 March 1902

No further war news. I thought Wil bach [his son Gwilym] would have been very delighted at the success of his friends. Did you tell him how the mules ran away when the Boers rushed amongst them. Then how the cavalry scampered away with the Boers chasing them like deerhounds.

We ought to have further particulars but nothing has come. We have not been told how many waggons the Boers captured. There must have been a very large number.

14 March 1902

Tell Uncle Lloyd I propose speaking in the debate on the war Thursday next—if I get a chance. Monday's debate on the contracts I am not disposed to touch. I have no interest in

---

[1] There's an Irish cheer for something or other.
[2] The English here are like things with their tails cut off.

it. There is not much of a case & personally I do not care a scrap how much they are swindled over their contracts. The one great crime is the war itself. All the rest follows.

17 March 1902

I have come finally to the conclusion that I cannot live happily without yr hen Fagi [old Maggie]. My hiraeth [longing] is getting worse & worse. Not the slightest symptom of convalescence. Tyrd yn dy ol, hen gariad [Come home, old darling].

Last night I went to Parkers.[1] He was in fine form. When the service was over I was asked to his private room. The old boy was delighted to see me. They put me in the pew in which Ld. Rosebery sat a fortnight ago.

Up to the present the contracts debate is not up to much. C.B. did not make a case. Labby is doing better. He has some facts but there is not very much in it at present.

18 March 1902

And so the reality was sweeter than the dream! It is generally the other way about & that is so disappointing is it not? The fat little woman you saw me with must have been a round little plump thing whom it is said I have got in the family way & packed off to an obscure little Welsh town in the wilds of Carnarvonshire. Do you know her?

(undated—apparently 20 March 1902)

Row ofnadwy yn y Ty [Terrible row in the House]. Chamberlain said Dillon was "a good judge of treachery". Dillon rose on a point of order. The Speaker declined to interfere. Then Dillon said "Mr. Speaker I say he is a damned liar". Row dychrynllyd [Frightful row]. Dillon suspended. I voted with the Irish. It is surely worse to charge a man with treachery than with lying. The Irish are all out now—probably conferring together. Harcourt is on now in an almost empty House. Dilke follows ac wedyn ceisio finna [and afterwards they want me]—altho' I wd. rather get up after dinner. The Speaker will try to shunt me as he is afraid I'll say something violent & produce another scene.

---

[1] Joseph Parker (1830–1902): leading Congregationalist, minister of the City Temple since 1869.

21 March 1902

Fe wnaeth dy gariad fusnes o honi neithiwr.[1] Several have told me that it was the best I ever delivered in this House. The Tories behaved on the whole very well. You must remember it was fel halen ar friw[2] to them. There were only just one or two who interrupted unfairly—the rest listened intently. Crowded benches of them. Dilke just tells me that this morning he thought I was like Shelley's Adonais. I had at last through toil & trouble got to fame. I haven't got the quotation but you can see it in Shelley's Adonais.

Channing[3] wants me in future to fly at higher game than Brodrick.[4] He wants me to seek a good opportunity of going for Chamberlain, watch for a really good chance sometime this session & then smash into him.

22 March 1902

I wish you would ask [D. R. Daniel][5] to spend y Pasg [Easter] & to discuss the Penrhyn business at some time. What a vindictive speech Ld. P. delivered the other day. Before I go down I mean to see the Woods & Forests people once more about that case. The strike must, so I am told, have cost him over £120,000 already. He took his son to the quarry so as to warn them they would gain nothing by killing him. It is one of the most desparate [*sic*] strikes on record.

Balfour introduced a major Education Bill on 24 March. Its main object was to place authority over elementary, technical, and secondary education in the hands of the county and county borough councils.

24 March 1902

Balfour is developing a most revolutionary Education Bill. Sweeps away School Boards. Creates the County Council the educational authority for the County & puts the Boards Schools & the Voluntary Schools under it. Llanystumdwy

---

[1] Your sweetheart made a job of it last night.

[2] Like salt on a sore.

[3] Francis A. Channing (1841–1926): Liberal member for East Northamptonshire, 1885–1910, a strong radical; created Baron Channing, 1910.

[4] St. John Brodrick (1856–1942): Conservative member, 1880–1906; Secretary of State for War, 1900–3 and for India, 1903–5; Earl of Middleton, 1901.

[5] David R. Daniel (1859–1931): secretary of the North Wales Quarrymen's Union from 1896; a close friend of Tom Ellis and Lloyd George in the 1880s.

School will be now under the County Council & a very great improvement it is. Up to the present I rather like the Bill. It is quite as much as one would expect from a Tory Government—in fact, more than anyone could anticipate.[1]

Whole thing destroyed by making the whole Bill optional —it is left entirely to discretion of each County Council! What a miserably weak thing this Government is.

Have doubts as to anything coming of the new peace movement. Schalk Burger[2] & the Eastern Transvaalers have always been fidgeters rather than fighters. They were disposed to give in over twelve months ago. They have now gone to see Steyn[3] to consult him as to terms of peace. They had better not talk too much about giving in to De Wet,[4] otherwise that truculent gentleman may perchance have them all sjamboked or shot.

25 March 1902

I meant to say a few words on the question of the peace negotiations today. But Morley & Bryce[5] are against it—they think the less said the better pending negotiations. My idea was to put in a general plea for a liberal and generous interpretation of the wishes of the people of this country & a hint that we must have no more niggling. However, I must not fly in the face of these men.

10 April 1902

Dined with Lawrence (the Echo). Delightful lunch. Told me today, or rather told the company, I was always quoting my wife's opinion—that evidently you were my ultimate Court of Appeal.

14 April 1902

Listening to a most interesting budget statement by Hicks Beach. Up to the present we have had another 1d. on Income Tax—rather hard on us who are pressed. Still the

[1] In fact, of course, Lloyd George's enthusiasm for the Bill evaporated almost immediately, although making the county councils the educational authority did give him an instrument for initiating the 'Welsh Revolt' in 1903.

[2] Schalk W. Burger, a member of the 'acting government' of the Boers, headed a peace delegation to Pretoria on 23 March 1902.

[3] M. T. Steyn, ex-president of the Orange Free State.

[4] General C. R. de Wet, commander of the Boer commandos.

[5] James Bryce (1838–1922): Liberal member, 1880–1906; Chief Secretary to Ireland, 1905–6, ambassador to Washington, 1907–13.

sacrifice is worth it if it helps to bring home to the people what war means. It looks to me as if one part of Beach's speech were going to produce friction with Joe. Beach made a very strong peace speech & recommended most generous grants towards rebuilding Boer farms. Joe you could see was angry & turned round to Balfour to say something sharp & decisive. Balfour was evidently upset. I fear if there is any difference of opinion in the Cabinet Joe will win. He knows his own mind & also knows how to get it.

Aha—a shilling duty on corn & five pence a hundred weight on all flour imported from abroad. This will help to bring it home to those who cried out for the war.

Frank Edwards was sponsoring a Bill to set up a joint board of the Welsh county councils. It was defeated on its second reading.

15 April 1902

Now Frank [Edwards] came up. His deputation [on the Local Government Bill] was an immense success & he is full of gratitude to me who have advised him all along. The Welsh M.P.'s seemed to know that & were green with envy. They dare not keep away. Had to be there but they cursed it all under their breath. Greaves[1] did uncommonly well. So did Sir Watkin.[2] The Bill did not go far enough for him! Just think of that.

Went with Frank now to Asquith to get him to speak tomorrow. He has promised to do so. Quite pleased to be asked.

Had a very nice letter from Dean Howell[3] giving me advice what to do with my throat gargle every night for a month with water & table salt—shut my mouth in going out—*peidio siarad llawer* [don't talk much].

17 April 1902

[Harold] Spender is not happy over the position at the Daily News. Paul has had to go & Spender feels his own head is not safe on his shoulders. He never knows what day he may be called upon to resign. I had to reassure him on that point. . . .

There is a great Irish debate on in the House tonight.

---

[1] J. E. Greaves, Lord-Lieutenant of Caernarvonshire.
[2] Sir Watkin Williams Wynn, of Wynnstay, Lord-Lieutenant of Montgomery-shire and the leading landowner in North Wales.
[3] Dean David Howell (1831–1903): Dean of St. David's from 1897, a Liberal.

What fools they are to provoke rows in Ireland, with the Nonconformists in England & Wales, in addition to war in Africa during the coronation year.

18 April 1902

The news from South Africa today is very promising. The Boers have asked for facilities to bring the terms before their commanders in the field. These facilities Kitchener has given & the Boer leaders have left Pretoria to consult their men. It is thought this will take 3 weeks. This looks as if the terms tendered by us were more generous than those we offered last year to Botha—that is the terms as finally cooked by Chamberlain then. Botha[1] refused if you remember when he got them even to submit them to his Government as they [were] not worth discussing. I think you will [see] the proposals we have now made are much more liberal & that as far as money for restocking farms is concerned they were fairly lavish. I wish peace would come so long of course as it brings fair treatment to these gallant chaps in the field.

21 April 1902

I am busy now in the Library getting up a *solid* speech for Swansea[2]—full of statistics. I shall surprise them by the character of the speech. They will expect brimstone. I will give them bread. . . .

Megan Lloyd George was born on 22 April

'Bore Mercher' (Wednesday morning—23 April 1902)

I cannot put into words the thrill of joy & affection which passed through me on reading the telegram announcing that all had passed off well. I am quite happy in thinking about it. . . . There was great delight as the news circulated. I was having my breakfast about five minutes to 9 when it came. The girls had already left for school. Dick was in the garden. He is full of a cwt ieir [chicken run] having soon forgotten all his worries even if ever [he] had any. I sent for him. He came with a troubled face expecting a scolding. When I told him the good news his face assumed a quizzical appearance as if he didn't

---

[1] Louis Botha (1862–1919): commandant-general of Boer forces, 1900–2; first Prime Minister of the Union of South Africa, 1910–19.
[2] For a free church rally against the Education Bill.

quite appreciate what I meant & he said "Be?" [What]? I repeated "Y mae gen ti chwaer bach" [You've got a little sister]. He was quite staggered & perplexed & that is how I left him. . . . Well Beggar bach dyna fo trosodd yn hapus iawn—tan y tro nesaf! [there, it's turned out very happily—until the next time!] . . . How I would cover your sweet & pure & tender face with kisses.

5 May 1902

[He is trying to speak on Second Reading of the Education Bill.] Haldane is now speaking in support of the Bill! It will help as far as it goes to damage the Liberal Imperialists.[1]

6 May 1902

Ellis Griffith spoke & he told me before getting up that he had a good speech—but it turned out to be a dismal failure. Sorry, considering all the trouble he has gone through. The members trooped out when he got up—of the few that remained several walked out after listening to him a few minutes. The hubbub of departing members was so great during the first minute or two after he got up that you could not hear a word.

16 May 1902

Last night was quite a triumph. Never have I spoken anything like it at Carnarvon. . . . At Crewe who should I see but Asquith returning from the great meeting at the Free Trade Hall, Manchester. We travelled up together. Yr oedd o yn glên iawn ac yn siaradus.[2]

21 May 1902 (from Cardiff)

Last night was an immense success.[3] The reception would have warmed your heart, & the speech was described by Spicer as "the finest I had ever delivered", "magnificent" &c. I have hardly ever seen an audience so completely in my hands. Herbert Lewis came before me & did better than I have ever heard him do, in his earnest way. It was rather difficult to follow so I had to start with some jokes at the expense of the Bill which brought down the House. Then I went on.

[1] Haldane, an apostle of Hegelian *étatisme*, was virtually the only Liberal Imperialist to support the Education Bill.
[2] He was very affable and talkative.
[3] A demonstration at Cardiff against the Education Bill, Spicer presiding.

23 May 1902

I was never more unhappy by your absence—cold coffee, cold grape nuts & eternal ham help to make you much more popular. I want to turn the present ministry at Trinity Rd. & bring back the old Prime Minister. Tyrd gynta gallwch chwi, hen gariad annwyl.[1]

People very excited here about the prospects of peace. The general opinion is that it is coming off. I earnestly hope so for the sake of Liberalism. I confess to being utterly at a loss to form any firm opinion as to what is going to happen.

24 May 1902

[He urges his wife to join him in London.]

Why the poor Boer women had often to trek on waggons through sun & rain over open rough country for days when baby was only a fortnight or 3 weeks old. I am not as hard as that. But the concentration camp on Wandsworth Common does need your presence.

28 May 1902

Rumours of a desparate [*sic*] row between Joe & Beach over the Corn Tax.[2] Hope it is true & that Joe will be beaten for he will pay them out for his discomfiture.

Saw Haldane now for the first time since I chaffed him on the Education Bill. He sent me a copy of his Education Book just out & he told me he meant to label it "Views from above the Snowline".

2 June 1902

Wel heddwch a'r diwedd ac ar delerau anrhydeddus i'r Boers.[3] The first intimation I received of the news was after I went to bed last night when I heard the Church bells of Shepperton ringing, shots fired & the sound of cheering crowds in the distance.

They are generous terms to the Boers. Much better

---

[1] Come as soon as you can, dear old darling.

[2] Hicks-Beach's 1902 budget introduced a new duty of 3d. per cwt. on imported grain and flour. It was rescinded by Ritchie in 1903.

[3] Well, peace at last and on terms honourable to the Boers. (The peace of Vereeniging was signed on 31 May.)

than those we offered them 15 months ago—after spending £80,000,000 in the meantime!

16 August 1902 (from Zermatt, Switzerland)

I am so pleased to know that you are attending to Uncle Lloyd. You know how deeply I love him—I don't know of any two men who ever loved each other so. So every kindness you show him goes straight to my heart & endears you more & more to me. I sometimes have doubts as to whether the children have been taught the reverence & affection for him that is his due. All that is best in life's struggle I owe to him first. You came on late on the scene. My ambitions & direction in life had then been settled. Even then I should not have succeeded even so far as I have were it not the devotion & shrewdness with which he without a day's flagging kept me up to the mark. He understands me—my strengths & weaknesses—as no other person did. It has often struck me how remarkable his confidence has been in my some time or other doing great things. I used to put his faith down to blind fondness. But when I recollect that I never thought myself of attaining the measure of parliamentary success which I have reached I often wonder whether he did not see more than—I will not say my best friends—but that I myself ever saw. With that amazing bump of perception projecting over his nose & the other faculty of knowledge of human nature which arches his forehead he saw deeper into my nature than anyone else. How many times have I done things—& successful things—in Parliament when I was on the point of shirking my duty—but done them entirely because I saw from his letters that he expected me to do them & I knew that if I failed it would give him pain, whereas if I did them it would give him joy. I was telling Frank Edwards about it the other day & I have often told Vincent [Evans]. Then I have never seen him press me to take any action which was not absolutely the wisest to take under the circumstances. His instinct is unerring & no man could have a wiser counsellor through life. Yes—how often have I kept straight from the very thought of the grief I might give him. You know how true he has been to you—true with a noble chivalry which I have never surpassed.

I sometimes—I often in fact feel that my busy tumultuous life I don't seem to pay him enough attention & when that thought comes to me it gives me great remorse & I despise myself. But he knows that there is no one on earth whom I esteem so highly.

I know perfectly well how tenderly you feel towards him & I want the children also to appreciate him as you do.

3 September 1902

I've been to the Trades Union Congress to plead for the Bethesda Quarrymen.[1] They suspended the standing orders to enable me to do so. Gave me a fine reception and passed a resolution unanimously to support them. I think they have been saved. But very severe things were said about [D. R.] Daniel I am sorry to say. Unions that had paid £10 a week regularly refused balance sheets saying how the money was being spent.

2 December 1902

Morgan Gibbon[2] told me last night a story of Joe Chamberlain. E. T. Reed of Punch[3] asked him what he thought of Lloyd George. He replied "Lloyd George is a very able man & will go far. It is a pity however that he is so provincial in his views!" What a comment for Joe.

4 December 1902

[Ll. G. has spoken on the Third Reading of the Education Bill.] What a handsome compliment Balfour paid me—& so did Asquith in his speech. The general cheering in the House was very remarkable—the Tories being nearly as hearty as our own men.

This afternoon I got a wire to go to Berkeley Sq^{re} to see Rosebery. He wanted to see me about the Education Bill. He took me for an hour's stroll in the Park. He was most complimentary.

The political situation, already increasingly favourable to the Liberals, was transformed on 15 May 1903 when Joseph Chamberlain called for tariff reform and imperial preference in a major speech at Birmingham. This shattered the unity of the Unionist Party henceforth.

[1] Lloyd George addressed the T.U.C. at Holborn Town Hall to appeal for financial assistance for the quarrymen.
[2] Rev. J. Morgan Gibbon (1855–1932): minister of Stamford Hill Congregationalist chapel, London.
[3] The famous *Punch* cartoonist, son of the member for Cardiff.

28 July 1903

[An interview] took me off a debate in the House. But on the whole I lost nothing by that. It was better perhaps to let the Unionists quarrel amongst themselves. Cecil & Gorst made a stinging attack on the Govt.[1]

29 July 1903

Prysur iawn gyda cwestiwn Addysg Cymreig.[2] Deputation up from Wales. I bullied the Board of Education. Herbert Lewis said I was very rough. I hate the dictation & the insolence of officials—as if no one knew anything but themselves.

11 August 1903

Wedi bod yn dyweyd gair ar yr[3] Appropriation Bill on Tariffs. The Speaker had ruled everybody out of order—but I managed to walk round him much to the amusement of the House.

13 August 1903

[He has been attending a session of the Public Works Loan Commissioners.]

Pwllheli is applying for £15,000 loan towards Harbours. Advantage of getting from Commissioners is that rate of interest is low & if Harbours doesn't pay then they excuse interest. Most important this as I should not like its cost to add to rates.

27 November 1903 (from Oxford)

Last night was a great triumph. Never has the Union been so crowded. 50 extra seats were brought in—a thing never done before—& not only were they full but scores stood at the door & round the walls. Galleries crowded with ladies & parsons. I dined with the President & Temple (the late Archbishop's son). Spoke for an hour. I could see I made a very deep impression. They gave me a great ovation when I sat down—& then thronged out to vote. Wouldn't listen to any

---

[1] Over the Sugar Convention Bill. In fact, neither Cecil spoke in the debate.
[2] Very busy with Welsh Education question. (At this time, Lloyd George was much preoccupied with trying to set up an educational council for Wales.)
[3] Have been saying a word on the . . .

reply. We carried a free trade motion by over 20. A few weeks ago the Union had carried a Chamberlain motion by 80. A large number of Tories wouldn't vote at all. Met today a retired Colonel who was there & said he knew the young Tory undergraduates had come there to scoff but he said "You made a deep impression on them. You took them the right way."

23 December 1903

Returned early train from Banbury. Perks[1] wanted to see me on a proposed agreement with the Duke of Devonshire & the Free Trade Unionists as to the Education Act. Glad I saw him for we cannot accept their proposals at any price & Asquith—who was prepared to agree—must be stopped at once.

11 January 1904 (from Fallodon)

Grey[2] met me at his private station. I had a very long walk with him in the morning & we had a very frank chat about the prospective Liberal ministry—if it comes off. He says I am certain to have a seat in the Cabinet. Told him I must bargain for Wales. His ideas are dangerous. Rosebery Premier & Asquith leader of the House. The former is possible but the latter I fear impossible as it means shelving C. B. & Morley. I told him that could not be done. He is more bent on an Asquith leadership of the Commons than on a Rosebery Premiership. He would prefer a Spencer Premiership with an Asquith leadership. Young Ridley thinks a dissolution possible & likely in February.

In February 1904 the Liberals swept to victory in every county council election in Wales. This heralded a new phase of Lloyd George's campaign of resistance to the 1902 Education Act.

8 August 1904

Am organising campaign to fight the Coercion Act[3] in Wales. Shall beat them. Feel sure of it. But it is taking my time & thought.

---

[1] Robert W. Perks (1848–1934): Liberal member for Louth, 1892–1910; a Wesleyan Methodist, known as 'Imperial Perks' for his views on the Boer War.

[2] Sir Edward Grey (1862–1933): Liberal member for Berwick-on-Tweed, 1885–1916; Foreign Secretary, 1905–16; created Viscount Grey of Fallodon, 1916.

[3] The 'coercion act' was the popular name for the Education (Local Authority Default) Act, passed in 1904 to try to combat the 'Welsh revolt'.

15 September 1904

Just had a telegram from Bishop of St. Asaph wants to see me after 10 at Atheneum tonight. "Important". Curious to know what it is about.

Yesterday's meeting was immense. Never saw such determination & enthusiasm. It was a great stroke bringing the religious denominations on the ground.[1]

27 December 1904 (from Naples)

Very glad to hear of the Diwygiad.[2] I hope the Garthcelynites[3] will not treat it in a critical spirit. There are many characters which can never be impressed except by eruption of this sort. You must take them to the brink of the crater & show them the boiling sulphur in the depths. I am genuinely delighted. You know I am an intense believer in the goodness of this Diwygiad.

4 January 1905 (from Menton)

[He has met Gibson Bowles[4] in his hotel at Genoa.] He was very very depressed about the political situation from the point of view of a Unionist Free Fooder & also from his own personal standpoint. "I have no future" *meddai* [he said]. "You have a great future before you". *Dyn a helpa Tommy. Gallu mawr iawn ond dim barn. Diffyg gras attaliol mewn ystyr wleidyddol. Mynd at Rendel yfory. Galw yn Monte Carlo ar y ffordd yno er mwyn gweld y lle.*[5]

[1] The Bishop at this time was engaged in negotiations with Lloyd George to try to secure a compromise over the Welsh Church schools issue; however, this came to nothing. The 'meeting' to which Lloyd George refers was the Welsh County Councils executive meeting at Shrewsbury which unanimously voted for a national policy of passive resistance. The councils would decline to levy an education rate themselves, leaving the government in direct conflict with nonconformist ratepayers in Wales. In the meantime, Welsh children would be withdrawn from Church schools and given instruction in chapel vestries on a voluntary basis. (There is a full discussion of all the issues in Lloyd George to Robertson Nicoll, 15 September 1904, Nicoll MSS. See also Kenneth O. Morgan, *Wales in British Politics, 1868–1922*, 2nd edn., 1971, pp. 191–8.)

[2] The religious revival which had swept Wales since October 1904.

[3] Garthcelyn was the Criccieth home of William George.

[4] Thomas Gibson Bowles (1844–1922): Unionist member for King's Lynn, 1892–1906, then Liberal member, 1910.

[5] God help Tommy. Very great ability but no judgement. No saving grace in the political sense. Going to Rendel tomorrow. Calling at Monte Carlo on the way there to see the place.

6 January 1905 (from Cannes)

[Ll. G. is staying with Lord Rendel at the Château de Thorenc, Cannes—they visit Monte Carlo.] Uffern o le—neu yn hytrach Paradwys wedi ei holl feddianu gan seirph.¹ The Casino haunts you. Men & women recklessly gambling away their whole fortune. The Grand Duke Sergius, a member of the Russian royal family, throwing hundreds away, walking from table to table, having placed a stake of £30 or £40 on each. And this on the very darkest hour of his country's trouble. No wonder Russia is on the brink of revolution. . . . Ld. Welby² here. He used to be at the Treasury. Had a long chat with him about the National Expenditure, as I intend speaking on the subject at Degannwy. But I have lots of figures to look up in turn. I cannot find the material at Criccieth.

6 July 1905

Llawer o siarad am fy araeth pnawn ddoe. Morley ac Asquith yn canmol yn arw iawn.

Cinio gyda Asquith neithiwr. Grand iawn. 3 neu 4 o Arglwyddi &c. Lord Rosebery there. He was very nice. . . . Holi yn arw am Evan Roberts.³

7 July 1905

Bishop of St. Asaph hanging around. We are in for another fighting—in Montgomeryshire this time—& he doesn't want [?it].⁴

George Kenyon (M.P.)⁵ wrote me a delightful letter as to my speech at Bangor on the neutral zone. He wants peace

---

¹ A hell of a place—or rather Paradise completely possessed by serpents.

² First Baron Welby (1832–1915): permanent secretary to the Treasury, 1885–94.

³ Considerable talk about my speech yesterday afternoon. Morley and Asquith praising it very highly. Dinner with Asquith last night. Very grand. 3 or 4 Lords &c. . . . Close questioning about Evan Roberts [the Welsh revivalist]. (Lloyd George still retained much admiration for Rosebery. In July 1904, he described him privately as 'the only possible man' for the Liberal leadership: D. A. Hamer, *Liberal Politics in the Age of Gladstone and Rosebery*, Clarendon Press, Oxford, 1972, p. 287.)

⁴ The Montgomeryshire county council was found to be in default over the non-administration of the 1902 Education Act.

⁵ Hon. George T. Kenyon (1840–1908): Unionist member for Denbigh District, 1885–95 and 1900–6.

now & says there is only one man in Wales can make it & that is y fi [me].

26 August 1905

Those Merionethshire fellows have broken away once more. What a worry they are. I don't know what to do with them on my honour.

In the autumn of 1905 Lloyd George had a serious operation on his tonsils. He then went to Italy to recuperate. While he was away, William George sent word that Balfour's government was likely to resign. Lloyd George arrived back in England on 3 December. Balfour resigned on the 4th.

(undated—some time in late 1905)

With Morley until after 4. Most important talk on situation. He said to me "If you take anything but Cabinet rank you will be a donkey. Told him I must first see Wales right. That I would stand by my people whatever happened. He liked my plan for them very much—self government including power to deal with temperance.[1]

[1] Lloyd George accepted the post of President of the Board of Trade in Campbell-Bannerman's new government on 8 December. He told his brother that he had insisted on guarantees over 'the extension of self-government for Wales' (William George, *My Brother and I*, p. 206). John Burns recorded in his diary for 17 December 1905: 'Walked to Wandsworth to see Lloyd George about Welsh questions, Education, Church, Devolution' (B.M. Add. MSS., 46323, Burns Papers). In the event, apart from the modest scheme to set up a Welsh department in the Board of Education in 1907 the government made no attempt to extend Welsh devolution, while Lloyd George's interest in disestablishment and other Welsh issues steadily diminished.

CHAPTER 7

A Radical in Office

(1906–14)

The new Liberal government was confirmed in office by a huge landslide victory at the polls in January 1906. Its new President of the Board of Trade was an unknown quantity in the executive, with no previous experience of office. But he soon showed himself to be an energetic and creative departmental minister, with a fierce determination not to be dictated to by his permanent officials. Over the next two years, he generated a steady stream of major legislation, notably a Patents Act, a Merchant Shipping Act, a Companies Act, and a census of production. In addition, he demonstrated a rare expertise in negotiations with organized labour; by the triumphant settlement of the national railway strike of October 1907 he established a special relation with the trade unions which was to serve him well over the next fifteen years. But these years of public triumph also brought crushing private grief. In November 1907 his favourite daughter, Mair Eluned, died at the age of seventeen. Lloyd George was prostrated by sorrow, while relations with Mrs. Lloyd George, who reacted with remarkable calmness to the tragedy, became almost imperceptibly more distant from this time onwards.

When Asquith became Prime Minister in April 1908, he appointed Lloyd George as Chancellor of the Exchequer to placate the radicals. This new appointment was accompanied by an angry complaint from the new premier about prior publicity in the press over the new ministerial changes. But thereafter his relations with his new Chancellor seem to have been entirely cordial. Both Asquith and Lloyd George were well aware of the slump in the government's electoral fortunes since the heady days of 1906, a slump symbolized by the recent by-election defeat of Winston Churchill at North-West Manchester. A new political initiative was required, and it was Lloyd George and Churchill, the Welsh radical and the renegade aristocrat, who supplied it. After Lloyd George returned from a visit to Germany in the summer of 1908, during which he examined the welfare schemes that had flourished in that country since the time of Bismarck, he promptly began to commit the Liberals to a far-ranging programme of social reform. A major address to the Welsh National Liberal Council at Swansea in October 1908 outlined an imaginative series of measures, including old age pensions, health and unemployment insurance, and labour exchanges. The whole content of Liberalism, a legacy of the days of Gladstone, was to be transformed.

The first stage was to provide a financial base for the new welfare measures. This came with Lloyd George's famous 'people's budget' of April 1909 which outlined a sweeping programme of direct taxes, including new duties upon the unearned increment on land. These proposals, which offered a radical alternative to tariff reform, were initially devised to meet a financial need rather than provoke a political crisis. But when it became clear that the House of Lords might commit the supreme folly of rejecting the budget, the first time this had ever been done, Lloyd George deliberately whipped them on to new heights of fury. His speeches were remarkable for their invective coming from a leading Cabinet minister: a speech at Lime-house (July 1909) became especially notorious. As a result, the Lords threw out the Budget, and Asquith dissolved parliament. The Liberals gained roughly equal representation with the Unionists in the January 1910 election, but Irish and Labour support enabled them to count on a safe working majority of 124. Asquith then introduced a Parliament Bill which would permanently restrict the Lords' veto on Commons' legislation to two years only. This required a further general election in December 1910 which left the Liberals with virtually the same working majority. Eventually in August 1911, under the threat of a royal pledge to create enough peers to carry the bill if necessary, the Lords passed the Parliament Bill. Radicals claimed it as a triumph for the People versus the Peers.

Lloyd George played a less prominent role in the later stages of this acute party warfare. Indeed, in the summer of 1910 he had seized the opportunity created by the accession of a new king, George V, to propose an all-party coalition which would by-pass the old partisan issues and give supreme priority to social reform and 'national efficiency'. This, however, inevitably foundered. Lloyd George, therefore, had to rely on his own party for pushing on with social legislation. He gained new stature in 1911 by passing an immensely complex National Insurance Bill, a comprehensive measure for health insurance with a more limited scheme for unemployment insurance. With new triumphs in labour negotiations during the industrial unrest of 1911 he seemed at his zenith as a radical reformer. But, in fact, his career ran into many difficulties in 1912–14. His public position was almost undermined by accusations of financial irregularity during the 'Marconi scandal'. The Liberal government was reeling under a sequence of hammer-blows — Ireland, the suffragettes, the Triple Alliance. Lloyd George's new land campaign of 1913–14 fell rather flat, while he himself was temporarily locked in conflict with Churchill, now at the Admiralty, over the naval estimates. In addition Lloyd George's domestic life was seriously affected by the entry into his life of Frances Stevenson, originally Megan's private tutor, who became his private secretary and intimate companion from the end of 1912.

Then his career was transformed anew by international crisis. In late July 1914 the threat of war between Britain and Germany suddenly became a reality. Lloyd George's reputation in foreign affairs was an ambivalent one. In the first place, he was still in some sense the voice of 'little England-ism' in the Cabinet, and a constant opponent of increased military and naval expenditure. He had clashed violently with Haldane, the former Secretary for War whom he had once dubbed 'the minister for slaughter'.

On the other hand, since his visit to Germany in 1908. Lloyd George had been increasingly alarmed at the mounting tension between the great powers in Europe. His Mansion House speech in 1911 contained a stern warning to Germany during the Agadir crisis. His membership of the Committee of Imperial Defence kept him in touch with international developments thereafter. In the final days of crisis, between 27 July and 4 August, his agonies of conscience are well illustrated by his letters to his wife. But there was scant prospect of his resigning or leading a 'peace faction' in opposition to the war. The German ultimatum to Belgium provided the occasion for a decision that he had long foreseen. Not merely did he stay in the Cabinet. Reinforced by the unexpected jingoism of the aged Uncle Lloyd in Criccieth, he soon found a fresh buoyancy and self-confidence in the new challenges of total war.

A general election was held in January 1906.

(undated–January 1906, from Leamington)

Row yn [in] Leamington. Our chaps last night refused Lyttelton[1] a hearing with the inevitable result that their roughs shouted us down today. There were about a hundred of them & we could do nothing but adjourn to the Club & talk there. As you know I have been dead against this policy of breaking up meetings. It leads to reprisals.

6 January 1906

I am sorry they are smashing up Naylor's[2] meetings. That won't do us any good although he thoroughly deserves it. He is a first-class bounder.

The election resulted in a Liberal landslide, with 401 Liberals, 83 Irish Nationalists and 29 Labour Party members returned against only 157 Unionists. In Caernarvon Boroughs Lloyd George won easily with a 1,224 majority over R. A. Naylor. However, the 1906 session was an unsuccessful one for the Liberal government. Their major measure, Birrell's Education Bill, was mutilated by amendments in the Lords, and other bills perished in the same way.

1 August 1906

Booked for Lisbon—taking a lady, a *real* lady with me— sweet & pretty. We've got a magnificent set of rooms on decks placed at our disposal. They cost 200 guineas but we get them at ordinary rates. Owen Philipps did this. So you will be quite spoilt on your first sea voyage for the future. Have booked for Uncle W. & Dick.

[1] Alfred Lyttelton (1857–1913): Unionist member for Leamington, 1895–1913; Colonial Secretary, 1903–5.
[2] R. A. Naylor, Unionist candidate for the Caernarvon Boroughs.

10 September 1906

I must have another talk with Roberts.[1] This courtship is doing him no good, although it ought to buck him up. I never neglected my practice when I courted you, did I cariad [darling]? And yet I managed to see you for hours every day.

29 December 1906 (from Biarritz)

Robson & Emmott[2] are staying here. Had a chat with Robson this morning. He has a poor opinion of Birrell's[3] fighting qualities. He saw a good deal of him during the Education Bill. "He is no fighter" ebo [says] Robson.

One source of encouragement for the government was Lloyd George's striking and consistent success at the Board of Trade.

31 July 1907

Willie Davies, editor of the Western Mail,[4] came up purposely today to see me. He says the commercial people of Cardiff want me to stand for Cardiff. If I do the Tories won't fight me!! They think I am the best President the Board of Trade ever had & that it would be a fine thing for Cardiff. He says his proprietor Riddell[5] is very favourable to me.

31 July 1907 (later)

Been lunching with Roberston Nicoll.[6] He is most friendly. Told me I was the only Minister who had made a reputation as a Minister & that everyone was talking of me as the next Liberal Prime Minister. He had a great contempt for Ellis Griffith & for all the Welsh M.P.'s—even poor Herbert Lewis.... Elfed had told him apropos of the Welsh Disestablishment agitation, "You may depend upon it, the Welsh people won't give up Lloyd George lightly—they are very proud of him &

[1] Arthur Rhys Roberts, Lloyd George's partner in their solicitors' firm.
[2] Alfred Emmott (1858–1926): Liberal member for Oldham, 1899–1911.
[3] Augustine Birrell (1850–1933): Liberal member, 1889–1900 and 1906–18; President of the Board of Education, 1905–7; Chief Secretary for Ireland, 1907–16.
[4] Sir William Davies (1863–1935): editor of the *Western Mail* since 1901.
[5] George Riddell (1865–1934): newspaper proprietor, chairman of the *News of the World*, 1903–34; very friendly with Lloyd George until after the war; bought him a car and a new house at Walton Heath.
[6] William Robertson Nicoll (1851–1923): editor of the *British Weekly* from 1886; Lloyd George's main champion in the nonconformist press.

besides they have no substitute". Go dda ynte [Pretty good, isn't it]?

2 August 1907

Just got the third reading of the Merchant Shipping Tonnage Bill. Was up with it until after one o'clock this morning. They threatened to fight all night but I soon cajoled them into reason & although they had 3 pages of amendments they only moved one. The Prime Minister was there part of the time & when one of the members who were opposing my Bill complimented me effusively, he said chaffingly, "I am just hearing too much of this sort of thing about you. Yesterday it was Sir William Lyne[1]—today it is this chap".

8 August 1907

A row in the Lords over my Tonnage Bill. If they throw it out it will mean setting the shipping interest in the country against them. Not a bad thing.

14 August 1907

I got 39 Clauses of my Companies Bill through today. Another day puts me through. Tomorrow I hope.

Got my Patents & my Patents Consolidation Bill through last night. I hope to be able to manage to get Companies' Bill on the statute book. That would be an enormous achievement. Everybody told me it couldn't be done & that put my back up, otherwise I shouldn't have attempted it.

20 August 1907

All night sitting. I was in charge until 6 this morning & I feel fairly cheap today. The Whips made a jolly mess of it & it looked at one time as if they had destroyed one at least of my bills. But at last by good temper—or rather a mixture of honey & wormwood—I got one bill through & came to an arrangement with the Tories to give me my Companies Bill in a couple of hours on Wednesday morning. So all my Bills are now assured. The Companies Bill is a huge one & they could easily have killed it had they gone about it in earnest & skilfully.

23 August 1907

I can't accept a post of £2,000 a year without attending

---

[1] The Australian Minister for Trade and Commerce.

to it. Ministers *must* be here to the end as a question affecting their departments may arise at any moment. And although my bills are through the Commons I must also see them through the Lords. I have to stand on the steps of the House to confer with Earl Granard & the Lord Chancellor on the amendments as they are moved. And then I have to propose in the House of Commons whether we agree or disagree as the case may be with the Lords amendments. Felly, paid ti a siarad nonsense [So, don't talk nonsense] Beggar. Your concert may be very important & probably more important to you than my work, but you will excuse me for taking a different view.

23 August 1907 (later)

There are only two thoroughly vicious amendments down to my Patents Bill. These I'll fight even to the death of the Bill—if necessary. But they won't dare to kill it. It is too popular on their own side. The rest of their amendments I care nothing about.

On 30 November 1907 Lloyd George's favourite daughter, Mair Eluned, died of appendicitis.

4 December 1907 (from Manchester)

I am so pleased to think you are joining me up in London tomorrow night darling. Your placid, brave spirit has a soothing effect on my turbulent & emotional nature. And, as John Owen so truly said, there is not a trace of the morbid about you. That is more than I can say of myself. I have always been disposed towards morbidity. We must help each other not to brood. Take warning from the sad example of poor Mr. & Mrs. Robert Thomas who were always towing each other out into the breakers. We did our best. It was the decree of fate which millions besides ourselves are now enduring. What right have we to grumble? More than that I have a profound conviction that cruel as the blow may appear & purposeless as it may now seem it will prove to be the greatest blessing that has befallen us & through us multitudes whom God has sent me to give a helping hand out of misery and worry a myriad worse than ours. I can see through the darkness a ray of hope. I am not sure yet what it will reveal but I am certain of its presence & promise. How nobly the Garthcelynites have all behaved. Whilst I know the tragedy was wringing their hearts they spent no sympathy on themselves but spared it all for us.

'Xmas night' 1907 (from Nice)

Last night the Kearleys[1] & I dined with Lord Glantawe[2] in Nice. I was glad to see him. He lost five of his children, in fact all his children by his first wife. One was a beautiful little dot of five, another when he had grown up into manhood, the rest very young. You may therefore imagine that when a man who had passed through such experiences assured me that time does heal the sore his word carried real consolation to my heart. He also lost the mother of the five of whom he was passionately fond. She was a beautiful but very delicate woman. He told me the whole story of their courtship & he was able to dwell on her beauty & the beauty and brightness of his lost children with pleasure. What an alchemist is time that it can turn sorrow into delight. The thought of them is now part of the joy of life to him.

5 January 1908 (from Nice)

Returned from Lord Rendel's. Very pleased to see me. Poor old Lady Rendel looks very much broken. They both inquired so kindly about you. They would have been so glad had you seen your way to take their villa at Valescure. So would I too cariad [darling]. Three weeks without your gentle and soothing influence have been very trying & often heartbreaking. I would rather have you—jealous old Maggie as you sometimes are—I would rather see you near me in my trouble than anybody else—you & Uncle Lloyd. You don't mind my bringing him in, do you? . . .

probably 6 January 1908 (from Nice)

I have been attending to Board of Trade business this morning & it has done me no good as I have been very depressed the last day or two. They have made a mess of things over the dispute in Lancashire. Smith, the moment I left, thought he would like to settle this new war[?] himself so he wrote the parties suggesting Board of Trade intervention.[3]

[1] Hudson Kearley, Viscount Devonport (1856–1934): parliamentary secretary to the Board of Trade, 1905–9.

[2] Sir John Jones Jenkins, Lord Glantawe (1835–1915): Liberal member for Carmarthen, 1882–6, Liberal Unionist member, 1895–1900; rejoined Liberals over free trade, 1903; created Baron Glantawe, 1906.

[3] A lock-out closed over half the cotton mills in Lancashire: the dispute was finally resolved, without mediation, on 27 January. H. Llewellyn Smith (1864–1945) was permanent secretary to the Board of Trade, 1907–19.

I felt it was a blunder the moment I heard of it & wrote at once to say so. Things are not ripe for us. Now both parties have refused Smith's interventions. I wired for the correspondence & they have come. No man of the world with a knowledge of men could have proceeded in such a blunt fashion. I have written Smith. It will do him good. These men think these things are easily & cheaply done, forgetting that the management of men is the rarest of all gifts.

10 January 1908 (from Nice)

There will be hard, difficult & anxious work awaiting me & I am glad to think that there is. There will be the great Lancashire lockout which Llewelyn Smith has messed so badly in my absence & there will also be the Port of London. I am not very sanguine as to Lancashire. Both parties are so keen about fighting & I shall have to clear out of the way the debris of Llewelyn's folly. Not an easy task. . . .

I am not going to accept the charity of the party come what may. I have made up my mind not to. Tom Ellis did it & he was their doormat. I mean to fight my way through myself. This is an offer[1] made to me because they find the jealousies & rivalries are so great that they cannot raise the status of my office & C.B. [Campbell-Bannerman] wants to do something for me. It is very kind of him but I won't have it. I'll take my chance & I know I can rely on your help.

In April 1908 Campbell-Bannerman resigned as Prime Minister, a dying man. Asquith succeeded him. On 12 April he appointed Lloyd George as Chancellor of the Exchequer. After a visit to Germany in the summer of 1908, Lloyd George embarked on a sweeping programme of social reform. Crucial to it was his budget of 1909 which was to provoke a supreme crisis between the Commons and the Lords.

15 March 1909

First Cabinet on Budget.[2] Good start. At it again to-morrow.

16 November 1909

Well the Lords have made up their minds.[3] The Lord hath delivered them unto our hands. That is my feeling. The

---

[1] Apparently of financial assistance. [2] i.e. the 'people's budget'.
[3] On 9 November it had become known that the Lords would reject the Finance Bill on the second reading.

Budget is quite safe as far as its leading features are concerned. We may have to come to terms with the Irish but that won't touch land.

Asquith dissolved parliament and a new general election was held in January 1910. Lloyd George retained his seat with a majority of 1,078. The Liberals stayed in power with a working majority of 124.

7 January 1910

Immense [meeting?] last night. Thousands outside. Just like St. Pancras. Tories tried to get a counter demonstration but horribly failed. Tree was there (Beerbohm).

13 January 1910

Very disappointed with Criccieth canvass. *Much the worst.* 43 "unseen" in a small town like that & only 20 in Bangor.

8 May 1910

Do not quite know what to think about this catastrophe.[1] It never entered into our calculations. What insolent creatures we all are. We reckoned without taking the Great Ruler into account.

9 May 1910

Summoned at 10.45 to an audience with the new King. I being the first minister to be called in. Grey came in after me. The King exceedingly nice. Talked a good deal about his father of whom he was evidently very fond. His eyes suffused with tears. Gave me some details of his last illness. We had an exceedingly frank & satisfactory talk about the political crisis. We got on excellently. He means to try his hand at conciliation. Whether he will succeed is somewhat doubtful. Much will depend on pending bye-elections.

10 May 1910

Cabinet over—adjourned until Thursday. Think I saved them from precipitating themselves into a 2nd blunder. They were all agreed & I swung them round. As Samuel[2] said to

[1] King Edward VII died on 6 May 1910 at a vital stage of the conflict with the Lords.

[2] Herbert Samuel (1870–1963): Postmaster-General, 1910–14 and 1915–16; President of Local Government Board, 1914–15; Home Secretary, 1916 and 1931–2; succeeded Lloyd George as Liberal leader, 1931; created Viscount, 1937.

me "For the second time this year you have succeeded in swinging round the Cabinet when they were on the wrong course."

We meet again on Thursday. Tuesday we have to receive the King's body at Westminster Hall. Today we bury the poor old boy.

8 September 1910 (from Balmoral)

The King is a very jolly chap ond diolch i Dduw does dim llawer yn ei ben o. Pobl syml gyffredin iawn iawn ydynt a hwyrach ar y cyfan fod hynny yn citha peth. . . .[1]

10 September 1910 (from Balmoral)

Sat between the Queen & the Prince of Wales at lunch. Quite a nice little fellow. After lunch when the cigars came on the Queen remained to smoke a cigarette, the boys began the game of blowing out the cigar lights—then little Princess Mary wanted to join in & got very excited over it—then the Queen & the rest of us all joined in & the noise was deafening until the little Princess set her lamp on fire. We thought then it was time to stop.

They were all pleased at the way the Welsh papers have taken the Investiture.[2]

Another general election was held in December 1910 as a mandate on the Parliament Bill.

14 December 1910

Had a breakfast party this morning, Ramsay Macdonald,[3] a French Socialist Deputy & Mr. & Mrs. Masterman.[4] Ciniawa heno gyda Winston. Gyda Vincent neithiwr.[5]

---

[1] . . . but thank God there's not much in his head. They're simple, very, very ordinary people, and perhaps on the whole that's how it should be.

[2] i.e. the news that the Prince of Wales would be invested at Caernarvon in July 1911.

[3] James Ramsay MacDonald (1866–1937): secretary of Labour Representation Committee, 1900–12; chairman of Parliamentary Labour Party, 1911–14; Prime Minister, 1924 and 1929–35.

[4] Charles F. G. Masterman (1874–1927): Liberal member for Ipswich, 1900–14; Chancellor of the Duchy of Lancaster, 1914; worked closely with Lloyd George over his social reform policies in 1909–14; quarrelled with him after the Swansea District by-election in 1914, but reconciled with him after 1923.

[5] Dining tonight with Winston. With Vincent [Evans] last night.

We have lost one seat today. That makes us all square once more. It looks like our ending "as we were". As you know that was my bet.

15 December 1910

Dr. Dillon (E. J.) the famous foreign correspondent here with me this morning. Says that on the Continent of Europe I have taken Gladstone's place. Much the best known name he says in all countries. Count Witte, the ex-Russian Premier was anxious to see me. He thinks my Budget opened a new era in finance & social reform. . . .

One Lib gain on balance today—so we are now one ahead. Rather fear tomorrow's results—but Rosebery's five seats down is not out of the question I think.

(undated—December 1910)

Elections on the whole quite up to my expectations. I reckoned on a nett loss of four yesterday. We only lost 3. We will probably lose 4 or 5 tomorrow. London has once more amazed everybody. The East End actually increased the Liberal majority. Ipswich doubled.

Well hen gariad [old darling] we are not to be turned out of Downing St. this time. Tell Megan that the people of England seem to prefer her to Austen Chamberlain's little girl.

The first results that came in were disconcerting & the Master [of Elibank] was thoroughly frightened but we both went to bed cheerful & elated. The N.L.C. people most enthusiastic.[1]

In 1911 Lloyd George was mainly preoccupied with the passage of his National Insurance Bill. He was also caught up in critical labour negotiations during the railway strike and delivered a major speech on foreign affairs at the Mansion House in July.

10 January 1911 (misdated 1910)

Went to see the Stepney St. [i.e. Sidney Street][2] house

---

[1] The election results were: Liberals 272, Unionists 272, Labour 42, Irish Nationalists 84, a working government majority of 126. In London, Liberals and Labour gained five and lost two overall.

[2] Churchill sent troops in to lay siege to some foreign anarchists in Sidney Street, Stepney, on 3 January.

with Rufus[1] & Elibank.[2] It is a sight. It confirms my conviction that the whole affair was disastrously muddled by the police. I strongly urged Winston to go into the box at the inquest & make it clear he had nothing to do with directing the operations.

20 January 1911

Saw Macnaughton this morning. Said I was much better but that there was still some inflammation in the throat & that I ought to give it complete rest for a few weeks so as to get rid of it altogether before I resume work.

I saw the Prime Minister & he urged me to go at once so as to be back before the actual work of Parliament began —that is immediately after the address was voted.

Macnaughton was keen on my going away from the climate altogether & away from the reach of work. As long as I am, he thinks I will insist on talking & that is quite true. I talked incessantly at Haldane's last night. Yr un fath yn y Cabinet heddyw.[3] I can't help it as long as I am in the melee.

21 April 1911

Daeth y Prif Weinidog ir Ty neithiwr mewn diod yn drwm. Ymddygodd y Toriaid yn foneddigaidd iawn. Balfour begged Elibank to take him home. Hugh Cecil yn ddigri iawn.[4] An amendment was coming on about the Protestant Succession. Cecil said privately to Winston "I rather object to the Government settling the fate of the Protestant Succession with the aid of a drunken Christian & two sober Jews"! Gresyn. [Pity]

26 July 1911

Still very busy. The Germans blustering a good deal about my speech.[5] Sent a despatch over about it. Ministry firm.

---

[1] Sir Rufus Isaacs (1860–1935): Attorney-General, 1910–13; Lord Chief Justice, 1913–21; Ambassador to U.S.A., 1918–19; Viceroy of India, 1921–6; Foreign Secretary, 1931; created Marquess of Reading, 1913; involved with Lloyd George in the Marconi scandal.

[2] Alexander Murray, Master of Elibank (1870–1920): Liberal chief whip, 1909–12; also involved in the Marconi scandal.

[3] The same in the Cabinet today.

[4] The Prime Minister came to the House last night in a very drunken state. The Tories behaved very honourably . . . Hugh Cecil was very amusing.

[5] Lloyd George made a strong speech at the Mansion House, 21 July, warning Germany about her provocative policy in the Agadir crisis in Morocco.

Knollys[1] writes that the King is most pleased with it. Llwydyn [Olwen] had tea on the terrace with the Maharajah of Baroda who wanted to see me. Asked Mrs. Asquith & Mr. and Mrs. Winston.

(undated—July or August 1911)

I told you Germany was climbing down. This time I have done the trick & they are very angry with me. They tried to induce the Government to repudiate me. Grey lost his temper with them & now they are all honey.

I am now engaged in arranging a deal with the Irish & Labour parties on my Bill.[2] The Irish are alright. Labour is also meek after (frightful crash of thunder—big storm outside) —after the way I stood up to them last week & beat them.

Believe Llwydyn & I are on the track of an excellent Governess for Megan. A nice German Swiss—simple, straight, kind looking but not good looking. . . .

31 July 1911

Cabinet, Insurance & Interviews. We are hesitating whether to go through now which we could do by *sitting up to the end of September* or having an autumn session & breaking up in a fortnight & then have a campaign in the autumn for our Bill. I am agreeable to either course so long as the Bill goes through this year.

4 August 1911

Made a long speech summing up the position—gave great satisfaction.[3] All full of admiration. . . .

The Sassiwn people want me to take the chair at the Young People's meeting at Carnarvon. That is the worst of going down to Wales. I get no mental & nervous repose. I need both.

---

[1] Francis, Viscount Knollys (1837–1924): private secretary to Edward VII, and to George V, 1910–13.

[2] i.e. the National Insurance Bill. The Labour Party promised to support it in return for the introduction of payment of members (J. R. MacDonald to the Master of Elibank, 4 October 1911, quoted in Frank Owen, *Tempestuous Journey*, Hutchinson, 1954, p. 207).

[3] A speech on the National Insurance Bill, summarizing progress so far (*Parl. Deb.*, 5th ser., Vol. XXIX, pp. 734–52).

To Megan Lloyd George, 7 August 1911

My darling little Megan

I thank you so much for sending me that sweet little tooth which had smiled so often on me. I hope you will soon get another which will last you at least ten times as long.

I am glad that you like your new companion[1] & that you get on so well together. I knew you would. I want you to learn French & music so that you can talk French like a petite Parisien [*sic*] & play the piano like Paderewski.

I am so looking forward to seeing your bright face.

7 August 1911

P.M. splendid today. Ellis Griffith delivered a very brilliant speech. Glad, for I am sorry in my heart for him & he looked so worn & ill today. He beat F. E. [Smith][2] at his own game of persiflage.

10 August 1911

Just made what I am universally told is the best speech I ever delivered in the House in introducing payment of members. Gave immense delight. Congratulated on all hands by Tories as well as Libs.

Fate of Veto Bill still doubtful. Chances are we carry it by a small majority. Rosebery delivered a powerful speech in favour of passing it. Knollys called to see me. He thinks it will go through by "skin of our teeth". Elibank is staying with me.

11 August 1911

Veto through.[3] I can hardly believe it. The dream of Liberalism for generations realised at last. Gladstone, Bright, Bannerman, Harcourt—all looking forward to this day but passed away heb weled yr addewidion.[4]

[1] Frances Stevenson (who eventually married Lloyd George in 1943) was appointed to coach Megan Lloyd George during the summer holidays (Frances Lloyd-George, *The Years that are Past*, Hutchinson, 1967, pp. 41 ff.).

[2] F. E. Smith (1872–1930): Unionist member for Liverpool (Walton), 1906–19; Solicitor-General, 1915; Attorney-General, 1915–19; Lord Chancellor, 1919–22; Secretary of State for India, 1924–8; created 1st Baron Birkenhead, 1919 and Earl, 1922; a close and convivial associate of Lloyd George after the war.

[3] On 11 August 1911, the Lords finally passed the Parliament Bill, 131–114.

[4] Without seeing their hopes fulfilled.

So pleased that I am responsible for it. The Budget did it.

15 August 1911

My motor trip to Wales on Saturday is off. P.M. summoned a second meeting of Defence Committee[1] on Wednesday. Foreign situation still anxious. Insists on my presence. He remains in town specially for it. Winston was to join his wife in Switzerland. He has had to put it off.

16 August 1911

In charge. Spoken on the labour situation. A most difficult speech to make. Had to hold the balance even. Our fellows exceedingly pleased. . . . Winston come in to consult on the sending for troops.

19 August 1911

Yn ghanol negotiations pwysig.[2] Got Railway Managers to meet me so that is at any rate an achievement I never hoped for. Favourable so far. Employers behaving well. I got workmen's leaders here & addressed about 40 of them. Made favourable impression. First time I have seen them.

Shall wire. Two men shot in a row at Llanelly.[3]

19 August 1911 (later)

Hardest struggle of my life but I won. I cannot even now realise quite how. As someone said "It is a miracle" & really it looks like it. The Railway Companies have agreed to something I thought quite impossible.[4]

22 August 1911

Fierce labour attack on Winston.

Just spoken—smashed Keir Hardie.

16 September 1911 (from Balmoral)

I shall be so glad to find myself in the car starting. I am

[1] The Committee of Imperial Defence. On 23 August Asquith was to call a special meeting of the C.I.D. to consider 'action to be taken in the event of intervention in a European war'.

[2] In the middle of important negotiations (i.e. trying to settle a national railway strike).

[3] In a riot during the strike.

[4] i.e. the recognition of the railway unions.

not cut out for Court life. I can see some of them revel in it. I detest it. The whole atmosphere reeks with Toryism. I can breathe it & it depresses & sickens me. Everybody very civil to me as they would be to a dangerous wild animal whom they fear & perhaps just a little admire for its suppleness & strength. The King is hostile to the bone to all who are working to lift the workmen out of the mire. So is the Queen. They talk exactly as the late King & the Kaiser talked to me if you remember about the old Railway strike.[1] "What do they want striking?" "They are very well paid", etc. I have made great friends with Sir Frederick Treves and Sir Francis Laking, the King's physicians. Treves is a fine fellow. He is disgusted with the conduct of the medical profession over the Insurance Bill. He wants to help me.

To Megan Lloyd George, 18 September 1911 (from Balmoral)

I am now starting for the faraway North of Scotland where I am going to stay with a much richer man than the King & a man who made all that money himself—or at least a man who collected it all himself.[2]

I shall expect a letter there from you. . . . The King is sending on to Criccieth a fine chunk of venison out of a deer he shot. You cannot eat it all so you must divide up with Auntie Garthcelyn[3] & some of your other friends.

21 September 1911 (from Edinburgh)

Elibank & I motored here through beautiful country. . . . Scotch people wherever we stay very interested. Rowntree,[4] the M.P. for York, who has been through the country motoring tells me this morning that they are interested in no other politician—friend & foe alike. Everywhere they went I was the topic of conversation—Liberals lauding me to the skies, Tories abusing me to Gehenna. The latter say I am entirely responsible for the labour unrest. One man said the workmen were satisfied with 11/- a week until I came along.

---

[1] A famous railway stoppage in October 1907 when Lloyd George first demonstrated his unique expertise in labour negotiations by persuading the railway companies to accept compulsory boards of conciliation.

[2] This presumably refers to the Master of Elibank, although his residence was actually in the lowland county of Peebles.

[3] Anita, William George's wife.

[4] Arnold Rowntree (1872–1951): Liberal member for York, 1910–18.

9 October 1911

Had three hours of doctors & friendly societies. Most useful. I am in the saddle—well in—& I mean to ride hard over hurdles & ditches—& win.

10 October 1911

Been lunching with Winston. He is so happy about his transference to the Admiralty & so gratefully [*sic*]—at least for the moment—to me for fighting his cause.

11 October 1911

Prysur [Busy]. Labour party lunched with me—their Insurance Committee. They mean to support a time limit for the Bill. That means an enormous lightening of my labours. They are thoroughly friendly. They have at last made up their minds to fight Hardie, Snowden & Lansbury.[1] They have had an actuarial report which completely supports my scheme.

12 October 1911

[He has consulted Dr. Macnaughten about his daughter, Olwen.] Deputationing. Lunched with Riddell & Robertson Nicoll. Breakfast Labour Party. Dinner with Grey & Haldane— a pretty full day. Grey coming here now. MacKenna [*sic*][2] won't go to the Home Office! Wedi sorri [in sulks]...

16 October 1911

As far as I am able to judge the speech has created an immense impression. The fighting note which I have hitherto rather repressed has roused the Liberal press to a support which they have not yet given. It has also frightened the others. There has been a great change even in the Mail.

12 January 1912 (from the French Riviera)

I want another week at Insurance. We mean to have a

[1] Keir Hardie (1856–1915), Philip Snowden (1864–1937), and George Lansbury (1859–1940), the members for Merthyr Tydfil, Blackburn, and Bow and Bromley respectively, led Labour opposition to the National Insurance Bill.

[2] Reginald McKenna (1863–1943): Liberal member for North Monmouthshire, 1895–1918; President of the Board of Education, 1907–8; First Lord of the Admiralty, 1908–11; Home Secretary, 1911–15; Chancellor of the Exchequer, 1915–16.

great campaign throughout the country—some thousands of meetings to explain the Act.

Morant[1] writes me that he is getting on admirably. The conference with the Trades Unions yesterday was a great success so he wires me.

Hamar Greenwood[2] dining with us here tonight.

In April 1912 Asquith introduced the third Irish Home Rule Bill. In the same month Lloyd George became embroiled in the financial scandal of the Marconi affair which almost ruined his career.

11 April 1912

Home Rule launched. Went off quite well but no enthusiasm. It is much too soon to form any estimate of its effect even on our party. My own opinion—rhyngwch chwi a fi [between you and me]—is that the Liberal party will by & by be looking in the direction of the Welsh hills for another[?] raid to extricate them out of their troubles.

Not yet heard Redmond.[3] Carson[4] delivering a most unequal speech. Bonar Law[5] rude & silly.

12 April 1912

Home Rule seems to be going well. If the bye-elections don't go heavily against us we shall pull through.

15 April 1912

So you have only £50 to spare. Very well, I will invest that for you. Sorry you have no more available as I think it is quite a good thing I have got.[6]

[1] Sir Robert Morant (1863–1920): permanent secretary of the Board of Education, 1903–11; chairman of National Insurance Commission, 1911–19.

[2] Sir Hamar Greenwood (1870–1948): Liberal member, 1906–22, 'Constitutionalist' member, 1924–9; Chief Secretary for Ireland, 1920–2.

[3] John Edward Redmond (1856–1918): leader of the Irish Parnellite M.P.s at Westminster after Parnell's death, and chairman of the Irish Nationalist Party after 1900.

[4] Sir Edward Carson (1854–1935): Unionist member for Dublin University, 1892–1918, and for Duncairn, 1918–21; First Lord of the Admiralty, 1917–18.

[5] Andrew Bonar Law (1858–1923): born in Canada of Scots–Ulster stock; leader of Unionists, 1911; Colonial Secretary, 1915–16; Chancellor of the Exchequer and leader of the House, 1916–18; Leader of the House, 1919–21; Prime Minister, 1922–3.

[6] This is apparently not a reference to the proposed purchase of shares in the American Marconi company. On 17 April, Lloyd George bought 1,000 shares from Sir Rufus Isaacs. This led to a major crisis which threatened to destroy the careers of both ministers.

18 April 1912

What a terrible disaster the Titanic sinking is. Poor old Stead.[1] His last regret must have been that he could not survive to describe so horrible a catastrophe. Extraordinary mixture of humbug & nobility of character.

Cabinet Committee appointed to enquire into the industrial unrest. I appointed Chairman.

19 April 1912

Well your spec. has come off & you have each of you made another £100. Llwydyn won't sell as she thinks that by holding out she will get more! I also made a few hundreds out of it so we are a little better off than we were at the beginning of the week.

19 April 1912 (later)

I got a cheque from my last Argentina Railway deal today. I have made £567. But the thing I have been talking to you about is a new thing.

26 July 1912

The Tories played us a dirty trick today. They got their men here at 12 & then challenged a division on a motion we had put down to carry out an arrangement with them. Our fellows were not expecting it & had not arrived & we were very nearly beaten. Rufus & I are going to the Opera tonight. Will that suit Madame?

27 July 1912

The split has cost us Crewe.[2] Just as well. We might have lost it without seeing to the disaffection of the Railway men. The Tory barely increased his vote but the Labour man took 2,500.

29 July 1912

I am waiting for a debate on Insurance. It looks now as if the Tories were doing their level best to prevent its coming

---

[1] William T. Stead (1849–1912): editor of the *Pall Mall Gazette*, 1883–90, and founder of the *Review of Reviews*; died in *Titanic* disaster, 15 April 1912.

[2] The Liberals lost Crewe in a by-election by 966; the Labour candidate, J. Holmes, polled 2,485.

on! How different it would have been had the Act been in a muddle. They would have insisted on a debate on its administration. Now they are actually obstructing to keep the debate off. All the same I think it must come on fairly soon.

12 August 1912 (from Marienbad)

I don't mind the Manchester election.[1] As Uncle Lloyd truly says, Hewart was a poor sort of hedging Liberal. He shunned the Land Question. You wait until I start my campaign.

(undated—August 1912)

Just heard the result of the Carmarthen election.[2] Much better than I anticipated. Towyn [Jones] was a thoroughly bad candidate. Heard last night from Llewelyn [Williams]. He has been in the constituency & tells me Towyn was deplorable—full of conceit & vanity. "Myfiaeth" [Egoism]. Llew. will be made a K.C. in October. That is a piece of news for you.

14 August 1912 (from Marienbad)

Insurance news continues good. I dreaded a holiday abroad this year as I pictured the Daily Mail & Telegraph every day full of letters & articles on the "Insurance Muddle". Instead of that they barely mentioned it. I never expected it to work so smoothly at such an early stage.

Lawson, the proprietor of the Telegraph, is here. He does not think the Insurance Act unpopular.

28 August 1912 (from Marienbad)

Doctor has just left me & assures me I am much better. He has given me a good deal of advice as to the future which I must leave to you to enforce. It chiefly relates to food. No sauces of any kind, or pickles. High game to be avoided, tomatoes to be avoided. I must take a great quantity of vegetables—not much meat—no internal organs like kidneys & sweetbreads—& above all plenty of stewed fruit. I must drink between meals twice a day a bottle of mineral water. Take at

---

[1] The Liberals lost Manchester North West in a by-election; their candidate was Gordon Hewart, later to be Lord Chancellor.

[2] The Liberals retained their seat in East Carmarthenshire with a majority of 2,728. Their candidate was the Rev. Towyn Jones (see p. 85, n. 1).

least an hour's exercise every day. That is as far as I can remember. He tells me that if you can take charge of me & enforce these rules I will be three times as healthy & extend my life many years. So I shall judge from the care you take to help me to keep these regulations whether you want to get rid of me or not.

I am surprised Dick should have taken the car down without as much as writing to tell me. I resent it very much. . . .

16 October 1912

Had a glorious row last night. Austen rushed on to the point of a cloaked sword.[1] Our fellows were delighted. They rose & cheered as I left the House. But it has definitely raised the Land Question & it gave the House a glimpse of the savage passions that will be raised by the campaign when it is well on. Home Rule & all else will be swept aside.

I ended deliberately on the word 'game'. This produced pandemonium.

16 October 1912

Just seen a friend of Roosevelt's.[2] Brought a letter from him to me. Says R. is fighting on the Lloyd George programme. He is breakfasting with me tomorrow.

The Pankhursts & Pethicks have fallen out over a fresh development of militarism [*sic*].[3] I wonder what it is? We shall soon know.

16 May 1913

My car has gone to the Newmarket election. We shall be beaten there. Rose was personally very popular in the constituency.[4]

12 August 1913

Ploughing through deputations. Ld. Hugh Cecil came

[1] A debate on the Land Tenure Committee of Inquiry. Lloyd George was in highly belligerent form.

[2] Theodore Roosevelt was campaigning as Progressive candidate for the U.S. presidency in 1912. His 'New Nationalism', with demands for regulatory commissions to deal with trusts and tariffs in a 'scientific manner', was in some ways similar to Lloyd George's programme for his proposed coalition in 1910.

[3] In the Women's Social and Political Union.

[4] The Liberals lost the Newmarket by-election, the Unionist, Denison-Pender being returned with a majority of 851. Lloyd George's car was a present from Sir George Riddell, chairman of the *News of the World*.

before me on a deputation today! He was just a wee bit shy but quite pleasant—so was Bob Cecil in a little passage I had with him over the Budget last night.

Had a very important chat on political situation with P.M. this morning. He told me things that he has not yet informed his colleagues of as to serious talk with King on Home Rule etc.

10 September 1913

We had a most successful breakfast in spite of some ominous rumblings from the Land Taxers—they were as pleasant as they possibly could be. Hemmerde whom we all dreaded was specially helpful. That is what comes of making troubles in advance.[1]

18 September 1913

Spender is coming to see me tonight. He is a flounderer but always good company.

22 September 1913

Winston been & left. I am to meet him also in Scotland. He has had a most remarkable talk at Balmoral with Bonar Law a'r Brenin ynghylch yr Iwerddon.[2] Can't tell you in a letter.

14 January 1914

I came back very late last night. Lunched in Paris with Caillaux[3] the French Finance Minister who was anxious to have a chat with me. He is the French Radical leader, shrewd, smart, but not a great leader.

15 January 1914

As you may imagine I am very fully occupied over this Navy tangle.[4] It is serious & may involve the smash of the

[1] Lloyd George was currently preparing a major new land campaign to deal with rural and urban land alike, and also housing. E. G. Hemmerde had recently won a by-election in North-West Norfolk as an advocate of a single tax on land.
[2] . . . and the King about Ireland.
[3] Joseph Caillaux, former Prime Minister of France, 1911–12.
[4] Lloyd George and Churchill were locked in fierce conflict in January and February 1914 over Lloyd George's attempts to reduce the naval estimates for 1914 and 1915.

Ministry. Last night I had Macnamara¹ with me up till midnight. Winston gave me two hours today. Up to the present I cannot see light. Tonight I am with Sir John Simon² who is entirely with me & if necessary will go with me. I wish you were here. Asquith is returning Monday, then I must take an all important decision—the same decision as Gladstone & Bright had to take.

7 March 1914

House very excited. P.M.'s speech went off very well. General impression *now* in the lobbies is that there will be a settlement. In another hour they may change. It is too early yet to form any judgment.

11 March 1914

I am so delighted to know you are coming up tomorrow. In spite of occasional sulks &c. I cannot do without my round little wife. I am so disappointed you were not in the House last night. By common consent I scored the greatest Parliamentary triumph of my life.³ The party are even today in a state of wild exultation over it. One Tory M.P. said "What fools our fellows were to take him on". F. E. was a ghastly failure. I pounded them flat.

War between Britain and Germany suddenly became imminent in the last week of July 1914 as a result of the Balkan crisis involving Serbia and Austria-Hungary. Lloyd George was widely believed to be the head of the 'peace party' in the cabinet.

27 July 1914

Crisis upon crisis. Ireland is serious but Austria-Servia is pandemonium let loose.⁴ I am off now to Cabinet to consider both.

¹ Thomas J. Macnamara (1861–1931): Liberal member for North Camberwell and then North West Camberwell, 1900–24; Financial Secretary to the Admiralty, 1908–20; Minister of Labour, 1920–22.

² Sir John Simon (1873–1954): Attorney-General, 1913–15; Home Secretary, 1915–16; later successively Foreign Secretary, Home Secretary, Chancellor of the Exchequer and Lord Chancellor in the National Governments, 1931–45.

³ Lloyd George crushed the Unionist motion which condemned 'his repeated inaccuracies and gross personal attacks upon individuals' with a slashing and brilliantly evasive speech (*Parl. Deb.*, 5th ser., Vol. LIX, pp. 1163–79; see Frances Lloyd-George, *The Years that are Past*, pp. 61–7).

⁴ On 25 July Austria-Hungary declared that the Serbian reply to her ultimatum was unsatisfactory and broke off diplomatic relations.

Lloyd George, Dame Margaret, and Megan at the Royal Wedding,
Westminster Abbey, February 1922

Lloyd George, Mr. and Mrs. Asquith at Victoria Station, January 1925

Lady Megan and some Welsh supporters, Llandrindod Wells, *c.* 1930

Lloyd George and
Megan, Cannes,
January 1922

28 July 1914

War trembling in the balance. No one can tell what will or will not happen. I still believe peace will be preserved. The Great Powers will hesitate before they plunge their countries into the hell of war.

Engaged settling Ireland with P.M., Birrell, Redmond & Dillon.

29 July 1914

Foreign outlook most menacing. Very grave Cabinet this morning.

Welsh M.P.'s dinner tonight.

30 July 1914

Overwhelmed with serious business. No light yet.

Found time to give Llwydyn a lunch at the Carlton. Percy & Donald joined us. Delighted to hear about apples.

3 August 1914

I am moving through a nightmare world these days. I have fought hard for peace & succeeded so far in keeping the Cabinet out of it but I am driven to the conclusion that if the small nationality of Belgium is attacked by Germany all my traditions & even prejudices will be engaged on the side of war. I am filled with horror at the prospect. I am even more horrified that I should ever appear to have a share in it but I must bear my share of the ghastly burden though it scorches my flesh to do so.[1]

Britain declared war on Germany at midnight on 4 August.

6 August 1914

In spite of the hardest week since the Budget of 1909— & the most responsible work I ever engaged in, I am glad & grateful to say that I feel quite fit. Last night after continuous conferences with the biggest bankers in this country I felt very fatigued. I have been working right on from 5 a.m. up till midnight.

[1] On 3 August Germany issued an ultimatum to Belgium. This convinced Lloyd George and other waverers in the Cabinet that Britain must intervene. After a Cabinet meeting on the morning of 3 August, mobilization of the British army and navy was sanctioned.

M

Gwilym's choice meets with my complete approval. Any other course would have marked him down as a shirker & he is much too brave & fearless a boy ever to be open to a suspicion of that kind. He must not be rushed by excitable youths around him to volunteering for the front without first consulting me before he takes so serious a step. If the country be in danger we must all make sacrifices but we are a long way off that. There is no dearth of men.

I am sending you the first issue of the new Bank Notes.[1] I can only get four. But these are the very first issued. I want to give one to Megan—Llwydyn—Gwilym & little William Garthcelyn. I have no time now to endorse them. They must not change them. The fact of their being the first will make them one day exceedingly interesting.

Fondest love

D.

The Governor of the Bank is waiting for me.

7 August 1914

My arrangements to save a financial panic have been a complete success—a real triumph—the first great British victory of the war.[2] I hear the Ship Insurance scheme is also doing first rate. . . . Belgians are doing brilliantly.

7 August 1914 (later)

Still "conferring and advising at great length" to quote language of Bills of Costs. Dined last night at Lord Granard's to meet Italian Ambassador & Kitchener. Former very Pro British.

The German defeat although greatly exaggerated in the extent by the papers is in its effect greater than they portray. It has delayed by days the blow against France & given the French time to perfect their arrangements—still more it has bucked them up tremendously & that counts more with Frenchmen than with any nation except the Welsh.

So far the fleet has not done well. The way they allowed the Goeben to escape is disgracefully inefficient.

[1] Lloyd George dealt in a masterful fashion with the financial emergency resulting from the outbreak of war. Among several other measures, new Treasury ten-shilling and one-pound notes were sanctioned on 6 August, and the Bank of England empowered to exceed the legal maximum fiduciary issue.

[2] A sign of this success was the reduction of Bank Rate from 10 per cent to 5 per cent on 7 August.

Still it is too early yet to form any conclusion. There will be many ups & downs in this hell wheel.

11 August 1914

Mewn gwaith diderfyn.[1] Bankers, Manufacturers, Discounters &c. . . . They are pressing the territorials to volunteer for the war. We mustn't do that just yet. We are keeping the sea for France—that ought to suffice here for the moment especially as we are sending 100,000 men to help her to bear the first brunt of the attack. That is all that counts for Russia will come in soon. I am dead against carrying on a war of conquest to crush Germany for the benefit of Russia. Beat the German Junker but no war on the German people &c. I am not going to sacrifice my nice boy for that purpose. You must write Wil telling him on no account to be bullied into volunteering abroad.

[1] In never-ending work.

CHAPTER 8

Wartime and Peacetime Leadership

(1914–22)

Until August 1914 Lloyd George's reputation was essentially that of a left-wing radical and a critic of society. Now that total war had begun, he rapidly acquired a far wider authority throughout the nation. This was heralded by a famous address to an audience of London Welshmen on 19 September 1914 in which he appealed for recruits to defend 'the little five-foot-five nations' against Germany, 'the road hog of Europe'. By the end of the year he was the one minister in Asquith's government whose standing had unquestionably been enhanced by the war. But by the following spring he was deeply disillusioned by the war policies of his colleagues. He appealed for 'a definite victory somewhere' and warmly supported the expedition to the Dardanelles as part of a wider, peripheral strategy against the 'soft under-belly' of the central powers in south-east Europe. Widespread criticism of the Asquith ministry reached a climax in 17–24 May 1915 when, after a sudden political crisis at the Admiralty, Asquith remodelled his government on a coalition basis, bringing in Bonar Law and the Unionists, and also the Labour Party. It was once claimed that this first coalition originated in a plot by Lloyd George and the Unionists. In fact, his letters show that he was basically loyal to Asquith and his own party throughout the affair. His agreement to move from the treasury to the Ministry of Munitions, against the wishes of his wife and of Uncle Lloyd, was of great service to Asquith, as the premier acknowledged.

At the munitions ministry, Lloyd George achieved brilliant success in revolutionizing the supply of shells and other weapons of war. He was also very active in transforming welfare conditions in government arms factories. But he was mainly concerned to promote a more vigorous prosecution of the war. For him, this was symbolized by the adoption of universal male conscription. After a lengthy crisis that dragged on from October 1915 to April 1916, this was finally implemented, but at grave cost to the unity of the administration and to the morale of the parliamentary Liberal Party. Relations between Asquith and Lloyd George became far more tense. Yet Asquith was still greatly dependent on his Minister of Munitions. It was Lloyd George whom he asked to attempt a final settlement of the Irish question after the suppression of the Irish republican rising in Easter 1916. Lloyd George failed to find common ground between the Irish Nationalists and the Ulster Unionists, but it was Asquith's rather than Lloyd George's reputation that suffered as a result.

The unity of the government was further undermined in June 1916 when Kitchener was drowned at sea on a mission to Russia. After some delay Lloyd George succeeded him as Secretary of State for War. The Allied forces continued to meet with persistent failure on land and sea, and Lloyd George became more and more pessimistic about the prospect of victory. From 20 November onwards, he met Bonar Law and Carson, the effective leader of the Unionist backbenchers, in an attempt to create a supreme War Committee to replace the existing Cabinet system. On 1 December their scheme was presented to Asquith who made many criticisms. However, by the end of 3 December Asquith appeared to have accepted a modified form of the scheme. Quite unexpectedly, Asquith threw it over early on 4 December. In the ensuing crisis, he lost his support among the Unionists, while some of his own Liberal backbenchers and also the bulk of the Labour Party made it clear that they preferred Lloyd George as a war leader. The outcome was that Lloyd George finally kissed hands as Prime Minister on 7 December, with Asquith staying outside the government, and the Liberal Party deeply divided.

Lloyd George's wartime premiership saw an almost endless series of crises at home and on the front. It was a time of considerable domestic strain for him. Frances Stevenson, who now lived in a new flat in central London, was firmly installed as his private secretary, and relations with Mrs. Lloyd George became increasingly frigid. His two sons, Richard and Gwilym, were both serving as officers on the western front. Most shattering of all, Uncle Lloyd who had guided Lloyd George's destinies from his earliest ventures into politics in the early 1880s, died in February 1917 at the age of eighty-two. Lloyd George now had to face a depressing sequence of disasters virtually alone. Little went right in 1917, while in February 1918 he almost fell from power during a crisis that led to the resignation of General Sir William Robertson, chief of the imperial general staff. Another crisis, resulting from disclosures by General Maurice in the press about the numbers of men serving on the western front, led to an anxious debate in the House on 9 May 1918. Only a brilliant counter-attack by the Prime Minister beat back Asquith and his other opponents. At last, in September the tide of battle turned in favour of the Allied armies in France, now reinforced by the Americans, while Germany plunged into internal turmoil. On 11 November an armistice agreement was signed in the forest of Compiègne. Lloyd George and Bonar Law then held an immediate election on a coalition basis, the notorious 'coupon election' which the government won with the largest majority of modern times. Lloyd George seemed at the height of his power, indeed almost impregnable.

His peacetime premiership went well at first. The peace conference at Paris was thought by many to be a success, combining retribution from Germany with liberal and honourable terms. At home, some enlightened social reforms were passed. But from the autumn of 1919, the Lloyd George coalition was struggling, and it is surprising that it survived as long as it it did. An attempt at 'fusion' between Coalition Liberals and the Unionists in March 1920 came to nothing, and rebellion by the Unionist rank-and-file became more and more dangerous. They found a reluctant leader in Bonar Law: he resigned from the government on grounds of ill-health in

March 1921, but unexpectedly recovered and became henceforth a focus for 'die-hard' rebellion. On most fronts, the Lloyd George government, totally dominated as it was by the imperious personality of its leader, met with scant success. Repeated international conferences, from Paris in 1919 to Genoa in April–May 1922, intended to secure a settlement of the political and economic dislocation of post-war Europe, largely failed. At home, unemployment mounted, the cost of living soared, and there were many lengthy strikes. In April 1921, with the Pyrrhic victory gained over the miners on 'Black Friday', a general strike was narrowly averted. Ireland was another intractable problem. The retaliatory policy of the Black and Tans there encouraged virtual civil war with the Sinn Feiners. Lloyd George finally concluded a settlement with the Irish leaders on 5–6 December 1921 but this only reinforced Unionist pressure for a break with the Coalition. In 1922 further problems mounted. There was disaffection in the Cabinet over Lloyd George's aim of granting formal recognition to Soviet Russia, while in the country the so-called 'scandal' over the sale of honours further sapped the government's reputation. The occasion for Lloyd George's downfall finally came with a crisis in Asia Minor after the Turks had smashed through the Greek armies and threatened war with Britain at Chanak. Lloyd George found little support overseas; while, for Unionist critics such as Stanley Baldwin, Chanak was the breaking-point. Even though war with Turkey was averted, at a meeting at the Carlton Club on 19 October the Unionist members of parliament voted down their own leaders, and broke with the Coalition. Alone, apart from his small band of loyal Coalition Liberals, Lloyd George resigned. He was never within measurable distance of power again.

5 September 1914

French & English have turned on the Germans & there is fierce fighting going on along the whole line. So far going well. Kitchener thinks Joffre's plan clever.

8 September 1914

The great French attack[1] is developing all right. But it is much too early yet. The best news is that the French have cashiered three of their generals & put better men in.

10 September 1914

The great fight is doing well so far but yet far from being decided.

I am getting on to a rattling good speech—at least I think so—for the Queens Hall Saturday week.

11 September 1914

Prysur [Busy]. The fight going on well especially at the

---

[1] On the German position on the Marne.

British end. The enemy there getting demoralized. We picked several of them up drunk.

19 September 1914

The meeting is over. Great meeting.[1] You can judge of the speech. I am engaged in a conference with Lord Plymouth & others, to raise a Welsh Army Corps.

28 September 1914

Row ofnadwy efo Kitchener heddyw ynghylch Noncon Chaplains.[2] Spoke out savagely. Carried Cabinet & got my way.

20 October 1914

Wedi dod yn ol yn fyw [Have come back alive]. Went right to the front—the Germans were shelling the village close by. We got into the French trenches which were not being shelled at that moment. Saw General de Castelnau who is in command of an Army of 350,000. He took me on to the battle line. The German trenches were 1400 to 1500 yards from the spot we got to. We also saw General Foch, the second in command to General Joffre. These three men are the greatest generals in the French army. I went to the English headquarters. Had a great time. Gave me a new idea of what is happening. It is *stalemate*. We cannot turn them out of their trenches & they cannot turn us out. They can only frighten Belgians — French & English stand their ground. The Belgians have been driven back today.

Dick is being sent to Carnarvonshire to recruit. You will see him.

26 October 1914

Diwrnod fel pob dydd prysur iawn.[3] John Williams

---

[1] This was Lloyd George's famous speech to an audience of London Welshmen at the Queen's Hall, 19 September, in which he called for recruits to defeat Germany, 'the road hog of Europe'. It enormously enhanced his national stature, although Lloyd George was at first disappointed by his reception (A. J. P. Taylor (ed.), *Lloyd George: a Diary by Frances Stevenson*, p. 2).

[2] Tremendous row with Kitchener today about Noncon. Chaplains. (At first Kitchener refused to appoint nonconformist chaplains to the armed services, on the same basis as Anglicans. Lloyd George forced him to give way.)

[3] A very busy day like every day.

Brynsiencyn[1] just left here. Glad Dick has arrived. Wales has done gloriously so far.

27 October 1914

News from front distinctly good. Just had a wire in from Sir John French[2] that Joffre hopes to attack them today & tomorrow. They think the Germans are discouraged by the last few days fighting. They have suffered frightful losses. So have we, but the French are bringing reinforcements up but the Germans are for the moment doing badly in the East & cannot spare men.

28 October 1914

Stand up fight with Kitchener today over Welsh army.[3] Cabinet with me. I gave it him quite straight from the shoulder.

30 October 1914

Returned from a most satisfactory interview with Kitchener. The row did him good. He conceded everything. All Dick's points are settled. He can start at once. Artillery & Engineers can be trained in England with regulars & rejoin the Army Corps. I asked him to make Owen Thomas[4] the Brigadier for N. Wales. He signed it on the spot. If Dick would like promotion, Thomas appoints his own officers.

Secret. The Welsh Territorials are to be sent to India so K. says. I hope Wil's regiment will be included.

2 November 1914

Just been on the phone with Dick. He is full of his job. General Owen Thomas ought to promote him—I think he is going to make him a Captain!

3 November 1914

Hot fighting at the front. By no means decided. We are being hard pressed.

[1] Rev. John Williams (1854–1921): Calvinistic Methodist minister of Brynsiencyn, Anglesey; he held belligerently pro-war views, and caused much resentment by preaching in Welsh pulpits in full military uniform.

[2] Sir John French (1852–1925): Commander-in-Chief of the British Expeditionary Force, 1914–15; created Earl of Ypres, 1922.

[3] Lloyd George vigorously attacked Kitchener's refusal to create a separate Welsh division; again he won his point.

[4] Brigadier-General Sir Owen Thomas (1858–1923): in charge of recruitment in North Wales in 1914; later Labour, then Independent member for Anglesey 1918–23.

4 January 1915

Been to the Bank of England. Fear I must go over to Paris to meet the French Finance Minister.

News that a great Zeppelin raid is being meditated on London within the next few days. I fear it is true. Winston has circulated a document saying so.

By the start of 1915 Lloyd George was severely critical of the strategy of stalemate on the western front and urging a new attack on the Austrians through the Balkans or the Levant.

6 January 1915

No news. Tomorrow am going to consider the whole plan of campaign at a War Council. I insisted on its being called & I have proposed a totally new plan of operations.[1] That will force them to look at the situation. The usual thing is happening. The generals have fallen out (K. & F.) & the Admiralty & War Office are quarrelling.

12 January 1915

I have seen Ivor Philipps[2] & confirmed Gwilym's appointment with him if P. gets the Generalship of the Division. Have seen K. about that now & think it will be all right. Shall feel relieved from a good deal of worry when it is fixed up. Am off now to see Sir John French who is over here.

6 March 1915

I have got K. to promise 100 rifles for each battalion of the first 12 (not for the extra 5). They will be there soon.

11 March 1915

Diwrnod prysur iawn iawn etto [Very, very busy day again]. Now the Cabinet have asked me to take in hand the Labour problems—in addition to Munitions of War.

[1] On 1 January 1915 Lloyd George submitted a major memorandum to the War Council in which he criticized Allied strategy and called for 'a definite victory somewhere'. At the War Council on 8 January, he urged unsuccessfully a new attack on 'southern Austria' (Martin Gilbert, *Winston S. Churchill*, Vol. III, Heinemann, 1971, pp. 243–5).

[2] Major-General Sir Ivor Philipps (1861–1940): Liberal member for Southampton, 1906–22; commander of the Welsh Division in France, 1915–16.

12 March 1915

McKenna has sadly muddled the Disestablishment business.[1] As a matter of fact he is giving nothing away in his Bill but he ought to have consulted the Welsh M.P.'s. That would have put it right.

Tomorrow night I dine with Winston & Kitchener. There are big things coming to a point during the next few days. Wednesday I have a great Labour conference here.[2] Cabinet forced me to take this job in hand. I wish I could come down instead as I need a week's rest.

15 March 1915

Just spoken on the Welsh Church Bill. Went for the Welsh M.P.'s. They are a poor lot of hounds. They thoroughly misrepresent the Bill. It is a *very* small concession for the sake of unity.

14 April 1915

Llew[elyn Williams] is here giving me a most interesting account of the machinations of the Welsh members. Dyn a helpo'r crachod bach.[3]

16 April 1915

Up to the eyes in *Liquor*.[4]

[1] The Welsh members protested fiercely at McKenna's proposal to postpone the operation of the Welsh Disestablishment Act until six months after the end of the war. In spite of pressure from Lloyd George, they forced McKenna to withdraw. Lloyd George tried to persuade his friend, Sir William Robertson Nicoll of the *British Weekly*, to explain the benefits of the settlement to his fellow nonconformists. Lloyd George wrote:

'It practically closes this long chapter. If this Bill goes through by consent religious equality is an accomplished fact in Wales, and the Tory Party will be as anxious as the Liberals to treat it as such. For the first time there is an atmosphere of settlement about the question, and it is a settlement on exceedingly cheap terms for Nonconformity. . . . I strongly urge that we should rather treat this Bill as a final disposal of the quarrel between Welsh Nonconformity and this alien Church.' (Lloyd George to Robertson Nicoll, 16 March 1915, Nicoll MSS.). In fact, the question dragged on tiresomely until 1919.

[2] This conference was to negotiate the so-called 'treasury agreement' with the unions.

[3] God help the little scabs! (Later in the year Llewelyn Williams quarrelled violently, and irrevocably, with Lloyd George over conscription and a friendship of over twenty years was shattered.)

[4] Lloyd George proposed various schemes to curb the drink trade, either through complete prohibition or through state purchase of the liquor trade. The sole legacies were the diluted quality of 'Lloyd George's beer' and the 'King's Pledge' of total abstinence (which the King was virtually alone in taking seriously).

19 April 1915

Endless difficulties about Drink. He is the toughest of all foes. But I am getting at him.

22 April 1915

Got on uncommonly well yesterday in the House. Kitchener delighted. Considering that I have been his severest critic on munitions I treated him generously in defending the War Office yesterday.

On 17 May 1915 a new political crisis developed, after Lord Fisher, the First Sea Lord, had resigned following repeated conflicts with Churchill. Bonar Law went to see Lloyd George to propose an all-party coalition. In the event, Asquith seized the initiative himself and formed a coalition under his premiership. Lloyd George went to the Ministry of Munitions.

20 May 1915

Our fate still trembling in the balance. Tories want me in War Office—*but I will not go.*[1]

21 May 1915

Still engaged as an assistant Cabinet maker to the P.M. All day at it & we meet the Tories at 11.30 tomorrow. What will happen afterwards no one can tell. So far I remain here. I have declined the War Office. Winston fighting hard to remain at the Admiralty—has been told peremptorily he must go. At last he accepts the situation.

24 May 1915

Yesterday I had a procession of callers all day—beginning with Lord Northcliffe(!)[2] who kept me all the morning—

---

[1] A complex political crisis exploded on 17 May when, after a clash between Churchill and Fisher at the Admiralty which led to the latter's resignation, Asquith entered into negotiations with Bonar Law to form a coalition government. Far from leading a plot against Asquith, Lloyd George, as these letters show, was of immense service to him by declining various Unionist offers (including a suggestion of the premiership) and in agreeing to accept the Ministry of Munitions, thus leaving the Treasury free for another Liberal, McKenna. (There is an admirable discussion of this crisis in Cameron Hazlehurst, *Politicians at War, July 1914– May 1915*, Cape, 1971, pp. 227 ff. Also see Martin Gilbert, op. cit., pp. 438–73; A. J. P. Taylor, *Beaverbrook*, Hamish Hamilton, 1972, pp. 92–5.)

[2] Alfred Harmsworth, Lord Northcliffe (1865–1922): founder of the *Daily Mail* and later owner of *The Times*; Lloyd George's relations with him went through many vicissitudes.

McKenna, Montagu.[1] Riddell came to supper. I had also a visit from the French representative of the War Office here urging the French were most anxious I should remain at the Treasury as Ribot was a weak man. He said they regarded me as the strongest man in the Ministry. We have not settled yet. They are fighting for Treasury or Munitions. I am opposed to their getting either. I have proposed that the P.M. should take this place temporarily whilst I organise Munitions or that Runciman[2] should take Munitions. They oppose both but I think the latter will be forced upon them.

25 May 1915

It was found impossible after all to arrange for the P.M. to hold Exchequer during the time I am occupied in organising Munitions so McKenna is to come here *temporarily*. I am to return as soon as I place the other business on a sound footing. I am glad of this. Exchequer & Munitions would have killed me—& that is not good enough. The *Tories* insisted that McK. should only hold this place temporarily—they would only agree on that condition. They were willing I should hold it but if I went altogether they claimed it for Bonar Law. 11 Downing St. I still occupy.

26 May 1915

Judging by your & Uncle Lloyd's letters you will disapprove of my action in taking this new job. I am quite convinced that I have done the right thing & that you will agree with me when I have time to put the matter before you.

I enclose a very affectionate letter Asquith sent me. He doesn't know that I refused the Premiership from the Tories.

(enclosed) *H. H. Asquith to David Lloyd George, 25 May 1915*[3]
My dear Lloyd George,
    I cannot let this troubled & tumultuous chapter in our

---

[1] Edwin Montagu (1879–1924): Minister of Munitions, 1916; Secretary of State for India, 1917–22; was about to marry Asquith's intimate friend, Venetia Stanley.

[2] Walter Runciman (1870–1949): Liberal member for various constituencies, 1899–1931; then National Liberal member, 1931–7; President of the Board of Education, 1908–11, of the Board of Agriculture, 1911–14, and of the Board of Trade, 1914–16, and 1931–7; created Viscount Runciman, 1937.

[3] Asquith's letter is printed in David Lloyd George's *War Memoirs*, Vol. I between pp. 234 and 235.

history close without trying to let you know what an incalculable help & support I have found in you all through. I shall never forget your devotion, your unselfishness, your powers of resource, what is (after all) the best of all things your self-forgetfulness.

These are the rare things that make the drudgery and squalor of politics, with its constant revelation of the large part played by petty & personal motives, endurable, and give to its drabness a lightning streak of nobility.

I thank you with all my heart.

Always yours affectionately

H. H. ASQUITH

10 August 1915

I am working through a series of conferences with Shell Committees from different areas. Most useful.

I am most disappointed not to have heard from you what the doctor's report was about Uncle Lloyd. Weeks of diarrhoea would pull down the strength of a man of 25 & he must have the constitution of a rhinoceros to have stood it. All the same he looked pale & I have been most unhappy about it ever since. James Venmore said his presiding over the Commission was the most impressive thing he ever heard. He said that he quite understood where the nephew had come from. I never heard anything that impressed me in the same way.

Insist on his seeing a doctor & taking the medicine. He must do it for my sake—otherwise I cannot go on with my work. I shall be so anxious.

11 August 1915

Dardanelles news not quite as satisfactory today. The Welsh Division been in action. How anxious we should have been if the boys had remained in the Territorial regiments. They were in the fighting & horrible fighting it has been.

16 August 1915

Just been giving an a/c of Munitions to a Cabinet Committee. They were appalled at the War Office delay. Dining with Winston tonight.

18 August 1915

Welsh Division rather badly cut up in Dardanelles & did

not do well. Had a fool of a general. So glad & thankful boys have left it.

To Megan Lloyd George, *14 September 1915*

The sunshine has gone since you left & now we have cloudy skies & a great dismal outlook. Bring the sunshine back as soon as you can, little sweet. I am sending you the Cloister & the Hearth. It is one of the most delightful stories ever written. . . . Today I had Winston Churchill, Sir Edward Carson, Bonar Law & F. E. Smith to lunch. We had a most useful & important discussion about the war. Tonight I dine with Lady Randolph Churchill. As it is so cloudy I mean to risk the Zeps.

Between October 1915 and April 1916, the Cabinet was deeply torn by conflict about the adoption of universal male conscription. Lloyd George was now an ardent compulsionist, but Asquith and most other Liberal ministers were very reluctant.

1 November 1915

Cabinet over. P.M. & Balfour between them kept us talking about something else for hours—*deliberately*.[1] We meet tomorrow morning for a further talk—or rather to begin the other topic.

Do you think I can honestly take any other course than the one I have indicated. Insist on his redeeming his pledge immediately & if he does not then say I cannot go on with him. We have it off for months. Wire me Downing St. whether you agree or not. Wire early as the Cabinet is at 11.30.

Off to dine with Rufus who is alone.

27 December 1915

Cabinet pwysig iawn y pnawn.[2] P.M. & his gang trying to sneak out of their pledges. If they do I wash my hands of the poltroons & come out. I have made up my mind. My path is clear in front of me & as you know under these conditions I am always happy, whatever happens. By 5 p.m. I may be plain Lloyd George.

---

[1] This Cabinet was preoccupied by the conscription issue. The following day, 2 November, Asquith gave a pledge that married men would not be called up under the Derby scheme until almost all unmarried men of military age had joined up, whether voluntarily or not. This failed to satisfy Lloyd George.

[2] A very important Cabinet this afternoon. (Later that day, Lloyd George wrote to Asquith threatening to resign unless all unmarried men were conscripted at once.)

28 December 1915

Cabinet satisfactory. P.M. dropped on the right side. Compulsion for unmarried men. There may be resignations. Not certain. Simon, Runciman & McKenna threaten—but [I] doubt it.

30 December 1915

This morning a Major Butterworth came to see me after breakfast at Downing St. He is a major of the Engineers & took Dick into the firing line for the first time. He was quite cool. He was taken first of all within 350 yards of the Germans but insisted on going to the front line—150 yards off the Germans. He placed his men, gave them orders & carried out his work calmly and efficiently. He had a very high opinion of him. The Germans shelled them but hit no one. Dick was to be 8 days on the job but as this was 10 days ago he thinks Dick must be out of it now. I feel so proud of him.

Sir William Robertson[1] told me last night he saw Gwilym.

31 December 1915

Cabinet yn mynd ymlaen. McKenna & Runciman yn ceisio tori'r ymrwymiad trwy drws y cefn.[2]

Saw Hamar Greenwood. Just back from France. Saw Dick. In very good form. Simon wedi resignio [has resigned].[3]

5 January 1916

P.M. delivered an adroit but not a powerful speech for compulsion. Simon a very able lawyer's speech. The opposition will be but a minority—and that not a large altho' very noisy one.

10 January 1916

Have to go to the House as there is to be a debate on suppression of Forward.[4] Have a clinking case.

---

[1] General Sir William Robertson (1860–1933): Chief of the Imperial Staff, 1915–18; in permanent conflict with Lloyd George after 1916.

[2] Cabinet going on. McKenna and Runciman trying to break their undertaking through the back door.

[3] Sir John Simon, the Home Secretary, resigned over conscription.

[4] The Glasgow journal of the I.L.P., edited by Tom Johnston.

11 January 1916

Last night was a smasher for the "harriers". They'll give me less trouble in future.

18 April 1916

I have made another great effort to keep them together.[1] Put a fresh proposal before them. So far things look promising —but I am not sure of success. If there is a break it won't be my fault & I think the Cabinet will feel that. We meet again tomorrow. Sir William Robertson just left. He fully approves my new plan. Henderson opposes & I have no doubt McKenna will fight hard against it. P.M. friendly—so far.

26 April 1916

All's well. Gardiner's[2] attack resented even by those who agreed with him.

28 April 1916

An important Cabinet summoned for tomorrow evening so I must put off my meeting for a week. I shall be down Wednesday or Thursday if I can manage it. There is great excitement over my speech. Press very excited. Yesterday's collapse in Parliament a complete justification of the line I took & the Cabinet feel it.

Few letters from Lloyd George to his wife survive for the later months of 1916. In May and June he was mainly involved in an unsuccessful attempt to resolve the Irish question. When Kitchener was drowned at sea, Lloyd George eventually succeeded him as Secretary of State for War on 6 July 1916. In the autumn he became more and more discouraged by the lack of success on the western front; between 20 November and 1 December he had a series of meetings with Bonar Law and Sir Edward Carson which led to a proposal to create a new supreme War Committee, of which the Prime Minister would not be a member, to conduct strategy. The outcome was a complex political crisis which led to Lloyd George's succeeding Asquith as Prime Minister on 7 December and the creation of an all-party War Cabinet. The Liberal Party was henceforth deeply divided. In 1917 the war continued to go badly on the western front; one lone source of encouragement was the entry of the United States into the War in April. Among many domestic difficulties was the enforced resignation of the leader of the Labour Party, Arthur Henderson, from the War Cabinet in August.

[1] Lloyd George was again very near to resigning over conscription. The next day, 19 April, over 100 Liberal members reaffirmed their support for Asquith's leadership. Nevertheless, in May complete conscription was finally introduced.

[2] A. G. Gardiner (1865–1946): editor of the *Daily News*, 1902–19, and a vehement partisan of Asquith.

Dame Margaret campaigning, Taunton, July 1922

Lloyd George launches his new Land Campaign, Killerton Park, Devon,
September 1925

Lloyd George and Dame Margaret, December 1920

4 August 1916

[He has been to see the King at Buckingham Palace.]

Had long chat on things at the War Office. He is much more interested in petty personal details here than he was in the turning out of hundreds of guns & millions of shells. Dining tonight with Winston to meet Sir Ernest Cassel.[1] I am anxious to know the situation in Germany.

26 August 1916

I am relieved to hear that the Manchester specialist is to see Uncle Lloyd. Couldn't you persuade him to spend the fortnight at Brynawelon & force him to *rest*. I want him to try rest. You will find it difficult to persuade him to give up his Criccieth jaunts—but they are bad for him. Rest is Nature's sovereign remedy & he has not really tried it. He might do it with you all about him. I also want *you* to see Dr. Brocklebank & tell him how anxious I am personally about Uncle Lloyd's condition & how very desirous I am to see him put right. Do hen gariad [old darling] put your back into this job & I will love you ten times as much if you pull the old boy through. . . . Tell Uncle Lloyd there is an article about him & me in the Figaro, the great French newspaper. Charming.

1 September 1916

I am very pleased with Dr. Brocklebank's report. It has given me great relief and satisfaction. Now you must feed him up. I am so very grateful for the way you are looking [after] the dear old boy. We were evidently on the wrong tack in assuming that his digestion was weak. Olwen tells me he is to get meat. Let him have it. What about chicken?

I am off to France on Monday for a series of conferences about guns, transport &c. David Davies[2] is spending Sunday with me.

I agree it would be better for Uncle Lloyd to go down for

---

[1] Sir Ernest Cassell (1852–1921): financier, patron of the arts and of horse-racing. At this period, Lloyd George was helping Churchill to collect material to be presented before the Dardanelles Commission.

[2] David Davies (1880–1944): millionaire Welsh industrialist and philanthropist; Liberal member for Montgomeryshire, 1906–29; a member of Lloyd George's 'garden suburb', 1916–17, but then quarrelled with him; later devoted most of his time to the League of Nations Union; created Baron Davies of Llandinam, 1932.

N

a part of the day. That is Brocklebank's view. But I want that room made more comfortable. I have bought him a nice new chair which he can set in rest his legs upon [*sic*] & read papers & books. I am sending it down addressed to you at Cric. Tell them to take it to Uncle Lloyd's office. Have a nice hearthrug for him also. You can buy it there.

2 September 1916

I love you so much for looking after Uncle Lloyd. I hear it makes him so happy & he has always been devoted to you—always.

22 December 1916

Dog tired. Yesterday was my hardest day & today I did not get my lunch until 2.20 having asked Dalziel & Neil Primrose[1] to lunch. . . . Clearing things up. Parliament up. General feeling we have started well.

Mrs. Asquith yn beio Bonham a John Gulland am y cwymp![2]

31 July 1917

Dyma fi yn ol etto ond yn nghanol helbulon diri.[3] Henderson has now put us into the soup & there is no knowing what will happen. All done during my absence.

2 August 1917

Had a great triumph last night. Henderson wretched performance—added to our difficulties.

3 August 1917

Gwilym left this morning in excellent spirits, not at all sorry to join his battery—& come what may I would rather have him there where so many gallant boys are risking their

[1] Neil Primrose (1882–1917): Liberal member, 1910–17, and a government whip, 1916–17; a son of Lord Rosebery.

[2] Mrs. Asquith blaming Bonham [-Carter] and John Gulland for the downfall! (Sir Maurice Bonham-Carter (1880–1960) was Asquith's private secretary, 1910–16: John Gulland (1864–1920) was the Liberal chief whip, 1915–17.)

[3] Here I am again in the midst of innumerable troubles. (Arthur Henderson had gravely embarrassed the government by attending a socialist conference in Paris with Ramsay MacDonald. He was forced to leave the government after 'the doormat incident' on 11 August.)

lives for their country than have him here in safety. So would you I know hen gariad [old darling].

9 August 1917

Neville Chamberlain wedi resigno a diolch i Dduw am hynny.[1]

11 August 1917

Turned Henderson out. He behaved abominably.

13 August 1917

Got through the Henderson business today well. Henderson a pitiable failure.

18 August 1917

Had a very trying time last few weeks. Fighting almost with back to wall. Think I have for the time beaten off the attacks.

5 January 1918 (misdated 1917)

I have been delivering the most important speech I have yet made—to the Trades Union Conference.[2] I read out a carefully prepared statement on War aims. This morning I breakfasted with Asquith. Very friendly both. The statement went off uncommonly well & pleased the delegates.

8 January 1918

The speech is still the sensation. It has rallied the Allies but it does not mean peace. Never thought it would. It has just placed us on the sound footing for war. It may weaken Austria.

5 February 1918

I am literally overwhelmed with work on my return. Rows with A.S.E.[3]—food—Ireland & a sulky military staff.

The dismissal of General Robertson as Chief of the Imperial General Staff led to another political crisis which Lloyd George barely survived.

[1] Neville Chamberlain has resigned and thank God for that. (Chamberlain had been director of Military Service. He and Lloyd George kept up a steady vendetta ever afterwards—down to May 1940.)

[2] A major speech on British war aims to the Trades Union Congress at the Caxton Hall, Westminster on 5 January 1918.

[3] The Amalgamated Society of Engineers.

11 February 1918

Revolution going on here. Robertson sent off to Versailles & Wilson brought here as Chief of the Staff.[1] "Wully"[2] kicking hard. But I had had enough of him for a long time. He was in constant intrigue with Asquith.

13 February 1918

Trying to throw off a bad chest cold whilst settling three or four bad crises. Yesterday in the House was unpleasant & I was not at my best. The Asquithites mean mischief. I have always thought they would when they had a chance. It will take me all my strength to fight them. But I mean to do it.

21 February 1918

The Asquiths were routed. Doctor *ordered* rest on Friday. I have had *none*.

22 March 1918

We are all here full of anxiety about this terrible battle—undoubtedly the greatest the world has ever seen.[3] So far nothing much has happened. We have been forced to retire from our front lines but that always happens in an attack of this kind. It will go on for weeks & might well end the war.

26 March 1918

Overwhelmed with work & anxiety over this terrible battle. Have had 3 or 4 days of the most worrying time of my life. At moments things looked desparate [*sic*]. Looking better just now. Germans are making for Paris. That gives us at any rate some breathing space. Our fellows have been fine.

27 March 1918

Just holding our own. Next three days—in fact next week most critical. If they get Amiens we shall be in the tightest

[1] Lloyd George manœuvred Robertson into having to choose between remaining as C.I.G.S. and moving to the new post of Military Adviser at Versailles. Eventually by 18 February it was announced in the press that Robertson would accept neither post; General Sir Henry Wilson succeeded him as C.I.G.S.

[2] Robertson.

[3] On 21 March the Germans began a massive offensive against the British position on the Cambrai–St. Quentin line in north-east France.

place we have ever yet been in. But they have not yet had Amiens.

30 March 1918

Still critical. I hear that there is another tremendous attack now being prepared by the Germans on the French reserves. Much depends on what happens to this.

Pasg ofnadwy [Awful Easter]. We are doing our best here. I am engaged in waking up the Americans—with some success.

1 April 1918

In the battle we are holding our own better. But we are not out of it yet.

I am getting America at last to do something. Hope [to] God it is not too late.

2 April 1918

Y peth goreu ddigwydodd hyd yn hyn ydyw'r trefniad gyda'r America. Cawn 300,000 neu 400,000 hwyrach o dynion i'n helpu ni o hyn i fis Gorphenaf—pery'r frwydr hyd hynny.[1]

4 April 1918

Back from France.[2] Arrived about 2 this morning. All the French generals, Clemenceau & Haig. The French were more confident about the situation on their side. Haig more anxious. I am still more anxious after seeing Haig & his Chief of Staff—both of them very second rate men.

10 April 1918

Had a hard task yesterday.[3] We shall have great difficulties with the Bill in the House & after. If we fail to carry it we should have to resign or dissolve—the latter is very difficult in the middle of a great battle.

Things not going well in France, but they may improve. Our generals are second rate men fighting first class brains.

---

[1] The best thing that's happened so far is the arrangement with America. We'll have 300,000 or 400,000 men to help us, perhaps, from now to the month of July—the battle will last till then.

[2] From a military conference with Clemenceau and Foch at Beauvais.

[3] On the Military Service Bill (which included conscription for Ireland).

15 April 1918

News better these last two days. No fighting today so far
& every day now counts in our favour as the French are hurry-
ing up. Saturday & Sunday's fighting saved us. But we are by
no means through. Will have anxious days & weeks still in
front.

24 April 1918

French news not quite so good. We have had just a little
'biff' south of Amiens. Had it not been so near Amiens would
have had no importance. The naval news good. Don't you
think so? We have a nasty situation over the air quarrel. *Very*
difficult.

4 May 1918

Came back full of fight over Ireland, finding all my colleagues except Austen had funked.

30 July 1918

News from the front very good. Believe the German offensive this year is broken. Irish offensive last night also a failure![1]

*In September the tide of battle on the western front at last turned decisively in favour
of the Allied forces. Lloyd George and Bonar Law then took steps to fight a general
election on a Coalition basis as soon as hostilities ended. The 'coupon election', which
saw Lloyd George's Coalition Liberals and the Asquithian Independent Liberals in
bitter opposition, took place in December. Mrs. Lloyd George played an active part
in the campaign.*

13 December 1918

You have done brilliantly. Your tours have been *the*
feature of the campaign. You have been flitting about though
so much that I found it impossible to know where to write you.

I think the election is all right. The Unionist headquarters
expect a majority of over 200. The factors are so uncertain that
I cannot form any estimate. I shall be very surprised if we are
beaten. I shall be surprised if we don't get a majority of over
100. If it is over 120 then I shall be content. If it is under that
I shall be disappointed. The real difficulty comes from the

[1] Dillon's motion on the government of Ireland was defeated 245–106.

popularity of the Government. No one opposes & candidates are pretending support who mean murder.

I hope the Labourites will get more than the Asquithians. There would then be a clear issue for the future.[1]

I settled the cotton strike yesterday—but it took a lot out of me. I feel rather tired today.

Fond love to my sweet old girl—& to the two little girls.

16 December 1918

Lecsiwn trosod yn y wlad yma. Ond y mae'r sowldiwr etto i dod.[2]

Difficult to foretell as there are no reliable data—no canvass. But I believe I have won.

19 December 1918

I am back from the Great Banquet in the Palace—to the victorious British Generals. They had a fine reception. I took Megan to the station. When I got there I saw the Asquiths, Elizabeth & Puffin [Anthony Asquith] on the border of the crowd. I went back & fetched them forward on the platform. Poor old Asquith was very touched. I am glad I did it. I asked Mrs. A. whether she would like to come forward. She replied "I should like it very much if I am allowed to."

The Coalition won the election with an enormous majority. Over 520 supporters of the government were elected (473 of them with the 'coupon') as against only 57 Labour and less than 30 Asquithians. In 1919 Lloyd George was until July largely involved with the peace conference at Paris.

'Spa Conference'[3] (undated—1919)

Had a complete breakdown on Saturday & Sunday— Sunday in bed with a temperature. Milligan attended me & told me I was very tired. So I was—I am afraid the last five years have almost finished me.

The Conference in a bad way—a very bad way. We are sending for Marshal Foch and [Field Marshal] Wilson to come here to confer as to the action we should take in the event of a break.

[1] In the event, 57 Labour members were elected as against 29 Independent Liberals. Some of the latter considered themselves to be Coalition supporters.

[2] Election over in this country. But the soldiers still to come.

[3] This may refer either to the Spa conference of 6–8 February or of 4–5 March 1919. At both the German delegates objected to handing over the entire German fleet without a guarantee of food supplies.

The Bolshevik negotiations, if they come off, will completely alter my holiday. There may be a Peace Conference in London some time in August.

14 February 1919 (from Paris)

President Wilson is off tonight so my visit to Paris is off. I have had a most strenuous week. Next week will be worse & the next even worse. The miners' strike is upon us. It is a fight with revolution using starvation as a weapon. But it must be faced.

27 March 1919

I am very hard pressed with the most important discussions of the Conference.[1] Papers all going for us. So I must be 'short'—& as I always hope to be 'sweet'.

Colonel Wilson from Mesopotamia lunched with me today. Full of admiration for Tom. He is very popular with the high class Arab & Jews & would make money if he settled down there.

12 August 1919

Isn't Llew[2] a hog? I wouldn't in the least resent his differing from my policy. That is his obvious right, but this intense personal bitterness is unpardonable.

15 September 1919

Why should you object to "the Future"? Is it your notion that Ministers should stand to be shot at & spat upon by every rapscallion who has a grievance against them & that they should never reply? I have just had enough of that & I mean to put up a fight. When every whippersnapper says we have done nothing why shouldn't we advertise what we have done?

26 September 1919

Well the big strike[3] has come at last—quite unexpectedly —as a thief in the night. It is the most serious labour war the country has ever seen & no one can foretell how it will shape.

---

[1] On 25 March Lloyd George produced the 'Fontainebleau Memorandum' which called for moderation towards Germany in relation to reparations and frontier settlement.

[2] Llewelyn Williams (see p. 92, n. 4) had now become a violent opponent of Lloyd George.

[3] A national railway strike began on 26 September and lasted until 5 October.

7 October 1919

The Railwaymen have been thoroughly beaten & they know it. It will save much trouble in future. It has been very good business.

5 January 1920 (probably a mis-dating for 1921)

Meeting Sinn Feiners. They want to get off contribution for the war—altogether. I'll see them in Hades first.

22 January 1920

Back from Paris after a most unexpected experience.[1] The defeat of Clemenceau upset all our plans. It is a monument of ingratitude. From the point of view of policy I have not yet decided what it means except that I shall be dealing with very inferior men.

9 April 1920

In the throes of the Franco German crisis ever since I came here. The French have played the fool & we must act firmly with them if we are to keep out of great trouble.

22 April 1920 (from San Remo)

Things are difficult here. The French mean to be troublesome I fear. They are anxious Allies. For the moment their papers & politicians are in full cry against me because I refuse to support their mad schemes for the destruction & dismemberment of Germany.[2]

3 August 1920

I have had another relapse. I broke down on Thursday—just like Spa. I am very fatigued & must get away.

13 August 1920

Here I am working & worrying. It is difficult to build when there are so many people not only hindering but pulling

---

[1] Clemenceau had been defeated by Deschanel in the French presidential election.

[2] At San Remo Lloyd George was in conflict with the French when he urged opening negotiations with Germany to fix a lump sum for reparations.

down what you have laboriously built up. France has upset us once more.

In the autumn of 1920 Lloyd George had to deal with several major strikes and with the deteriorating situation in Ireland. Meanwhile by-elections were going very badly for the Coalition and there were sounds of rebellion from the Unionists.

2 September 1920 (from Lucerne)

We are here in the Cathedral to hear Welsh hymns played on the great organ. You remember coming with us to hear the Storm in the Alps played on it. The organist offered to play anything I liked. I gave him a number of old Welsh hymns—Dorcas, Rhyddid, Moriah, Rhosymedre, Brynhyfryd, Aberystwyth. . . .

The Lord Mayor of Cork business[1] is most unpleasant but if you let him off you might as well give give up Ireland altogether. You couldn't imprison anybody if they started hunger striking. Still it will rouse fierce feelings if he dies. You & Megan need not be anxious. There has never been a case of assassination of wives & daughters. Of course they will try to kill me & may succeed. I must do my duty. Hen gachgi ydi'r brenhin.[2] He is frightened to death & is anxious to make it clear that he has nothing to do with it. . . .

Kerr[3] writes me today that he had had a breakdown & that Bertrand Dawson has ordered a 2 or 3 months rest for him. He has worked no harder than I have—not as hard, for he gets the Sundays off and I don't except rarely. It will be a great loss to me to get on without Kerr. He & I fit in so absolutely in our ideas. I miss him here when there is work to be done. . . .

The papers have been very nice to you. I must see that all the cuttings are collected & pasted in a book. You deserve it all hen gariad [old darling] for your sincere & unselfish work all done with great dignity for good causes.[4]

Downing St. was never put to as good use. Heavens! What a contrast to your predecessor [Mrs. Asquith]. Isn't she making a fine exhibition of herself in her autobiography. . . .

[1] Terence McSwiney, the Lord Mayor of Cork, was on hunger strike as a protest against British policy in Ireland; he eventually died.

[2] The King is an old coward.

[3] Philip Kerr (1882–1940): Lloyd George's private secretary, 1916–21, who played a major part in the Paris peace conference; became 11th Marquess of Lothian, 1930; Ambassador to the United States, 1939–40.

[4] Mrs. Lloyd George was created Dame of the Grand Cross of the British Empire in 1920.

11 September 1920

Ireland is a hell's broth. Potas y Diafol [Devil's broth]. I dare say there is a good deal of damnable business on both sides. This is inevitable & may end in forcing the moderate men on both sides to seek a settlement.

15 September 1920

Trying to settle strikes & prepare for them. Now the London Electricians threaten to go out & leave us without tube trains or lights! This to come off on Saturday. Bonar, Horne[1] & I have failed to persuade the employers this time.

Lord Mayor of Cork about the same although getting gradually weaker. Police are convinced that if he dies the Irish will try to kill me. That makes Cobham a little risky for some time.

24 September 1920

After a great struggle I succeeded this morning in persuading the miners to put off their strike for one week in order to meet the owners to examine the Government proposals. They meet tomorrow morning to make a start. I have great hopes that it is now off altogether, but we are not yet out of the wood.

29 December 1920

Sorry to hear Megan has caught a cold. . . These late nights are too much for her—night after night of theatres & dances. . . . Glad you like your fur. I thought it would suit you & I always like to see you look nice. You are one of those who bear dressing well so long as the colours suit you.

31 January 1921

I have asked Sarah to send you the [bed] jacket down. Take it with the real affection of an overworked, much harassed old man, who the harder he works for the public the more is he abused.

When are you going to Cardiganshire?[2]

[1] Sir Robert Horne (1871–1940): Unionist member, 1918–37; Minister of Labour, 1919–20; President of the Board of Trade, 1920–1; Chancellor of the Exchequer, 1921–2; created Viscount Horne, 1937.

[2] Dame Margaret took a very active part in the bitter by-election in Cardiganshire in February 1921, in which Ernest Evans, Lloyd George's private secretary and a Coalition Liberal, narrowly defeated Llewelyn Williams, an Independent Liberal.

13 August 1921

Back again after a hard time. Rushed the French into a first rate decision.

These Irishmen are once more most troublesome. It looks for the moment as though they mean to refuse.[1]

19 August 1921

Feel just about quite exhausted. Had as trying a week as you can well imagine. Three big speeches & endless Cabinet Conferences, lunches & dinners (Welsh Members last night at which Robert J. Thomas exhibited his asinine qualities to the full, much to the disgust of all his fellow members). They all gave you a cheer—hearty iawn i [very hearty for] Dame Margaret! Hughes Australia[2] was there. Thought Criccieth very beautiful.

29 September 1921

I miss you so much. I very nearly came with you & should have done so but for Dawson's express orders. . . . Tomorrow Hilton Young[3] & the experts arrive & I leave Tuesday. Jolly glad to do so although I am back to face trouble.

Threw all the Cabinet over on De Valera & sent my own reply which they had rejected.

You don't tell me whether you like the Hindhead site.

Just received De Valera's acceptance.[4]

24 November 1921

I am so sorry I cannot get down for the weekend. The Irish negotiations have taken a turn for the worse—seriously. This

[1] In August 1921 De Valera and the Irish Dail repeatedly refused to enter into negotiations with the British government on the terms of reference proposed by Lloyd George.

[2] William Hughes (1864–1952): born at Llandudno, Labour Prime Minister of Australia, 1915–23; holder of various other Cabinet offices, 1923–41.

[3] E. Hilton Young (1879–1960): Liberal member, 1915–23, 1924–9, then Conservative member, 1929–35; Financial Secretary to the Treasury, 1921–2; National Liberal Chief Whip, 1922–3; Minister of Health, 1931–5; created Lord Kennet, 1935.

[4] De Valera accepted Lloyd George's proposal for a conference, provided no prior commitment to any specific settlement was assumed.

time it is the Sinn Feiners. Last week it was the Ulsterites. They are both the sons of Belial![1]

The treaty with the Irish delegates was finally signed on 6 December, and accepted by the Dail by a narrow majority. But in early 1922 Lloyd George's political position continued to deteriorate, as the Unionist rank-and-file, led by Sir George Younger, the party chairman, became more and more restive.

5 January 1922 (from Cannes)

I am now at the Conference waiting for the translation of my speech—a very plain spoken discourse. French don't like it. They are behaving very badly. Last night I had to write to Briand that unless he publicly disavowed an interview he & Loucheur had given to a Belgian paper my colleagues & I would refuse to attend the Conference. I sent the letter at midnight— *Reply 3 a.m.* repudiating the interview. . . . No idea when the Conference will end. There is a good deal of explosive material about.[2]

28 March 1922

Crisis is distinctly off.[3] Carried the Cabinet. Winston put up a fight but I got F. E. so Winston was left alone & realised it.

The downfall of the Lloyd George government, which had seemed imminent for many months, was finally triggered off by the crisis in Asia Minor. In September war threatened between Britain and the Turks at Chanak. Although this was averted at the Treaty of Mudania on 11 October, the majority of the Unionist party now declared its opposition to remaining in the Coalition. They found a leader in Bonar Law, who had retired on grounds of ill-health in March 1920 but now returned to lend his authority to the revolt.

29 August 1922

I am worried by much bigger issues which may alter the whole course of things. The Coalition is breaking up over

[1] The Irish talks ran into deadlock on 23–24 November when the Sinn Feiners raised objections to the position of the Crown under the proposed Treaty of Association.
[2] This episode is described in A. J. Sylvester, *The Real Lloyd George* (Cassell 1947), p. 70. At Cannes, Lloyd George again tried unsuccessfully to reach agreement with France over German reparations. The conference was ruined by the resignation of Briand (after a fateful game of golf with Lloyd George) on 12 January.
[3] Over the resolution to be presented to the Commons relating to the Genoa conference. But Lloyd George was defeated in the Cabinet over the *de facto* recognition of Soviet Russia.

the Tory revolt. I am off with Shakespeare[1] *alone* to Churt.

6 September 1922

I am here for 2 or 3 days for Cabinet conferences. I have not had much of a holiday. The Greek situation & Poincaré & the political situation at home have occupied me very much.[2] I have had a series of conferences at Churt Ministers coming down with their experts. Last night I had 5 Ministers. I really cannot stand this much longer. I don't believe my nerve & spirits can sustain the constant wear & tear. I feel depressed, dejected & very much in the mood to chuck the whole thing up. Weather medium—not raining but dull.

I lunched with Bonar today. He cheered me up as usual by telling me I looked very much older than he did & as to the political situation it was so bad as to be quite irretrievable. I don't like the outlook & as I am not clear what to do I am worried & unhappy.

7 September 1922

Prysur iawn heddyw [Very busy today]. Cabinets, Conferences. Always the case during a holiday. Crisis after crisis.

8 September 1922

Criccieth is impossible in August & Sept. I am like a beetle in a glass case or a tiger in a menagerie. There is no nerve relaxation for me.

28 September 1922

Cabinets all day—yn union fel yn y rhyfel[3]—adjourned now until 7. Then we all meet to dine at Winston's. The Greek Revolution[4] has changed the situation. I think it just possible God may now take a hand. It looks like it.

On 19 October the Unionist M.P.s at the Carlton Club voted by 185–88 to break with the Coalition. Lloyd George resigned the same day. The family now had to leave 10 Downing Street after nearly six years.

[1] Sir Geoffrey Shakespeare (born 1893): Private Secretary to Lloyd George, 1921–2; Liberal member, 1922–3 and 1929–31, then National Liberal member (Simonite), 1931–45.

[2] The Turkish army smashed through the Greek lines in Asia Minor in the last fortnight of August, sacked Smyrna on 9 September and advanced on the British position at Chanak.

[3] The same as in the war.

[4] King Constantine of Greece abdicated on 27 September after a bloodless revolution.

Dame Margaret to Olwen Carey Evans, 25 October 1922

We are very very busy packing to go away. . . . I have never seen such a lot of rubbish collected in all my life. The general election will be a rest after this. I can't see myself oping [*sic*] all these cases if I live to be a hundred. I leave here for Cric. & B'dawelon after this. We have taken a furnished house, it is Sir Edward Grigg's & Tada is in such a fever haste to get there but I am not going until I return from Wales. It is in Vincent Square. . . . I hope we shall have a house of our own by then or back in No. 10 perhaps. I can't see Bonar Law lasting *too* long.

Megan Lloyd George to Olwen Carey Evans, ibid.

We are packing as hard as ever we can. The mess is indescribable—books, papers, photos, caskets, over-flowing waste paper baskets, men in aprons, depressed messengers, abound in rooms in the house in vast numbers. . . . Newnham[1] walks about with the air of a man whose sufferings are so intense that he hopes he may not have long to live. He stays on with B[onar] L[aw] of course; his only reason for not resigning is that he may be here, when we come back, if ever we do!

The crisis came about, as I expect you know, very suddenly —with the exception of Father, stunned everyone. No one was expecting Bonar to act as he did—least of all poor Mr. Chamberlain. I am far sorrier for him in this business than anyone. It is such a humiliation for the recognised leader of a party to be thrown aside as he was by his own people. Tada had wonderful receptions both at Manchester & Leeds & made wonderful speeches in both places. The people are absolutely with him, altho' very tired of the government, more particularly because of its being a coalition than anything else. Whatever happens Tada will be the power. He will be tremendous in opposition—& Bonar knows it.

[1] Lloyd George's personal valet.

CHAPTER 9

The Last Crusades

(1922–36)

In the last phase of his career, Lloyd George lived at 'Bron-y-de', a country house at Churt in Surrey which he had bought in 1921. Dame Margaret, however, continued to live in Criccieth, at the family home, Bryn Awelon. Lloyd George's political position was now highly anomalous. Although his 'National Liberals' numbered only 57 he made little attempt at a reunion with the Asquithians, and gave first Bonar Law's and then Baldwin's governments general support. The relations between the two Liberal factions were still uncertain when Lloyd George set off on a lecture tour in the United States in September 1923. But, during this visit, Baldwin unexpectedly proclaimed his conversion to protection of the home market. The Liberals at once reunited under the leadership of Asquith in the defence of free trade. He and Lloyd George fought side by side in the December 1923 general election, in which the Liberals improved their position considerably and won 157 seats. However, the first Labour government was a disastrous time for the Liberals. There was constant internecine bickering over the distribution of the 'Lloyd George fund' and over policy. At the polls in October 1924, they lost over 100 seats, and finished up with only 40 members. Their problems were underlined by the General Strike in May 1926 when Asquith (now in the Lords) publicly rebuked Lloyd George for excessive sympathy with the trade unions. It was widely believed at this time that Lloyd George was bidding for a new 'fusion' between the Liberals and Labour. In fact, the bulk of the party rank-and-file backed him, and Asquith had to resign the leadership.

Far from being a spent force, Lloyd George largely dominated politics in the late 1920s. There were constant rumours that he was about to form a new political combination either with Labour, or with Rothermere and other press lords in forming a 'centre party'. More important, he transformed political and economic debate with his exciting new programmes. With the aid of Keynes and other economists, he produced a striking series of new blueprints for the revival of the stagnant British economy. *We Can Conquer Unemployment* in 1929, with its new plans for public works and counter-cyclical public spending programmes, commanded widespread attention. A generation later, these schemes were to become the conventional wisdom, but in the 1929 election they met with scant reward. The Liberals raised their total vote to over five millions, but finished with a mere 59 seats. The second Labour government of Ramsay MacDonald was disastrous for the Liberals as well as for Labour. When MacDonald resigned as Labour premier in August 1931 and took office as head of a 'National' government instead, barely half of the parliamentary Liberal Party was still loyal to Lloyd George. He himself had been recovering from a major operation at the time of the political crisis. But he soon made it clear that, in contrast to the bulk of his fellow Liberals, he opposed the 'National' administration, staffed as it was with many of the men of 1922. The October 1931 general election, however, saw Lloyd George isolated and impotent, at the head of a family group of only four Welsh 'Independent Liberals'.

For the rest of the 1930s, he was increasingly withdrawn from politics. Until 1936 he was busy refighting old battles in his *War Memoirs*. He made a last bid for power in January 1935, proposing a 'Council of Action' and proposals similar to those of 1929. He was asked by the government to submit detailed schemes for economic recovery, and in April 1935 it seemed possible that he might join the administration. But the hostility of Baldwin and Chamberlain was inexorable, while the 1935 general election resulted in all the Liberal factions opposed to the government totalling a mere 21. Lloyd George was still a figure of major stature. His enthusiastic report on Germany after a visit to Hitler at Berchtesgaden in September 1936 created an immense stir. His fierce attacks on the government's policy of 'appeasement' in Abyssinia, on the Munich settlement and on the guarantee to Poland in March 1939 all shook the government and gave new heart to its critics. His fierce onslaught on Neville Chamberlain on 7 May 1940 played some part in bringing about the Prime Minister's downfall. With his old colleague, Churchill, as the new premier, it was widely expected that Lloyd George would enter the government, even at the age of 77. But it wasn't his war. He turned down Churchill's offers of the ambassadorship in Washington and other posts. In 1941 he was a major advocate of a negotiated peace. Subsequently he was a jaundiced critic of the government's mistakes, mordantly compared by Churchill on one occasion to the aged Marshal Pétain in France. He had, however, a reconciliation with Churchill in the House in May 1944, and the premier delivered a superb and moving tribute to him at the time of his death.

Lloyd George's links with Wales and with his family in Criccieth became more and more tenuous in this final period. But they never snapped entirely. He was still much involved in Welsh affairs; his annual Thursday address at the national eisteddfod was a major event. He still visited his wife intermittently at Criccieth, and there was never a formal separation, even after Frances Stevenson gave birth to a daughter, Jennifer. Dame Margaret died in January 1941. Lloyd George, now rapidly breaking up, married Frances Stevenson in October 1943. The final accolade of an earldom on 1 January 1945 meant nothing. Lloyd George died on 26 March without taking his seat in the Lords; many in Wales regretted that their Great Commoner had given in to the blandishments of the English establishment at last. His old seat at Caernarvon Boroughs fell to a Conservative in the 1945 general election, ironically the one Conservative gain in that election, compared with 1935. The Lloyd George tradition in politics was upheld by his son, Gwilym, and his daughter, Megan. Gwilym moved right, became

o

a 'National Liberal and Conservative' member, and served in the Churchill and Eden cabinets of 1951–7. Megan, always far more radical, joined the Labour Party in the mid-1950s, after losing her Liberal seat in Anglesey in 1951; she won Carmarthen for Labour in a famous post-Suez by-election in February 1957. She died in 1966, her seat then being won from Labour by a Welsh Nationalist. In some ways, it was an appropriate final comment on the Lloyd George political tradition. Little else remained. Lloyd George's one surviving daughter, Olwen, and his second wife, Frances, Countess Lloyd-George (alive and active in 1972 at the age of 84), were the last direct links with a tumultuous career that had remoulded and revitalized British politics and society for over half a century.

(undated—probably late November 1922)

Most difficult & baffling fight. My chief aim is to keep the Tory numbers down. I don't care much who gets in as long as Bonar does not get a working majority. I am working for a break 2 or 3 years hence after we have formed a Centre party with a strong progressive bias.[1]

The Conservatives won the election and Bonar Law became Prime Minister. Lloyd George's 'National Liberals' numbered only 57. They continued to be on very distant terms with the Asquithian Liberals, the 'Wee Frees'. Baldwin succeeded Bonar Law as Prime Minister in May 1923.

29 March 1923

Grigg[2] scored a great triumph last night. So far our men have beaten the Wee Frees out of sight. Have you seen Mrs. Asquith's characteristically foolish ebullition in Spain? Asquith in power in 2 years. No unity unless I am left out.

(undated—perhaps June 1923) (from Cherkley)

Been weekending here. F. E., Winston & Rothermere. No agreement possible with R. He is just wildly pro-French over the Ruhr.[3] W., F. E. & I are not. Still it may produce a more friendly atmosphere in his papers. He promises to give me a good show over America. I hope his friendship will last so far and so long. Meanwhile they are all attacking Baldwin.

In 1921, Lloyd George had bought a new country house at Churt in Surrey, together with sixty acres of land. He named it 'Bron-y-de' to imply that it faced south.

[1] In fact, Bonar Law was returned with an overall majority whereas the dream of a Centre Party rapidly disappeared.

[2] Sir Edward Grigg (1879–1955): Lloyd George's private secretary, 1921–2; Liberal member for Oldham, 1922–5; Conservative member, 1933–45; created Baron Altrincham, 1945.

[3] France had occupied the Ruhr in January 1923.

Dame Margaret to Olwen Carey-Evans, undated (possibly 1923), from '*Bron-y-de*'

The only part of the house facing de (south) is the front door, the dining room, drawing room & all good bedrooms face north west, so pen ol [behind] & not bron [breast] is the best name for it. My dear, they are altering it now, making it bigger in less than a year after it was built, in fact alterations here started 6 months after its completion. Megan & her father have gone out for a walk but as they drag across heather up hill & down dale I did not go. . . . Lady Mond is chaperoning Megs out, she is quite keen to come. Tada has been very severe on her lately, once at Seville when the child had done nothing, we were at a Hotel she knew no one there & could not talk Spanish. One night or rather morning he asked her when she went to bed & she said about midnight & he flew at her & asked her what she had been doing. She said I went to write a p.c. & then I went to my room to write an account of what she had seen during the day at Seville. He never said well that's alright, you know he never will admit that he has made a mistake, since then Megan is not very happy. It will be nice for her to get right away. I shall miss her terribly, I shall be very lonely, perhaps Dick will lend me Valerie[1] for a while.

27 August 1923

Wheldon refused to stand & I am having difficulties over the American publishers of my book[2]—so that altogether I am not in a very happy mood.

Still we are making some progress over our political discussions. They are leaving this morning & tomorrow I get a fresh lot—McCurdy,[3] Hilton Young &c. I want to know where I am before I go to Llandrindod.

In September 1923 Lloyd George embarked on a triumphant lecture tour in the United States. While he was away, Baldwin unexpectedly announced his conversion to protection of the home market in a speech at Plymouth on 25 October. This immediately reunited the Liberal Party. When Baldwin called a general election in December, Asquith and Lloyd George fought side by side in defence of free trade. The Liberals

[1] Richard's eldest daughter, now Lady Valerie Daniel.
[2] *Is It Peace?* (Hodder & Stoughton, 1923).
[3] Charles A. McCurdy (1870–1941): Liberal member for Northampton, 1910–23; Coalition Liberal Chief Whip, 1921–2; chairman of United Newspapers, 1922–7; joined Empire Free Trade 'crusade', 1930.

recovered to win 157 seats at the polls but it was Ramsay MacDonald who became
Prime Minister in January 1924 at the head of the first Labour government, a
minority administration.

11 December 1923

Things are interesting.[1] There will be a Socialist Govt
in a month's time—or another Election! Had a long talk with
Asquith last night. Simon comes to Churt on Sunday.

17 December 1923

I came up today for a chat with Asquith. He was most
friendly & helpful. The old boy & I get on well together always
when mischief makers are kept out.

To Megan Lloyd George, 4 February 1924

What changes are taking place. A socialist govt. actually
in power. But don't get uneasy about your investments or
your antiques. Nothing will be removed or abstracted. They
have come in like a lamb. Will they go out like a lion? Who
knows? For the present "their tameness is shocking to me".
They are all engaged in looking as respectable as lather &
blather will make them. They are out to soothe ruffled nerves.
When you return you will find England quite unchanged.
Ramsay is just a fussy Baldwin—& no more.

The Liberals were bound to turn Baldwin out & the King
was bound to call Ramsay in & we are all bound to give him a
chance. That is the situation.

To Megan Lloyd George, 25 March 1924

[He is dismayed to learn that Megan is not due back
until the autumn.]

Here the situation is growing more & more difficult. To
use the words of a provincial mayor "the future is dark &
obscene"—meaning of course "obscure". I am not sure how it
is going to work out. The Liberals are in a tight place & for the
moment things are not going too well for them. I am lying low
—deliberately—but the time will come &c. So look out—but
not just yet.

Megan Lloyd George to her father, 22 May 1924 (from Simla, India)

I hear that Ramsay is growing more unpopular with his

[1] The result of the election was: Conservatives 259; Labour 191; Liberals 157.

own people every day—that his private consultations with his ministers become further speeches—the situation doesn't seem very hopeful for the future of the Labour party & I am so very glad that the Liberals are drifting away from them. I suppose if we cling for any length of time to any other party, our chances of establishing ourselves as a political force become less? Anyway I hope any idea of a rapprochment between the two parties is dead!

I was delighted to see you were on the war-path once more. I love to see you as "the disturbing element", darling.

24 July 1924

You talk as if my affection for you came & went. No more than the sea does because the tide ebbs & flows. There is just as much water in it. . . . You like me better sometimes when I am nice to you. So do I you when you are nice to me. But if at the worst moment anybody is not nice to you I am as murderous towards him as Patrick Mahon. I would readily hit them with an axe.

You say I have my weakness. So has anyone that ever lived & the greater the man the greater the weakness. It is only insipid, wishy washy fellows that have no weaknesses. Would you like to marry Tim!! He is sober & sternly good in all respects.

You must make allowances for the waywardness & wildness of a man of my type. What if I were drunk as well? I can give you two samples you know of both the weaknesses in one man & the wives do their best under those conditions. What about Asquith & Birkenhead? I could tell you stories of both—women & wine. Believe me hen gariad [old darling] I am at bottom as fond of you as ever. . . .

To Megan Lloyd George, 29 July 1924

Not much exciting news to record. The great International Conference[1] is lumbering along—bumping badly. No knowing yet how it will turn out. Ramsay has made every conceivable mistake of commission & omission—mostly the latter. But they all want the Dawes Report[2] so the chances are that in the end

---

[1] A conference in London attended by the Prime Ministers of Britain, France, Belgium and Italy, and later by the German Chancellor. France agreed to evacuate the Ruhr.

[2] A report in 1924 which proposed the slowing down of German reparations payments.

they will blunder through. No election just yet. If Ramsay had scored a prompt & clear success he would have tried his luck.

5 August 1924

Just finished an hour's speech on the Conference in the House of Commons. A quiet interrogative speech. Our people very pleased. Ronald McNeill[1] called it a remarkable speech. Wedgwood Benn[2] said it was bombs for Ramsay wrapped in cotton wool.

Tomorrow I speak at the Oxford Summer School. Thursday important debate on Irish Treaty. Asquith not here. So must be here.

Megan Lloyd George to her father, 7 August 1924 (from Simla)

Are you glad the Session is over? I should think that it must have had its intensely irritating moments for you. You must be frightfully tied & restricted by the O.M. 'Squith.

To Megan Lloyd George, 2 October 1924

So now for politics—the greatest and most varied stage in the world. It looks now as if we were in for another General Election. I have done my best to precipitate it. Labour had its chance & with a little more wisdom & what the old Puritans sagely called the "Grace of God" they could have remained in another three years & formed a working alliance with Liberalism that would have ensured a progressive administration of this country for 20 years. But they lost their heads as men & women will from sudden elevation. Hence their fall.

The October 1924 election was disastrous for the Liberals. Their total of seats fell from 157 to 40. Baldwin again became Prime Minister. Asquith was defeated at Paisley and Lloyd George led the Liberals in the House.

19 December 1924

Last night I dined with the Asquiths & on my way home it was snowing. They were all most pleasant—Mrs. A, Lady Bonham & the old boy.

---

[1] Ronald McNeill, Conservative member for Canterbury, a 'die-hard' in 1922.

[2] William Wedgwood Benn (1877–1960): Liberal member, 1906–27, then Labour; served in Labour Cabinets of 1929–31 and 1945–6; became Viscount Stansgate, 1941.

You can see they are economising. None of the old sumptuous dinners. Drank Cider or Whiskey. Very good for us all.

2 January 1925

Meeting y blaid [of the party]. Passed off well altho' I spoke plainly to them on factionalism.

Edge[1] & Macnamara & I worked hard at a Report the last two days. . . . Got another silly letter from Mrs. Asquith. She is miserable & so buzzes about like a mosquito in the room with her wings bedraggled but her sting active & indiscriminate.

15 January 1925

Interesting news. Very confidential. Asquith yn mynd i Dy'r Arglwyddi.[2] I have just left him. He is much better & fitter.

21 January 1925

Megs & I are going to see "The Farmer's Wife". Mr. & Mrs. Pringle[3] joining us! A sign of the [times?]. Had an excellent meeting at the the N.L.C. today. But Liberalism is by no means alright—not by a long way.

4 August 1925

The coal mess of the Government is their biggest & may bring Baldwin down.[4] The Tories are furious I mean to have a go at them Thursday. Spoke yesterday.

The Shadow Cabinet passed my land scheme today![5]

27 August 1925

I have been working here on the Land hard so as to get out the Report in time for the late autumn campaign. Gwaith ofnadwy arno etto [Tremendous work on it still].

[1] Captain William Edge (1880–1948): Liberal member for Bolton, 1916–23, and for Bosworth, 1927–31; National Liberal member for Bosworth, 1931–45; junior whip, 1919–22.

[2] Asquith going to the House of Lords.

[3] William M. R. Pringle (1874–1928): Liberal member, 1910–18 and 1922–4; a bitter opponent of Lloyd George during the war years.

[4] The government had decided to give a nine-month subsidy to the coal industry.

[5] This was the scheme later embodied in the 'green book', *Land and the Nation*. Its controversial plan for 'cultivating tenure' led to Mond's leaving the Liberal Party, but younger Liberals were generally very enthusiastic.

Tonight I go down to Surrey with Philip Kerr, J. L. Garvin(!)[1] & Martin Conway.[2] The latter wanted to see me. He says there is a real revolt against Baldwin's latest surrender. They want me to lead it. I am in no hurry to get mixed up with that gang again.

27 December 1925 (from Naples)

[He urges his wife to spend a week with him in Rome.]
Mussolini wants to see me. He will be back in Rome by then. The Fascists are very friendly to me.

9 February 1926

Convention[3] over. Great triumph.
One regrettable(?) episode. Pringle said something offensive to Hore Belisha.[4] H. B. said "Come out & I'll talk to you." Pringle refused, upon which H. B. hit him in the face, a great whack. Serve the bounder right. He has behaved scandalously right through.
There was great commotion. H. B. explained. The audience was with him. Pringle came out of it very badly.

18 May 1926

Things are very difficult here. The party think I took a much too pro Labour line in the strike. But I did it deliberately —& I mean to stick to it.[5]

22 September 1926

I am up in town trying to put a little spunk into the Chronicle & Sunday News. Since I saw the Express had passed us in circulation I have been most uneasy & I have been at it hard trying to put things right. I had them all at Churt last week. In the end I sent for Morris—the lawyer—found

---

[1] J. L. Garvin (1868–1947): editor of the *Observer*, 1908–42.
[2] Sir Martin Conway (1856–1937): Conservative member for the Combined Universities; art critic and explorer; created Baron Conway of Allington, 1931.
[3] A convention held to consider Lloyd George's land policies.
[4] Leslie Hore-Belisha (1893–1957): entered Parliament as an ardent supporter of Lloyd George in 1923; turned National Liberal in 1931; Minister of Transport, 1934–7; Secretary of State for War, 1937–40; Minister of National Insurance, 1945.
[5] This led to a final breach between Asquith and Lloyd George. In the event, the National Liberal Federation and the Liberal Candidates' Association tended to back Lloyd George; Asquith resigned as leader shortly afterwards.

what my powers were, then gave a fairly plain intimation that unless immediate steps were taken to put things right I should reconstruct the Board—that is sack the lot. Perris is right. McCurdy is lazy & flabby, Gwilym indolent. They have too many duds in high places on the staff. The property is a good one but it requires ceaseless activity & watchfulness. Perris spends too many of his evenings at the Kit Kat Club. It will do good to stir them up & frighten them. I mean to keep at it.

I have been offered poor Howard Spicer's shares. Would you like a few? You will have to pay 21/– for each but they are worth it. . . . This weekend I have *14* professors at Churt. . . .

Asquith resigned as Liberal leader in October 1926 and Lloyd George succeeded him. Lloyd George was now much involved with Keynes and others in devising new and imaginative schemes to promote economic recovery. The fruits of this came in Britain's Industrial Future, the 'yellow book', in 1928 and We Can Conquer Unemployment, the 'orange book', in 1929. Lloyd George and his wife were also engaged in trying to find a parliamentary seat for Megan.

6 March 1928 (misdated 1927)

Back from Middlesboro'. Wish you had been there. You never saw such a sight. 37,000 packed in the square. Think we are going to win. If we do that will console me for Mrs. Runciman's victory[1] which I hear is likely. Yr hen b— [the old b—].

30 March 1928

A word for the big M. first. Your speech at Penrhyn Hall was excellent. In spite of the success of the little M. the old girl is not by any means on the shelf yet. She has the knack of getting straight to the point. She is what is known at the Bar as a good verdict getter. . . .

Now as to the little M.[2] I am very anxious about her programme, next week more especially. Llanelly is a bad blunder & I am most unhappy about it. It involves 3 days very uncomfortable & exhausting travel. At the end of it she has to deliver the most crucial speech of her Anglesea [*sic*] campaign. Amlwch may "troi y fantol" [turn the scales]. A tired person cannot do justice to herself. R. J. [Thomas][3] is a practised

[1] The Liberals retained Middlesbrough West with a majority of 89; Mrs. Runciman gained St. Ives by 763.

[2] Megan Lloyd George was now contemplating the Liberal candidature in Anglesey.

[3] Sir Robert John Thomas (1873–1951): Liberal member for Wrexham 1918–22, and for Anglesey, 1923–9.

speaker. He also knows Megan but with a cruel selfishness & conceit he insisted on her coming because it inconvenienced him to put it off. I can assure you his conduct has put him finally off my register of friends. Megan has done him a great disservice by obeying his orders. It has put a man like Tweed[1] whom I consulted definitely against R. J. He has shown himself quite ready to ruin not only Megan's chances but her health in his own interest. I begged him to postpone & [said] that I would pay all loss. He said his Committee would not agree. Bunkum—if he had urged it they would have done so. Can you imagine Geoffrey behaving like this. But no. Had it been a bye election they would have been forced to give it up. After all this is practically a bye election.

Still I pleaded no more with Megan & R. J. His influence over her is complete. All you can do now is to see that her health does not suffer. You ought to go with her. She will beg you not to. Take my tip & go.

Insist that she must not stay for the night meeting. She won't get to Aberystwyth by 8. Get her to rest in the train with a slightly open window otherwise the stuffiness will poison her blood.

We must do our best for the fascinating little monkey. She is excelling my highest expectations. But we must see she gets fair play & Llanelly is a foul deal for her by a self centred vain fellow suffering badly from swelled head.

26 April 1928

Glad you are putting some punch into the fight. As W. J. (the Chairman)[2] puts it you must be certain of 300 delegates even to win. That is a big lack.

When you speak either privately or publicly—you M. No. 1—you ought to call attention to the unexampled training Megan has had. She has come in direct contact with the leaders of *all* the political parties—Libs. Cons. & Labour & heard them all discuss public affairs.

To Megan Lloyd George, 22 May 1928

I only want to write you to wish the best [of] luck on

---

[1] Lt.-Colonel T. F. Tweed (1890–1940): Lloyd George's political adviser from 1920; Liberal chief organizer, 1927–31.
[2] William Jones.

Thursday. It seems according to all accounts to be a "cert". You have no cause for nervousness or anxiety about your speech. I know you will do well. So don't worry about it my sweet.

I have caused it to be hinted to Walter Jones for use *after* the vote that if E.W.R.[1] behaves decently I will do my best to help him to find a constituency to fight. But I have warned him that this must on no account be used *before* the vote as an inducement for him to withdraw. But it will be helpful with several good fellows who had promised him already before you came out. R. J. [Thomas] urged it on me.

You have fought a splendid fight & I am prouder of you & the old girl than ever.

You might say in your speech in reference to Land that the special conditions of Wales must be taken into account in drafting any Land Bill. That the special circumstances of Scotland had been considered & that you feel certain Wales will have the same consideration.

To Megan Lloyd George, 24 May 1928

HWRE! HWRE!! The estimate I made this morning of the division is not far wrong. I'll show it to you. You two Megs. did it all yourselves against great odds. A fortnight ago you'd have a majority of three. Three weeks ago you would have been beaten. A month ago you had no chance.

Hallelujah. Hallelujee!!

To Megan Lloyd George, 28 August 1928

I wish you had been with us over the weekend. I had a first rate discussion on the political prospects & how to deal with the probable situation after the next general [election]. Keynes,[2] Ramsay Muir[3] & Tweed—with Snowden in the evening. The latter is pessimistic about the electoral outlook.

---

[1] Ellis W. Roberts. At a stormy meeting on 24 May 1928 the Anglesey Liberal Association at Llangefni adopted Megan Lloyd George as prospective candidate by a majority of 325 to 245 votes over Roberts.

[2] John Maynard Keynes (1883–1946): resigned from the peace delegation in Paris to write *Economic Consequences of the Peace*; reconciled with Lloyd George and worked with him on his reform programmes, 1926–8; created Baron Keynes, 1942; founder of modern economics.

[3] Ramsay Muir (1872–1941): historian, director of the Liberal summer school from 1921; later chairman and president of the National Liberal Federation.

Theirs & ours. He does not expect Labour to get more than 225—& as for me he puts us at 50 or 60(!). That would mean another 5 years of Tory Rule.

The S.W.D.N. is a gross betrayal & a sordid betrayal at that. I am getting thro' to Cardiff to get the late editor up tomorrow.

Hope to get down about Thursday of next week. Philip Kerr & Ramsay Muir coming down to Churt to settle manifesto for General Election (N.L.Fed.). Tell your mother that her wheat beats mine. I am looking forward to her whole meal bread.

The Liberals captured only 59 seats in the 1929 general election, Labour winning 287. Ramsay MacDonald formed a second minority government.

3 January 1930

Back here at work. Daily Chronicle—a tremendous mess. St. David's[1] is putting his back into it. He is at his best. Coal Mines amendments. Interviews until late last night—at Ld. Reading's today again & Saturday. We meet on Monday altogether. Sorry but it must be attended to.

20 February 1930

I lunched today to meet the Soviet Ambassador. Tonight I meet the great Ramsay at dinner! Am I not a proud man?

Politics are in a more queer state than they have been in my day. Never seen such a mix up. Come up soon hen gariad [old darling].

?2 September 1931

[He has had a little local trouble after his operation, but it is not serious.] Gwilym is to be offered a post today. He was very disinclined to take it when I saw him Friday.[2] I offered no opinion but I am expecting to hear from him.

Unemployment & trade figures getting worse. It is a dreary prospect for the new Govt.

Ramsay MacDonald had formed a 'National' government in August 1931: it won a huge majority at the polls in October. Lloyd George was withdrawn at this particular moment, as he was recovering from a major operation. Afterwards, he led a family

---

[1] John Wynford Philipps (see p. 46, n. 1), was now chairman of the trustees of the Lloyd George Fund and one of L.G.'s financial advisers.

[2] Gwilym Lloyd George in fact remained an Independent Liberal member.

group of four 'independent Liberals' into opposition. His main concern for the next four years was the writing of his War Memoirs.

13 December 1935 (from Marrakesh)

[He is enjoying a delightful and restful time in Morocco —'the French Government has been very attentive & obliging'.]

The Government seem to be making a horrible mess of the Abyssinian business.[1] It is the greatest outrage on decency & fairplay ever perpetrated by a British Govt.

18 December 1935 (from Marrakesh)

I am assuming that by the time this reaches you Megs will be down there. I have just read her speech[2] in Hansard. It is first rate. It is a real debating speech & therefore a real parliamentary achievement. I cannot tell you how pleased I am with it. . . .

I am getting on with my book[3] at a very satisfactory rate. I cannot get paid even for what I have already published unless I finish this last volume. Had I remained in England I could not have written a line. I should have inevitably been drawn into that frightful shemozzle over Abyssinia. What a muddle it it. It is quite incredible that any Government of ordinary intelligence & common honesty could have been guilty of what these fellows have done. What a fraud & a humbug that man Baldwin is. And yet he took in hundreds of thousands of decent Liberals.

1 February 1936

Here is another begging letter. As you know, I don't subscribe to chapels outside my constituency because I cannot afford it. But this is a special case. I was taught solfa at this chapel & here was my first prize as a child. I have an affectionate recollection of it. It is here also I attended my first Sunday school So I put Moriah in a category of its own.

But I would like you to find out from Lloyd Jones what they expect. I must not give anything which if published will bring down on me requests from every quarter. I might give them £20 as a special donation. Do you think that would do?

---

[1] The Hoare-Laval pact was concluded, 8 December 1935.
[2] A speech on Distressed Areas, 11 December 1935.
[3] Volumes V and VI of the *War Memoirs*.

Will you find out & let me know? You might sound Lloyd
Jones & see what he expects. Tell him I have to earn my money
by hard work. I am going up to town to be sworn on Tuesday.
But afterwards I am going to finish my book. I can see from
the advertisement in the paper that Haig's book will attack me.[1]

To Megan Lloyd George, 1 December 1936 (from Jamaica)

Your joint telegram as to the action taken by the Government in reference to the bombing school incident gave me a
great shock, and I immediately wired you my first impressions.[2] I think it an unutterable piece of insolence, but very
characteristic of this Government. They crumple up when
tackled by Mussolini and Hitler, but they take it out of the
smallest country in the realm which they are misgoverning.
It is the way cowards try to show that they are strong by bully-
ing. They run away from anyone powerful enough to stand
up to them and they take it out of the weak. In the worst days
of Irish coersion [*sic*], trials were never taken out of Ireland into
the English Courts. They might be removed from Roscommon to
Dublin, but they were never taken to the Old Bailey. I cannot
recall a single instance in the past of its having been done in
the case of Wales.[3] Certainly not in a criminal case. This is the
first Government that has tried Wales at the Old Bailey. I wish
I were there, and I certainly wish I were 40 years younger.
I should be prepared to risk a protest which would be a defiance. If I were Saunders Lewis I would not surrender at the
Old Bailey; I would insist on their arresting me, and I am not
sure that I would not make it difficult for them to do that.
This Government will take no heed of protests which do not
menace it. I hope the Welsh Members will make a scene, and
an effective one, in the House.

[1] Presumably a reference to Dorothy, Countess Haig, *The Man I Knew* or to the
second volume of Duff Cooper's life of Haig.
[2] On 8 September 1936, three Welsh Nationalists, Saunders Lewis, D. J. Williams, and the Rev. L. E. Valentine, committed arson at Penrhos aerodrome in
Caernarvonshire and then informed the police: it was a protest against English
military rearmament. Their case was transferred to the Old Bailey as it was claimed
that a Welsh jury would probably be prejudiced. They were finally imprisoned
for nine months.
[3] A somewhat similar case, which Lloyd George himself ought to have remem-
bered, had occurred during the Welsh tithe riots in 1887 when the case of thirty-two
men accused of riotous behaviour during a tithe distraint sale was transferred from
Ruthin county Court to Queen's Bench in London by a writ of *certiorari*.

It is a supremely foolish thing to have done; the majority of the Jury were in favour of a verdict, and they might at any rate have had a second trial, or removed it to some other part of Wales, but to take it out of Wales altogether, and, above all, to the Old Bailey, is an outrage what makes my blood boil. It has nothing to do with my views as to the merits of the case. It will reinforce the pacifist movement in England.

I am very disappointed not to have had a word from you as to the position; either you or Gwilym might have sent me letters by Air Mail telling me something of the gossip in Parliament. It cannot be your absorption in your Parliamentary duties, for I am disappointed to find that you have not yet taken any part in the Debates. You really ought to do so. It is a first-class mistake, because you are neglecting a great opportunity, and no-one can do it better, and very few as well, when you choose to do so. Could one or other of you not spare me ten minutes to write me by air Mail?

To Megan Lloyd George, 9 December 1936 (from Jamaica)

I assume that painful squalid business is over. At the moment it is not clear whether it has been terminated by abdication or withdrawal from the marriage.[1] The woman Simpson is not worth the price the poor infatuated King was prepared to pay. There are not in her any of the elements that can possibly constitute a tuppeny romance. All the same if he wished to marry her it could have been arranged quietly after the Coronation. By that time he might have been persuaded not to make a fool of himself. I agree with Gallagher. If the King wants to marry his American friend—why not? I cannot help thinking the Govt. would not have dealt so brusquely with him had it not been for his popular sympathies. The Tories never really cared for the little man. Labour have as usual played a cowardly part. Everybody here very sad about it.

From this time on, Lloyd George was increasingly withdrawn from politics, emerging now and again to deliver a formidable indictment of the National government's foreign policies. In May 1940 he took a leading part in the debate that saw the downfall of Neville Chamberlain. He refused various offers of government posts from

[1] The crisis had begun with the Bishop of Bradford's outburst on 1 December 1936; on 10 December Edward VIII abdicated. On Christmas Eve, Lloyd George sent the ex-King a cable in which he deplored 'the mean and unchivalrous attacks' upon 'a monarch who sympathized with the lowliest of his subjects'.

Churchill, including the British ambassadorship in Washington. Dame Margaret died in January 1941; Lloyd George married Frances Stevenson in October 1943. On 1 January 1945 it was announced that he had accepted a title as Earl Lloyd-George of Dwyfor. But he was now a dying man. He died on 26 March 1945 in the presence of his second wife, Frances, and his daughter, Megan. His grave stands beside the river Dwyfor at Llanystumdwy, the scene of his boyhood, of his earliest education in politics, and of his meeting with Maggie Owen of Mynydd Ednyfed.

SELECT BIBLIOGRAPHY

The primary and secondary sources relevant to the study of Lloyd George's career are immense: a complete bibliography would fill several volumes. I have listed here merely a selection of some of the more helpful recent studies.

For Lloyd George's career as a whole:

Malcolm Thomson, *David Lloyd George*, Hutchinson, 1948.
Thomas Jones, *Lloyd George*, Oxford University Press, 1951.
Frank Owen, *Tempestuous Journey*, Hutchinson, 1954.
A. J. P. Taylor, *Lloyd George: Rise and Fall*, Cambridge University Press, 1961.
Kenneth O. Morgan, *David Lloyd George: Welsh Radical as World Statesman*, University of Wales Press, Cardiff, 1963, second edition, 1964.
A. J. P. Taylor (ed.), *Lloyd George: Twelve Essays*, Hamish Hamilton, 1970.
Kenneth O. Morgan, *The Age of Lloyd George*, Allen & Unwin, 1971.

For Lloyd George's family and private life:

William George, *Richard Lloyd*, Western Mail, Cardiff, 1934 (in Welsh).
Viscount Gwynedd, *Dame Margaret*, Allen & Unwin, 1947.
A. J. Sylvester, *The Real Lloyd George*, Cassell, 1947.
William George, *My Brother and I*, Eyre & Spottiswoode, 1958.
Frances Stevenson, *The Years that are Past*, Hutchinson, 1967.
A. J. P. Taylor (ed.), *Lloyd George: a Diary by Frances Stevenson*, Hutchinson, 1971.

For Lloyd George's career to 1905:

D. A. Hamer, *Liberal Politics in the Age of Gladstone and Rosebery*, Clarendon Press, 1972.
Watkin Davies, *Lloyd George, 1863–1914*, Constable, 1939.
Kenneth O. Morgan, *Wales in British Politics, 1868–1922*, University of Wales Press, Cardiff, 1963, second edition, 1970.
Viscountess Rhondda and others, *The Life of D. A. Thomas, Viscount Rhondda*, Longmans, 1921.
T. I. Ellis, *Thomas Edward Ellis*, Vol. II, Brython Press, Liverpool, 1948 (in Welsh).

For Lloyd George's career after 1905:

Roy Jenkins, *Asquith*, Collins, 1964.
Randolph Churchill, *Winston S. Churchill*, Vol. II, Heinemann, 1967.
Martin Gilbert, *Winston S. Churchill*, Vol. III, Heinemann, 1971.
Lucy Masterman, *C. F. G. Masterman*, Nicholson & Watson, 1939.
Asa Briggs, *Seebohm Rowntree*, Longman, 1961.
Bentley Gilbert, *The Evolution of National Insurance in Great Britain*, Michael Joseph, 1966.
Trevor Wilson (ed.), *The Political Diaries of C. P. Scott, 1911–28*, Collins, 1970.
Cameron Hazlehurst, *Politicians at War, July 1914 to May 1915*, Cape, 1971.

Trevor Wilson, *The Downfall of the Liberal Party, 1914–35*, Collins, 1966.
Lord Beaverbrook, *Politicians and the War, 1914–1916*, Collins, new edition, 1960.
—— *Men and Power, 1917–1918*, Hutchinson, 1956.
—— *The Decline and Fall of Lloyd George*, Collins, 1963.
A. J. P. Taylor, *Beaverbrook*, Hamish Hamilton, 1972.
S. D. Waley, *Edwin Montagu*, Asia Publishing House, Bombay, 1964.
Robert Blake, *The Unknown Prime Minister*, Eyre & Spottiswoode, 1955.
Kenneth O. Morgan, 'Lloyd George's Premiership', *Historical Journal*, XIII, No. 1 (1970).
S. W. Roskill, *Hankey, Man of Secrets*, Vol. I, Collins, 1970.
—— *Hankey, Man of Secrets*, Vol. II, Collins, 1972.
Joseph Davies, *The Prime Minister's Secretariat*, Johns, Newport, 1953.
A. M. Gollin, *Proconsul in Politics*, Anthony Blond, 1964.
K. Middlemas (ed.), *Thomas Jones: Whitehall Diary*, Vols. I–III, Oxford University Press, 1969–71.
The History of the Times, Vol. IV, Times Publishing Company, 1952.
Nancy Maurice (ed.), *The Maurice Case*, Cooper, 1972.
D. G. Boyce, *Englishmen and Irish Troubles*, Cape, 1972.
Maurice Cowling, *The Impact of Labour, 1920–1924*, Cambridge University Press, 1971.
Robert Skidelsky, *Politicians and the Slump*, Macmillan, 1968.
Thomas Jones, *A Diary with Letters, 1931–50*, Oxford University Press, 1954.

Index